UNDER THE SHADOW

OF

THE RISING SUN

The true story of a
missionary family's survival and faith
in a Japanese prisoner-of-war camp
during WWII

Donald E. Mansell with Vesta W. Mansell

Pacific Press® Publishing Association
Nampa, Idaho
Oshawa, Ontario, Canada
www.pacificpress.com

Designed by Dennis Ferree

Additional copies of this book are available by calling toll free
1-800-765-6955 or visiting http://www.adventistbookcenter.com

Library of Congress Cataloging-in-Publication Data

Mansell, Donald Ernest, 1923-
Under the shadow of the Rising Sun : the true story of a missionary
family's survival and faith in a Japanese prisoner-of-war camp
during W. W. II / Don and Vesta Mansell
p. cm.
ISBN: 0-8163-1976-6
1. Mansell, Donald Ernest, 1923- 2. World War, 1939-1945—Personal
narratives, American. 3. World War, 1939-1945—Prisoners and prisons,
Japanese. 4. Missionaries—Philippines—Biography. 5. Missionaries—
United States—Biography. 6. Seventh-day Adventists—Missions—
Philippines. 7. Mansell family I. Title

D811.M3386A3 2003
940.53'17599'0922—dc21
[B]   2002045035

03 04 05 06 07 • 5 4 3 2 1

DEDICATION

To our grandchildren:
Donald Ernest Mansell II,
Dora Erika Mansell,
Elizabeth Lynn Draget,
Charles Everett Mansell,
Monica Jennifer Draget,
Emily Robin Mansell,
&
Taylor Allene Wood

ACKNOWLEDGMENTS

Over the past fifty-seven years, family members and friends have urged me to write a book about my experiences in the Philippines as a civilian POW under the Japanese during World War II. I kept putting off these appeals until I got a telephone call from Tim Lale, acquisitions editor of Pacific Press Publishing Association, encouraging me to submit such a manuscript. I agreed and, once committed to the project, determined to do as thorough a job as possible while the memory of events was still clear and vivid in my mind.

In working toward this objective I am indebted to several of my fellow internees. Chief among these is Dr. Marshall P. Welles, who, at the age of ninety-five, still has a sharp, clear mind, and who in prison camp was a spiritual inspiration to me. He not only has helped set the spiritual tone of this book but has also offered many helpful suggestions.

I am deeply indebted to James J. ("Jim") Halsema, a newspaper reporter by profession and training, who founded and published the *Camp John Hay Daily News* and its successor, the *Camp Holmes Daily News*. He has corrected factual errors and offered many helpful suggestions based on his broad and intimate knowledge, not only of what was going on in our camp but also (as one of those privileged to be in the secret "radio loop") of events that were going on outside in a world at war, of which we internees were largely unaware. I am also most grateful for his objectivity and dogged persistence in the pursuit of truth.

I am indebted to Lt. Col. Lee Allen, U. S. Army ret., who read the manuscript carefully and made many helpful suggestions. I am indebted to his cousins, John Ream and Katie Ream Sobek, who corrected many typos that might have inadvertently slipped by. I am also indebted to my brother, Charles G., and his wife, Mary Catherine ("Kay") Bell-Mansell, for helpful suggestions.

I am indebted in a special way to Robert and Richard Foley, who have graciously allowed me to quote from *Keepsake,* authored by their mother, Betty Halsema Foley. In addition, they have made an invaluable contribution to this book in allowing me to reproduce photographs that their father, Rupert Foley, took surreptitiously of my brother and me in the very act of smuggling radio tubes into camp.

When one records history, one must inevitably be selective. There is no such thing as a "complete history" of anything. It is therefore impossible to be totally unbiased. But this is no excuse for not trying to be as accurate and objective as possible. In aiming toward this goal, the diaries and books published by fellow internees have been most helpful. These individuals and their publishers and descendants have been gracious and generous in allowing me to quote or draw from their diaries, both published and unpublished.

Chief among these has been the unpublished diary of Dr. Ralph E. Longway, my best friend in camp, who has allowed me to quote freely from it. Lynn Bloom, editor and co-copyright holder of Natalie Crouter's book, *Forbidden Diary,* and Natalie's children, Frederick ("Bedie") Crouter and June Wortman, her heirs, have also been most generous in allowing me to quote from this book. Blue Dolphin Publishing, copyright holder of William R. Moule's *God's Arms Around Us,* and Jim Moule, William Moule's son and heir, have granted permission to quote freely from the book and reproduce one drawing from it. Fellow internee Fern Harrington Miles, who has been most generous, not only granted permission to quote from her book, *Captive Community,* but has allowed me to reproduce several of her drawings that appear in her book. Last but by no means least, the children of Elmer and Ethel Herold, William ("Billy") Herold and Elizabeth ("Betsy") Herold Heimke, who have granted permission to quote freely from their mother's unpublished manuscript, *Ethel's Diary,* which has proved to be an invaluable source of information.

I would be remiss if I failed to include in this list of contributors my loving and patient wife and best friend of fifty years (we celebrated our golden wedding anniversary on November 9, 2002), who read over this manuscript countless times. Although she did not go through the internment experience, she has lived it vicariously, and her suggestions and corrections have been most helpful.

Although an attempt has been made to present the history of our internment experience as accurately as possible, this author recognizes that nothing human is free from mistakes. For these errors he apologizes and assumes full responsibility.

Donald Ernest Mansell
October 7, 2002

CONTENTS

Don Mansell
two months after liberation
April 1945

CHAPTER

1

"The Battle of Manila Is On!"

"The battle of Manila is on!" Mom shouted above the staccato of machine-gun fire.[1] The next instant Mom, Dad, my sister-in-law Kay, and I threw ourselves on the concrete floor and crawled toward the opening in the wall that had once been a window on the second story of the hospital building of Old Bilibid Prison.[2] We peered over the sill toward Far Eastern University's administration building where the *rat-a-tat-tat* of automatic fire was coming from. Tracer bullets streaked off the cement façade of Far Eastern two hundred yards away. The building's large windowpanes fell like melting icicles. From the second floor of Far Eastern, the Japanese continued a furious fusillade at the American tanks on Quezon Boulevard.

"They're shooting at me!" shouted Charles, my brother, above the confused chatter of machine gun and rifle fire as he leaped through the empty window frame into the relative safety of our "cubicle."[3] A few minutes before, he had gone out on the balcony just outside our sleeping quarters to look around. Now bullets were zinging off the walls of our building.

The shooting that was coming our way stopped momentarily. Hearts pounding, we considered briefly what to do. Were we safe behind the foot-and-a-half-thick walls of our building, or should we go downstairs where we would have the added protection of the reinforced concrete of the second-story floor as a "roof"[4] over our heads? We were discussing our options when Johnny Black, a member of our camp Safety Committee, made the decision for us. "Everybody downstairs right away," he ordered. Crouching, we dashed toward the stairs and hurried down. We no sooner reached the lobby when Doc Walker, acting chairman of the camp Safety Committee, announced, "No one is allowed upstairs unless it is absolutely necessary. Stray bullets are flying through the windows, and they can kill."

Moments before the battle began, I was sitting on my makeshift bed writing about the day's events. My notebook-diary was still in my hand when I reached the safety of the lobby. As we internees stood or crouched in the central hall of our building, we could tell from the shorter and shorter intervals between explosions and bursts of machine-gun fire that the violence outside was intensifying.

After a bit, I located Ralph Longway, my best friend, and we crept cautiously toward the entrance to the lobby and looked over the sixteen-foot-high wall surrounding Old Bilibid complex.[5] We could already see fires breaking out beyond the walls, and we could hear an occasional stray bullet hit the ground. We decided we were safer inside our building and retreated to the lobby.

As we crouched in the middle of the central hall of our building, one of our Japanese civilian guards, Tenabe-San, strode in carrying a Samurai sword in his hands. He ordered Ralph to hold his weapon. As Tenabe unbuckled his belt to fasten his sword to it, I noticed his fingers twitching. He was visibly nervous as he fumbled to secure the weapon. After it was fastened in place, he left our building to join his compatriots in the adjacent compound. We never saw him again. A good guess is that he was killed in the fighting that followed.

I don't know where Ralph went after that, but I found what I thought was a secluded spot about a third of the way up the steps leading to the second floor where I could resume writing up the day's events. It seems incredible, but the city's electrical system was still functioning and, although dim, the 40-watt bulb above me gave enough light to see the pages with some difficulty. I took out my pencil stub and opened my diary to February 3, 1945. As I collected my thoughts, I was interrupted by a shout from someone down in the lobby, "Make way for the guards!"

The next thing I heard was the *clump, clump, clump* of hobnailed boots. Here came a squad of our guards in full battle dress, rifles at port arms, bayonets fixed, helmets strapped to their heads, bandoleers bulging with bullets slung over their shoulders. The last soldier carried in his arms a tray of hand grenades and Molotov cocktails. They obviously meant business. I scooted down the steps as fast as I could to get out of their way. The soldiers continued up the stairs on their way to the third floor of our building, which served as its roof. From that vantage point, which overlooked Quezon Boulevard, our guards could take potshots at the Americans 200 yards away.

After the guards disappeared around the corner of the stairs, I resumed my place on the steps and once again opened my diary. Not a minute passed before Albert Ofner, one of our older internees, came walking down the stairs, gritting his teeth and gripping his bleeding right forearm with his left hand. In the darkness he had been stabbed by the bayonet of one of the guards. Had he obeyed the order to go down to the lobby when the rest of us did, he could

The author standing on the stairs where he sat to write in his diary on the night of Feb. 3, 1945. Photo taken Feb. 1991.

have avoided being injured. Moaning, he continued past me down the steps to get first aid. I still hadn't written a word. *War is hell,* I thought.

I opened my diary for the third time, but before beginning to write, the realization suddenly struck me: *If the tanks breech the wall surrounding Old Bilibid, and we are caught in the crossfire, we could be dead ducks.* My mind raced back to the events that had plunged our family into this life-threatening situation.

We weren't supposed to be in the Philippines at all. Mom and Dad and Charlie and I were on our way to Africa as missionaries when Pearl Harbor was bombed, America was plunged into World War II, and three weeks later we were taken prisoners by the Imperial Japanese Army. During the intervening thirty-seven months we had never doubted that one day our country would liberate us, but it wasn't supposed to happen *this* way. Many imagined liberation coming with the United States Marines charging into camp—and no one getting killed or even wounded! This, in fact, was the way Daphne Bird, our camp artist, pictured liberation in a poster she drew for Christmas 1943, with internees rushing out to greet the tanks, and with boyfriend and girlfriend Charlie and Kay, my brother and his future wife, prominently portrayed in the group.[6] How different reality was turning out to be.

* * * * *

More than three-and-a-half years before, the General Conference of Seventh-day Adventists had appointed my father, Elder Ernest P. Mansell, to the presidency of the Mozambique Mission in Portuguese East Africa. At first the plan was for my parents to sail to Africa from the East Coast of the United States, but on April 16, 1941, the German raider, *Atlantis*, sank the Egyptian liner *Zamzam* in the South Atlantic. Several Seventh-day Adventist (SDA) missionary families traveling on that vessel were taken prisoner, and plans changed. Because our family was visiting relatives in Southern California at the time, the General Conference instructed us to sail from Los Angeles to Africa by way of the Pacific.

A letter from church headquarters in Washington, D.C., dated July 13, 1941, urged "the Mansell family to go to Portuguese East Africa," "without delay."[7] Arrangements were made for us to sail on August 29, 1941, on the *President Monroe*.

What a difference it would have made if we had sailed on that vessel! However, matters beyond our control made sailing on that date impossible. There were too many loose ends to pull together—securing permission from the U.S. government to leave the country under wartime conditions; obtaining passports from the State Department; getting visas from the Portuguese government to enter Mozambique Colony; ordering tickets and purchasing things we would need when we arrived in Africa.

Because World War II was raging in Europe and North Africa, the State Department was reluctant to issue passports. But the biggest hurdle was the foot-dragging by the Portuguese government regarding visas for Mozambique. As a result, our sailing date was postponed until November, when the *President Grant* would sail from Los Angeles.

In the meantime, another obstacle arose. I would turn eighteen on October 7. Would the Selective Service allow me to leave the United States when involvement in World War II seemed imminent? I was in excellent health, and if I were not allowed to leave the country, there was a good possibility I would be drafted. What would happen to me if America were drawn into the war? On the other hand, if I were not drafted, where would I continue my education?

While we wrestled with these problems, the General Conference phoned Dad and told him that, contrary to expectations, the State Department raised no objection to my leaving the country. But now, even though free to leave the United States, I seriously considered staying to attend school. What tipped the scales in favor of going with my parents were my love of adventure and the prospect of traveling to new lands. As for my education, I could attend Helderberg College, an SDA educational institution in South Africa.

Now, as I sat on the stair steps of Old Bilibid, I wondered about the decision I'd made. A loud explosion outside jerked me back to reality. I still hadn't written a thing. The noise outside was making it more and more difficult to concentrate. During a lull, I went to the latrine. Above the walls of our prison the fires hissed like a steak sizzling in a huge frying pan. Clouds of burning embers filled the sky, and ashes kept sifting down like snow into our compound.

After attending to nature's call, I went over near the open cells that served as our camp hospital. Several other internees were standing within the shelter of one of the cells. A spent bullet thudded into the ground some ten or twelve feet from me. I wanted that slug for a souvenir but decided I'd better get back into the shelter of the main building before another projectile found me. I would pick up the bullet in the morning.[8]

---

[1] Donald E. Mansell, transcribed diary, from Jan. 1, 1944, to Feb. 4, 1945, p. 142. (Hereafter designated D. Mansell.)

[2] Old Bilibid Hospital, constructed in 1908 to take care of the health needs of sick prisoners, was in the process of being torn down when the war broke out.

[3] A "cubicle" was what we called the assigned sleeping area allotted to each family or group.

[4] The razing of the building had begun at the top. This was why the third floor served as a "roof."

[5] The main part of the prison was separated from the hospital section where we lived.

[6] Kay was given this drawing as a souvenir.

[7] T. J. M[ichael], associate secretary of the General Conference of Seventh-day Adventists (SDA), letter to E. P. Mansell, dated July 13, 1942.

[8] When I looked for it the next day, it was gone. Someone in the cell block must have gotten it before I did.

CHAPTER

2

Sailing Into a Maelstrom

By mid-October 1941 our sailing date had been set for November 5. Our family would travel on the SS *President Grant*. Beginning at San Pedro, the port for Los Angeles, our itinerary would take us to San Francisco, Honolulu, Manila, Shanghai (if wartime conditions permitted), Singapore, Calcutta, Bombay, and finally Cape Town. From there Mom and Dad would go to Munguluni Mission in Mozambique, and Charlie and I would enroll in one of the SDA secondary schools in South Africa in preparation for attending Helderberg College.

As mentioned previously, the General Conference (GC) had been trying for months to obtain our travel documents, but on November 1 we still didn't have passports or visas, nor had we purchased all the things we would need when we arrived in Africa! During the last two weeks of October a flurry of airmail letters and telegrams flew between Dad and the GC, and between the GC and various agencies, foreign and domestic, that were working on the needed documents, but the wheels of progress turned exasperatingly slowly.

Adding to the frustration of all concerned, the President Line's office notified Dad that the sailing date of the *Grant* had been advanced from November 5 to November 3. Still confident that we would have our passports and visas before we left U. S. territory, the Travel Department of the

GC bought and airmailed our tickets, and sent money for Dad to make necessary purchases. But, if November 5 was a tight schedule, being ready by November 3 seemed impossible.

On November 1, Dad and I went to a second-hand store and bought some old steamer trunks and a used, but very good, Rolleiflex camera. At a gun shop Dad purchased a firearm and ammunition for it.[1] At an appliance store, he bought a state-of-the-art Hallicrafter radio receiver. Mother's entry in her diary for November 3 reflects the pace of our activity. "Much confusion. Returned home to finish packing & closing trunks at 6 P.M. instead of one o'clock. Hurrying! Hurrying! Hurrying! Hungry, tired, & nervous. Aboard at 10 P.M. in the nick of time."[2]

We almost missed the boat. How different our lives would have been if we hadn't made it. But, as I look back on our experience, I believe that what happened was providential. If I had stayed in the U.S. and been drafted and sent to one of the combat zones, I might not have survived the war,[3] and if I had, there is a great probability I wouldn't be a Christian today.

That first night on the *Grant*, we were almost too tired to sleep. Next morning, when we woke up, our ship was sailing north off the California coast en route to San Francisco. In spite of the fact that we still did not have our passports, visas, or shots for overseas travel, the GC kept assuring us that everything was on track and would work out all right. They would make sure we got our vaccinations in San Francisco. If we didn't get our travel documents there, they would be sent airmail-special delivery to Honolulu, and, if worst came to worst, and they didn't reach us in Honolulu, they would be sent to Manila airmail-special delivery on the Pan American Airways *China Clipper*.

We docked in San Francisco at 10:00 A.M. on Friday, November 6. The *Grant* was scheduled to leave port two days later on Sunday evening at 6:00 P.M. Trusting that our travel documents would arrive in time, we all went ashore to do last-minute shopping. Among other things, I bought a diary in which to record events.

On Friday afternoon Dad received a telegram from the GC stating that our passports and visas had been airmailed special delivery to San Francisco in care of a local SDA physician. On Saturday evening the doctor came aboard, handed Dad our travel documents, and gave us the shots needed for overseas travel. We'd made it! What a relief!

UNDER THE SHADOW OF THE RISING SUN

Next day, Sunday, promptly at 6:00 P.M., the *President Grant* loosed its moorings and we were on our way. As our ship churned out through the Golden Gate, we were a bit apprehensive over the tensions building between the United States and the Axis powers, especially Japan. But the latter menace had been alternating between war and peace for months, and we hoped calm would prevail until we reached the Indian Ocean. We were aware, of course, that war was raging in North Africa, but when we reached Africa, we would be at the southern end of the continent. The war would be far away. And yet we couldn't help feeling a bit concerned when we remembered that German raiders had sunk Allied ships in the Indian Ocean. But, as the balmy breezes wafted over the *Grant*, there were times when we almost forgot there was a World War going on in a large part of the planet. The Pacific seemed to be living up to its name—peaceful. We never dreamed that what we were experiencing was the calm before the storm. Even as we sailed, Japan had made the fateful decision to attack the United States.

We were reminded that a war was raging in other parts of the world when we became acquainted with several of the fifty engineers on board the *Grant*. They had contracted with the United States government to build the Burma Road to help China in its war against Japan. Also on board was a family by the name of Middleton. Mr. Middleton was the British consul in Shanghai. He and his family were returning to China from a vacation in America. Charlie and I became friends with their son, André, a young man about our age. We also became acquainted with his sisters, Mireille and Jeanne.

André told us what he knew about the so-called "China Incident" on the Marco Polo Bridge in Shanghai. It was there that Japan started the Sino-Japanese War on a trumped-up charge. We also learned about the absolute ruthlessness of the Japanese military in its infamous "Rape of Nanking." And of course, he had to bring us up-to-date on the war in Ethiopia from the English perspective by singing a ribald ditty about Mussolini being kicked out of Abyssinia at bayonet point by the British.

Our parents made friends with some of the missionaries on board, among them the A. George Rodgers family, British SDA missionaries on their way to India. The Rodgerses had a five-year-old son, Marcus. We also became acquainted with Woody and Sarah Bartges and the Frederick W. Brandauers,[4] Church of the Brethren missionaries bound for China. There were other missionaries on their way to Ceylon (now Sri Lanka), whom we also came to know as friends. Also on board was an SDA businessman, Wolfe Ismond,[5] who had lived in Shanghai and was returning to that city to settle up his business affairs before returning to his wife and children in British Columbia.

In addition to these passengers, there was a passel of English children who, because of the war, were being sent to India to live with relatives. A thirteen-year-old girl in charge of these youngsters did a remarkable job of shepherding them. The youngest of these kids, a mischievous six-year-old named Janet Bruce, enjoyed playing school with Marcus Rodgers. The latter drove the passengers to distraction by shouting over and over at the top of his lungs, "Teacher, teacher, teacher!"

We arrived in Honolulu about sunrise, Monday morning, November 16, and were told that our stay would be brief, so we should not wander far from the ship. As the *Grant* coasted up to the pier to dock, Charlie saw a steel hawser snap and whip around, killing one crewman outright and seriously injuring another. We watched the dead man's body being lowered to the dock, wrapped in a gray blanket and laced into a kind of wire body basket. The wounded man was carried down the gangplank on a stretcher. These tragedies didn't seem to bode well for the future.

The *Grant* was scheduled to sail that evening, but its departure was rescheduled for noon the next day because of the accident. This delay gave Charlie and me, and our friend André, time to go swimming on famous Waikiki Beach. We went ashore with Mom and Dad and stopped at a clothing store, where we bought some dark blue athletic shorts. These shorts had a narrow white stripe down the sides. Before leaving for the beach, Dad gave us strict orders to be back on shipboard before noon. We promised we would be back in plenty of time.

After a refreshing dip in the ocean, we headed back to our vessel, only to learn that the *Grant* had been delayed another day, ostensibly because of the accident, but very possibly because a convoy was being assembled. Whatever the reason, the *Grant* wouldn't be sailing before noon the next day. We boys thought this was wonderful news. Early next morning we again went to Waikiki Beach for a swim and scampered back to our ship well before midday.

The *Grant* left Honolulu on November 17 at about 2:00 P.M. I stood on the starboard side of the ship as it slowly pulled away from the pier. As we passed Pearl Harbor, I admired the mighty U.S. Pacific Fleet anchored in Battle Ship Row. Little did I dream that in less than three weeks most of these ships would be smoldering wrecks, and 2,403 service personnel and civilians would lose their lives. And, of course, I never imagined that our family would become victims of the armed conflict that followed.

As the *Grant* steamed out onto the high seas, I noticed other ships gathering near our vessel—the *Cape Fairweather,* the *American Leader,* the *John Lykes,* and the *Doña Nati,*[6] the latter a Filipino vessel painted gray. All the other ships, including the *Grant,* were painted black. Next morning we awoke to find a United States warship was convoying us. For two days we didn't know its identity, but early on the morning of the third day, it raced up through the middle of our convoy and we were told it was the cruiser, USS *Boise.* We were ordered not to take pictures for security reasons. The presence of this warship made us feel safe.

The food on the *Grant* was delicious and plentiful, and after a week, when I weighed myself, the scale registered 143 lb.[7] This was the most I had ever weighed in my life up to that time. However, it wouldn't be long before I lost all that avoirdupois. Charlie, André, and I spent much of our idle time watching men play cards, oblivious to the possibility that war could break out at any moment. This possibility became a little more real when William S. Tyrrell, captain of the *Grant*[8] (probably at the behest of Captain S. B. Robinson of the *Boise*), ordered a blackout of our ship. That evening the ships were not only under blackout, but our convoy began to zigzag. The purpose for these movements was, of course, to make it more difficult for submarines to sink us, if war should break out. By mid-November, tensions between the United States and Japan were near the breaking point.

On November 25, Thanksgiving Day, we crossed the international date line and "lost" a day. I remember wondering what our family would have done if we had arrived at the 180th meridian on Friday at sundown, the beginning of the Bible Sabbath. Would we have observed the following day, Sunday, along with the Sunday keepers? I should have asked Dad but didn't. I was a teenager and reckoned I could figure it out without his help. Years before Dad had read a little book to our family for morning worship, titled *The Marked Bible,*[9] which told how some people had solved the international date line problem for Sabbath keepers.[10]

On November 27, a rumor went around among the passengers that our convoy was passing through the Caroline Islands, an archipelago under

Japanese mandate, in the midst of which was the island of Guam, an American possession. Jack, one of three sailors on loan to our ship from the *Boise*, pointed out to me a mountain on the horizon and said it was Guam.[11] The reason these navy men were on our ship was to teach semaphore to the engineers going to Burma. Any passenger who wished was encouraged to join the class. Charlie and I attended several sessions and learned the rudiments of spelling out messages by wigwagging flags.

Mom's diary entry for November 29 says, "International situation extremely grave."[12] It was far graver than we had any idea. Only as I write have I learned that our convoy came "close to going right through the Japanese Fleet, which was then assembling for attack [on Pearl Harbor!]."[13] Had the *Boise* intercepted this Strike Force, our naval escort would have alerted the U. S. Navy. The Japanese would then have faced three terrible choices: (1) abort the Pearl Harbor mission; (2) go through with the mission with cover blown; or (3) go to war then and there. If they chose either of the first two alternatives, there is every reason to believe that America would not have been caught napping at Pearl Harbor. If they took the third option, it is unlikely I would be writing this book. I believe God was watching over us, but I mourn the tragic loss of life at Pearl Harbor, which resulted from the Japanese surprise attack on our naval base.

This is what happened from our then limited perspective. While eating dinner, we felt the *Grant* begin rolling from side to side as it slowed to a stop. We wondered why it was slowing down. Our steward said a German raider had been spotted on the horizon. He was wrong. It was the Japanese cruiser *Katori*.[14] Charlie immediately went up on deck and saw the *Boise* catapult a seaplane to investigate. All at once the "raider" puffed a plume of black smoke and disappeared over the horizon. When I finally got up on deck, I saw only the black smoke, but Charlie saw the *Boise*'s hydroplane fly in the direction of the "raider" and return.

The seas were heavy, and while the hydroplane was observing the "raider," Charlie saw the *Boise* turn in circles to calm the waters and make a smooth "landing strip" for the plane. According to witnesses, the plane missed the wake and was damaged when it landed, but remained afloat.[15] When I arrived at the ship's railing, the pilot was standing on the wing of the aircraft, and the *Boise* was in the process of recovering him and the plane.

Vincent Langelo, radioman on the *Boise*, says that his ship's two scout planes patrolled "the area 200 miles ahead of the ship,"[16] but he does not mention that one of these hydroplanes checked on the mysterious ship we saw. However, he seems to allude to this incident when he says:

At 6:40 P.M., *Boise* lookouts sighted a darkened ship . . . at an estimated range of 16,000 yards. The *Boise* immediately went to general quarters and set material condition Affirm. The other ships were alerted by signal light. The ship was hull down, and after a few minutes it appeared on the horizon. [Apparently, this is what Charlie saw.]

In accordance with . . . International Rules and Regulations . . . the *Boise* signalmen sent out the query, "QRA? DE NAQG," which meant, "What is the name of your ship? This is the USS *Boise*."

There was no reply. . . . After five minutes, the *Boise* challenged once more. Still no answer! The *Boise* changed course and speed and got between the unknown ship and the convoy, to be in a better position in case anything happened.

Darkness was setting in fast, and the *Boise* could not identify the flag of the ship. Its silhouette was similar to that of a destroyer, and of course it was presumed to be Japanese. The darkened ship changed course to the left and increased its speed, disappearing over the horizon in a few moments.

This was an ominous situation. If the ship had made a move against any of the ships of the convoy, the *Boise* would have had a fight on its hands. Of course, this would have been a provocation of war, and the *Boise* would have been part of it. It is possible that the Japanese saw our patrol planes and decided to investigate by sending out destroyer patrols.

The *Boise* and the other ships were secured from alert and general quarters, and the rest of the evening transpired without event until 10:53 P.M. The darkened ship was sighted again . . . at a distance of about 13,000 yards. Again, the *Boise* went to general quarters and alerted the other ships. Again, the *Boise* changed to various courses and speeds to interpose between the convoy and the darkened ship. It again challenged the ship with no reply. *Boise* guns tracked the ship wherever it went.

At 11:00 P.M. the darkened ship passed abeam to port of the *Boise* at about 8,000 yards. . . . The ship then increased speed, and a few minutes later disappeared into the darkness. In retrospect, it is quite apparent that the *Boise* came close to going right through the Japanese Fleet which was then assembling for attack [on Pearl Harbor]. This mysterious ship has since been identified as the Japanese cruiser *Katori*.[17]

After sighting this ship shortly before sundown, our family went to bed. Thus, we were completely unaware of the cat-and-mouse maneuverings of the *Katori* between 10:53 and 11:00 P.M., or the fact that "the *Boise's* guns tracked the ship wherever it went." Looking back on what the *Boise's* lookouts saw, it seems almost certain that the mysterious movements of the *Katori* were intended to divert attention from the strike force then assembling to attack Pearl Harbor. I happen to believe that a merciful Providence spared us from death in what could easily have been the beginning of World War II for the United States.

About sundown, December 3, the convoy slowed and began to break up as it neared the San Bernardino Straits. In the northwest and off to our right we could see cone-shaped Mt. Mayon, with a wisp of volcanic smoke rolling upward. Any uneasiness we might have felt crossing the Pacific was quickly dispelled when we entered Philippine waters. The mighty United States was in control here.

That night the *Grant* proceeded slowly along the coast of Southern Luzon. During the early morning hours, while we slept, our ship must have reached the entrance to Manila Bay and stopped. When Charlie and I went up on deck, our ship was dead in the water. As I looked eastward, I could make out Corregidor Island, ahead and slightly to the left. It was silhouetted against the predawn sky. To the right was another smaller island, which we were told was Fort Drum.

After it became light enough to see more clearly, the *Grant* threaded its way slowly through what must have been a minefield. Past this gauntlet, we sailed into Manila Bay and could see in the distance the "Pearl of the Orient"—Manila, capital of the Philippines. About 9:00 A.M. our ship docked at Pier 7, the longest wharf in the Far East at that time.

As soon as the *Grant* tied up to the pier and sailors lowered a gangplank, our family joined the passengers debarking and we walked into Manila. Dad hailed a taxi and directed the cabby to take us to Manila Sanitarium and Hospital, an SDA institution located in the suburb of Pasay. When we arrived there, we were introduced to the Wilcoxes and several other missionary families who lived in cottages on the compound.

While we were visiting with Mrs. Hazel Wilcox,[18] Ralph Longway, wearing suntan shorts and shirt and matching sun helmet, walked in. He and his brother, David, and their mother, Mrs. Inez Longway, had left China for the safety of the Philippines, as recommended by the American government. Elder Ezra L. Longway remained in unoccupied China. Mrs. Longway and David had gone up to Baguio in Northern Luzon, where they lived in a rented apartment. Ralph, fifteen at the time, was boarding at the Wilcoxes' and was attending Manila American High School. I also became acquainted at that time with Wendell, the Wilcoxes' teenage son. Mrs. Wilcox graciously invited us to have lunch at her place, and we gladly accepted.

On Saturday, December 6, our family attended church at Philippine Union College. Dad was asked to preach, and I was asked to tell a mission story for the children's Sabbath School.[19] After services Dr. Louis M. Stump, president of the college, invited our family to have lunch at his home. Later that afternoon, after enjoying a siesta, I took a stroll with some of the students. Most were Filipinos, but some hailed from other countries in the Far East. After an evening of roller-skating at the college gym, Charlie and I spent the night at the homes of a couple of faculty members.[20] I stayed at the home of the M. C. Dyers, who had a daughter, June. Mom and Dad returned to the *Grant* and spent the night on board.[21]

On Sunday morning I went to the college library and read *The Manila Tribune*. A front-page article told about a young man my age, the son of a local chief in the Celebes, who lost his life while pearl diving. Unbeknown to his fellow divers, a giant clam closed its shell over one of his feet and held him fast. When his body was recovered, the clam contained a giant pearl, the largest discovered up to that time. Reading this article made me realize a little better that eighteen-year-olds were not immune to death.

That afternoon our family was taken on a tour of Manila. We saw ROTC cadets drilling on the grassy mall along what was then Dewey Boulevard. In a few weeks many of those young men would either lose their lives on Bataan, die on the Death March, or perish from disease and malnutrition in infamous O'Donnell and Cabanatuan prisoner-of-war (POW) camps.

Sailing Into a Maelstrom

That night Mom and Dad stayed at Manila Sanitarium while Charlie and I returned to the *Grant*. Dad gave us some spending money. On the way to the ship we stopped at a vendor's stand, bought some green coconuts, and drank the delicious juice. This was the first time we had had such a treat since we had been small boys living in Brazil. After discarding the husks, we hired a calesa[22] and rode to the entrance of Pier 7, where we boarded the *Grant* and went to bed.

---

[1]These were bought for the purpose of defending ourselves from wild animals in Africa.

[2]Edith W. Mansell, unpublished diary, from Friday, Oct. 31, 1941, to Friday, Sept. 12, 1942 (in the possession of Donald E. Mansell), p. [1] Fri., Nov. 3, 1941. (Hereafter designated E. Mansell.)

[3]For instance, the Bergamini family, who were interned with us in the Philippines, lost their eldest son, John, in the battle for Guam in 1944.

[4]*American President Line: Guest List.* SS " 'President Grant,' Sailing from Honolulu. November 18, 1941, William S. Tyrrell, Commander," p. 1. (Hereafter designated Guest List.)

[5]Ibid.

[6]E. Mansell, p. 3, Nov. 19, 1941.

[7]Ibid., p. 16, Jan. 30, 1942.

[8]Guest List.

[9]This book is still available at Adventist Book Centers.

[10]A little more than three years later, when I returned to America after liberation, the ship I was traveling on, the *Jean LaFitte*, crossed the international date line on Friday afternoon going from west to east. This time I faced the problem of what to do with two Sabbaths in succession. I reasoned that if people could set the international date line at the 180th meridian (actually the line zigzags from north to south to avoid certain island groups), why couldn't I set it a few hundred miles farther east and have one Sabbath followed by two successive Sundays? Right or wrong, I kept the first day as the Sabbath and washed my clothes the next day.

[11]Vincent A. Langelo, *With All Our Might: [The WWII History of the USS Boise]* (Austin, Tex.: Eakin Press, 2000), p. 28. Until June 5, 2002, I had always assumed that our convoy sailed south of Guam. After reading this book, I realized that our convoy "passed north of Guam Island" (Langelo, p. 37). An overcast sky on the day the island of Guam was pointed out to me is the reason for my misconception.

[12]E. Mansell, p. 4, Nov. 29, 1941.

[13]Langelo, pp. 27, 28.

[14]Ibid., 28. Edwin T. Layton, Rear Admiral U.S.N. (Ret.), with Captain Roger Pineau, U.S.N.R. (Ret.), and John Costello, *And I Was There* (New York: William Morrow, 1985), p. 212: "That evening [Nov. 28, 1941], some eight hundred miles from Japan, out in the northern Pacific, the ships of Admiral Nagumo's *Kido Butai* (literally Mobile Force but more accurately Striking force) were rolling and pitching their way eastward. Despite the rising heavy seas the *Kido Butai*'s oil-hungry destroyers and four carriers had successfully completed their first scheduled refueling operation.

" 'A good beginning,' Commander Tomatsu Oishi noted in his diary. Lookouts had been increased after the Kwajalein radio relayed a report from cruiser *Katori* that an American light cruiser, escorting five transports, had been spotted east of Saipan. This was *Boise* shepherding a convoy of troop reinforcements toward the Philippines, but her captain [S. B. Robinson] did not make a sighting report of the Japanese ships until his force reached Manila a week later on 4 December."

[15] E. Mansell, p. 4, Dec. 1, 1941: "[We] saw the airplane crash into the water."

[16] Langelo, p. 27.

[17] Ibid., pp. 27, 28.

[18] E. Mansell, p. 4., Dec. 4, 1941.

[19] Ibid., p. 4, Dec. 6, 1941.

[20] Ibid., p. 5, Dec. 7, 1941.

[21] Ibid.

[22] A light, horse-drawn vehicle used in the Philippines for transportation.

"Pearl Harbor Has Been Bombed!"

About sunrise Monday, December 8,[1] Charlie and I awoke to the sound of rapping on our cabin window. It was André. When we opened the shutter, he said, "The radio just announced that Pearl Harbor has been bombed." André was such a jokester that we didn't believe him. However, minutes later all doubts vanished when our steward knocked at the door of our cabin and told us Japan had bombed Pearl Harbor and Captain Tyrrell had ordered all passengers off the ship. That was the last time we saw André. We never learned what happened to him and his family. Because his father was a diplomat, the family may have been repatriated to England.

As soon as Charlie and I heard that America had been attacked and we had been ordered off the ship, we leaped out of bed, dressed, and raced up to the purser's office, where I phoned Dad at Manila Sanitarium. I told him that Pearl Harbor had been bombed. He already knew. I told him that all the passengers had been ordered off the ship. What should we do? Dad told us to pack the things in our cabin and stay on board if at all possible. He and Mom would come shortly. He further instructed us that if we had to get off the ship, to stay on Pier 7 as close to the gangplank as possible. If ordered off the pier, we were to meet him as close to the entrance to the dock as possible.

As Charlie and I left the purser's office, we heard the roar of planes. They were coming from the north. We were on the south side of the ship. If the planes were Japanese, I hoped the bulk of the ship would shelter us from exploding bombs. Five or six fighters flew over. As they passed to our left, I was relieved to see a blue star in a white circle on their wing tips. These were the first and last American planes we would see for more than a thousand days. After the planes disappeared over Cavite Navy Yard, Charlie and I hurried down to our cabin and began packing our hand luggage as fast as we could. Somehow we managed to stay out of sight, or at least we were not again ordered off the ship.

Mom and Dad arrived about 9:00 A.M. In the meantime Charlie and I had heard that many of the passengers were transferring from the *Grant* to the *President Coolidge,* which was docked on the opposite side of Pier 7. Among those changing ships were the fifty engineers headed for the Burma Road, the English children going to India, and the missionary families bound for Ceylon. The *Coolidge* was building up steam in preparation for leaving port in a few hours. Dad realized that if we were going to transfer to that vessel, we would have to let the authorities on the *Grant* know our plans immediately.

Dad and I went over to the starboard side of the *Coolidge.* Dad was not one to make snap decisions. He didn't say anything for several minutes, but I knew he was praying. The ship's crew was working feverishly to get their vessel ready to sail. Dad studied the activity for several minutes. When at last he spoke, he was decisive. "We stand a better chance on land than at sea." And that was that. Dad had been a soldier in World War I, and his experience in all probability had a bearing on his decision. The safety of his family came first. His mind made up, Dad asked the *Grant* authorities to off-load our baggage as soon as possible, explaining that our church organization in the Philippines would look after us.

Looking back with hindsight—and from the human standpoint—what a difference it would have made if we had transferred to the *Coolidge.* We didn't know then, and in fact didn't know until after the war, but both the *Coolidge* and the *Grant* made it safely out of the war zone.

Because of the hazards these ships faced, we felt sorry for those passengers who had no choice but to transfer to the *Coolidge* or stay on the *Grant.* From a purely human point of view, they faced the terrible risk of losing their lives if their ships were sent to the bottom. Yet they made it out safely. Thus, from the human point of view, they were the "lucky ones," and we who opted to get off the ship and were taken prisoners three weeks later, were the "unlucky ones." But, from the spiritual viewpoint, I know God led Dad to make the right decision. I have every reason to believe I would not be a Christian today if I had not gone through the internment camp experience. "God never leads His children otherwise than they would choose to be led, if we could see the end from the beginning."[2]

While Dad returned to the ship to oversee the off-loading of our baggage, he sent me to the customs office to keep an eye on our baggage when it arrived. Because we were only passing through the Philippines, Dad hoped the inspection would be over by early afternoon. In the meantime, our SDA leaders in Manila decided to evacuate their families to Baguio, and recommended we do the same. They feared that Manila would be bombed and that, if the Japanese succeeded in landing, the capital would become the focus of vicious house-to-house fighting. No one imagined that Manila would be declared an open city, or guessed that the main Japanese landings would be on Lingayen Gulf, just twenty miles west of Baguio.

Dad hoped we could take the express train leaving Manila for Damortis on Lingayen Gulf that afternoon. So, to hurry things along, he spoke to Elder Samuel L. Frost and asked if he could possibly take our hand luggage and me to the train station. Elder Frost was happy to oblige, and early in the afternoon he drove me to the depot, where he dropped me off, then left to attend to personal business. Meanwhile Dad went to the train ticket office to buy tickets for our family and arrange for our baggage to be transported to Baguio the next day. But there were too many delays and loose ends to gather up, making it impossible to leave that day.[3]

The plaza in front of the train station was swarming with Filipinos, all anxious to get out of the city. Everyone seemed convinced that the Japanese would bomb the station at any moment, and, of course, I was thinking the same thing. To get my mind off the danger, I chatted with a Philippine Constabulary soldier standing nearby. He was short and sported a gold crown with a white, heart-shaped center on one of his incisors. The white enamel heart showed through when he smiled. I'd never before seen that kind of dental artistry and was fascinated. Although he appeared outwardly calm, I discovered that he was just as nervous as I and everyone else was, if not more so.

The Filipinos milling around the plaza intrigued me. The younger women were charming in their blouses of light-colored chiffonlike material with little peaks on the shoulders. The young men wore colorful shirts called *barongs*. Some of the older women smoked cigarillos with the lighted end in their mouths. How they kept from burning their tongues, I still don't know. The incidence of mouth, throat, and lung cancer among them must have been high.

It was about dusk when Dad at last arrived in a taxi to pick me up. He said he had only been able to purchase tickets for a train that would leave the next morning.[4] He and I helped the driver load our suitcases into the trunk of his vehicle, after which the cabby whisked us off to Manila Sanitarium. On the way Dad made arrangements for the driver to pick us up at four the next morning and bring us to the station.

I had eaten nothing since breakfast, and neither had the rest of the family. William E. ("Ed") Guthrie, manager of the Sanitarium, arranged for us to have supper in the cafeteria. The Philippine government had decreed a nationwide blackout, so we ate by a dim blackout light, shaded according to the regulation issued that day. After we ate, Mr. Guthrie and Edna Stoneburner, the head nurse, showed us to a large room on the second floor at the front of the Sanitarium building where we could bed down for the night. The stiflingly hot and humid air made it difficult for us to sleep, but after a while we dozed off.

We were awakened around 2:00 A.M. by the wail of air-raid sirens. We got up in our nightclothes, dashed to the windows at the front of the building, and looked out. The whole city was cloaked in darkness, but the stars were out and the moon was shining. Mr. Guthrie, Miss Stoneburner, and other hospital personnel soon joined us. Above the wail of sirens we could hear the distant hum of planes approaching. In a few minutes we saw the blazing trails of what we assumed must be antiaircraft rounds rising high into the sky.

Months later we were told that what we saw were rockets sent up by fifth columnists (traitors) to mark out the location of Nichols Field. True or not, these fireworks reassured us that the armed forces of the United States were on their toes. As we watched, we saw the flash of exploding bombs and heard their terrifying rumble seconds later. After the fires that the bombs ignited were doused, we went back to bed, but sleep wouldn't come.

We got up at 3:30 A.M., washed and dressed, and went downstairs to a breakfast of papaya, toast, and Postum. A few minutes after we finished, the taxi driver arrived and we hurried out to help load our suitcases into his vehicle. We had only gone a few blocks when a squad of soldiers at a roadblock stopped us. The corporal in charge refused to let us proceed. Reversing course, our cabby worked his way through the streets trying to find an alternate route. Again we were stopped and turned back. Our driver tried a third route. This time he was successful in getting us through. When we arrived at the train station, we off-loaded our baggage, Dad paid and tipped the cabby, and we looked for a place to wait until the great iron gates opened.

"Pearl Harbor Has Been Bombed!"

By now it was six o'clock, two-and-a-half hours before our train was scheduled to depart. The plaza was almost empty that early in the morning, so we easily found a place near the large, wrought-iron gates leading into the marshaling yards. As the minutes dragged by, the plaza began filling rapidly with people. In less than an hour thousands of Filipinos, streaming in from all directions, filled it completely. Everyone was obviously anxious to leave the city.

While we waited, Dad quietly gave us instruction about what to do in case the train was bombed or strafed. He warned us not to take seats inside the coaches. If the train were attacked, he said, those inside the coaches stood less of a chance of surviving than those near an exit. Besides, he continued, if we were inside, and even if we didn't get killed by bullets or shrapnel, we risked being trampled to death by panicky passengers desperate to get out.

The station portals swung open promptly at 8:00 A.M. and the mass of humanity gathered in the plaza surged forward. Although Dad had purchased first-class tickets, we had no idea how far up the station platform the first-class coaches were, nor did we know whether the train would pull out promptly at 8:30 or perhaps would even leave ahead of schedule because of the outbreak of war. So, lugging our heavy suitcases, we struggled along until we came to one of the first coaches at the tail end of the train. Dad felt sure we could locate the first-class cars at the next stop. Following Dad's advice, we let the coach fill up before we took our places by the exits.

Mom found a place on the little verandah at the front end of the coach. Charlie and I waited until our two adjacent coaches filled up, then grabbed the handrails and stood on the steps. Dad took a place on the coupling between our two coaches and held onto the end of the coach where Mom was standing. Typical of Dad, he insisted on taking the most dangerous place. As a young man, he had "hopped" many a freight.

The engineer must have been in a hurry, because when the clock struck 8:30,[5] the whistle blew, the train lurched, crept out of the station, and gained momentum as it chugged along. At last we were on our way up into the mountains and safety—or so we thought.

---

[1] Sunday, December 7, on the American side of the date line.
[2] Ellen G. White, *The Desire of Ages* (Nampa, Idaho: Pacific Press, 1898), p. 224.
[3] E. Mansell, p. 5, Dec. 9, 1941.
[4] Ibid.
[5] Edith W. Mansell, *The Fall of Baguio by a Participant,* unpublished monograph (in possession of Donald E. Mansell), p. [1], "Taken from [her] Diary." (Hereafter designated E. Mansell, participant.)

CHAPTER
4

Flight to the Mountains

While our family waited for the coaches to fill up, Dad quietly gave us final instructions about what to do in case the train was attacked. He said we should jump, cover our faces, roll into a ball, and try to find cover in the ditch beside the tracks. But now, as the train sped along, we could see that the depression along the tracks was thick with vegetation and in places was littered with garbage. Not only that, but we didn't know what else we might find in the ditches to "welcome" us if we jumped.

The tropical sun beat down mercilessly, and the humidity must have been above 90 percent. As the train moved along, our Filipino fellow travelers kept up a constant chatter in Tagalog, a language we didn't understand. There were no other Caucasians on board. We concluded we must look like a bunch of crazy Americans—which we were. The Filipinos were friendly, and if this was what they thought of us, they politely said nothing. From time to time the train made brief stops,[1] but never long enough to get off and find the first-class coaches because of our heavy suitcases. So, we stayed where we were. It was better to ride third class than not ride at all.

About 3:00 P.M. our train came to a stop in the middle of rice fields. We wondered why. After a while the people on all the coaches began getting off, and a kind traveler told us in Filipino English that "De Japs hab bombed de tracks, sir." He added that our train was just south of Tarlac, the midpoint of our journey. We would have to walk across the rice fields on the dikes to Highway 3. Buses would take us from there to the train station where we would board another train that would take us to Damortis, the end of the line. We were glad to hear this and thanked our friend.

From the train to Highway 3 was more than half a mile. We got a little help from some of our Filipino friends, who also had their own loads to carry. Even so, by the time we reached the highway the trek seemed like fifty miles. When we finally reached the highway, our friends helped us heave our luggage onto one of the waiting buses. We thanked them, then climbed aboard and sat down—tired, sweaty, and hungry.

When we arrived at the Tarlac train station, we were met by our shipmates, Woody and Sarah Bartges and the Brandauers. They had been riding first class all the way and wondered why we hadn't ridden first class as well. Hadn't anyone from our mission helped us find the first-class coaches? We had to admit that no one had.

In Tarlac, we found an empty first-class coach all to ourselves and settled in a compartment near an exit. Because the train was behind schedule and was expected to leave at any moment, we decided not to risk getting off to buy food.

Out on the station platform we heard a young man hawking some wares. *"Balut! Balut!"* he cried. Dad caught his attention, and he came over to the window of our coach. Dad saw he was selling eggs and asked, "Are the eggs boiled?"

"Oh, yes, sir," the fellow assured Dad. "They are beetty [very] good, sir."

Dad bought a dozen eggs. After the young vendor had gone his way, Mom cracked open one of the eggs.

"Look at this!" she exclaimed. "A chick! This egg must have been pulled out from under a setting hen!" The chick was almost ready to hatch.

We all stared in surprise and disgust. Dad cracked open a second egg. Another chick! Moments later Charlie cracked open a third egg. A third chick! We assumed, correctly, that the remaining nine eggs were in the same condition. Who would rob a clutch of eggs from under a brooding hen, then boil and sell them? Was this some kind of a joke?

Hungry as we were, and knowing full well that a chick develops from the contents of an egg, we simply could not overcome our feelings of revulsion. It was those eyes that kept staring at us. About this time someone informed us that *baluts* were a Filipino delicacy. A hen was allowed to sit on a fertilized egg for twenty days. (It takes twenty-one days for a chick to hatch.) On the twentieth day the egg is boiled and eaten as a *balut*.[2] We chuckled at our predicament and decided it was either learn to eat *baluts* or go hungry. We never learned. About sunset the train pulled out of Tarlac and headed for Damortis. I don't remember, but we may have given the *baluts* to some of the Filipino passengers, or more probably, we tossed those eggs out the train window when we were "far from the madding crowd."

We reached Damortis around nine or ten that evening and detrained. While Mom, Charlie, and I waited by our suitcases, Dad looked around for a taxi to take us to Baguio. Someone who claimed he was acquainted with the roads, warned us not to go up Naguilian Road at night. It was winding, narrow, and extremely dangerous, especially at night and in a blackout. I don't know, but maybe the man was a local hotel owner. Meanwhile, Dad returned with a taxi. The driver assured us that there was no danger and that he knew the road like the palm of his hand. We had no choice but to believe him, since we had no intention of staying in a hotel in Damortis. After stowing our luggage in the trunk of his vehicle, we began the "perilous" ascent. The moon was full, the sky cloudless, and, contrary to what we had been told, the road was in good shape.

We arrived at the police station in Baguio at exactly midnight. When the officials were satisfied that we were who we claimed to be, Dad asked one of them where we could find lodging for the rest of the night. He said that Pines Hotel was full. Another official volunteered that Washington Hotel on Session Road had vacancies. Our taxi driver took us there and helped us take our luggage into the lobby. Dad paid and tipped him, and he left.

A sleepy night clerk handed Dad a registration form. Dad filled it out and handed it back. Before the clerk showed us to our room, Dad mentioned that we hadn't eaten anything since early the previous morning and asked if we might have a bite to eat. The clerk wakened a young hotel employee, who served us a light meal. When we finished, he showed us to a room on the second floor on the street side of the building. As soon as the door was closed, we put on our pajamas, fell exhausted into bed, and were soon asleep. At last we were safe—or so we thought.

---

[1]E. Mansell, p. 5, Dec. 9, 1941.

[2]Many years later a Filipino friend confided that although he enjoyed *baluts*, he ate them in the dark. They tasted oh so good, but he couldn't stand the sight of the chick looking at him.

CHAPTER
5

The Enemy Lands Twenty Miles Away

Our family woke up about 7:30 A.M. to the roar of approaching planes. We heard no air-raid alarm, only the roar of motors. Dashing to the window overlooking Session Road, we threw open the curtains, expecting to see American planes. The belated wail of what sounded more like a foghorn than an air-raid siren answered our question. Looking up, we saw three twin-engine fighter-bombers in formation flash across Session Road at rooftop level. They were so close that we could clearly see the rising sun[1] under their wing tips. We only glimpsed them for an instant, but it was long enough to know they weren't American planes. The buildings on the other side of the street obscured our view beyond. We waited to hear the report of exploding bombs, but none came. But, bombs or no bombs, the war was coming uncomfortably close.

Soon the all clear sounded, we showered, dressed, and went downstairs for breakfast. After the first full meal we'd eaten in many hours, we gathered around the radio in the hotel lobby and listened to the news. Reports coming in from KZRH in Manila and KGEI in San Francisco gave continuous updates of what had happened at Pearl Harbor and elsewhere on the "day of infamy." Among other announcements, we learned that the U.S. Congress had declared war on Japan. But the reports that concerned us most were those coming in from Radio Manila telling about Japanese landings at various points in the Philippines.

When we tired of listening to the discouraging news, Dad and I left the hotel to look for a store where we could buy staples. Although this was only December 10, we found the stores on Session Road virtually empty of food. The locals had naturally bought up almost everything. At last we did find a Chinese store near the lower end of Session Road that still had a few expensive items left on the shelves, but about all we bought were some small glasses of chipped beef. The price was exorbitant, but Dad purchased several glasses anyway.

On our way back to the hotel we met several SDA missionaries—elders Frost and William Hilliard, and nurses Pauline Neal and Emma Pflug. Elder Frost introduced us to them. The women told about a harrowing experience some of the China Division women secretaries had had two days before. Eighteen Japanese planes had dropped bombs on Camp John Hay, a U. S. Army post used by Army personnel for rest and recreation situated about a mile southeast of the hotel. Eleven men had been killed and twenty-two wounded.[2] One plane in the formation that scouted the Baguio airfield dropped more bombs. One of these missiles fell between the house where the secretaries lived and the house next door, where several missionaries of other denominations were living. Fortunately, none of the missionaries were killed or injured, but tragically, the owner of the latter house, Mr. Rivera,[3] was decapitated by a shrapnel fragment, and a servant girl was badly wounded in the cheek and face. Mary Ogle, one of the secretaries, helped her get to the hospital for emergency treatment. Nurses Neal and Pflug were on their way to Manila, where, they believed, it would be safer.

A few doors up the hill from Washington Hotel was a Philippine Army recruiting station. After leaving the chipped beef with Mom, I walked up there. A young Filipino about my age, smartly dressed in a suntan uniform, was standing in front of the station, holding a Springfield rifle. When I spoke to him, he urged me to volunteer.[4] It was my patriotic duty, he said. My first impulse was to sign up, but calmer judgment prevailed.

Just before I turned eighteen, Dad had told me that war isn't a game. Death is for keeps. Without proper training, about all a raw recruit is good for is "cannon fodder." The expression stuck with me. Besides, Dad had said, while SDAs should be the best of citizens and should support their country to the best of their ability, we drew the line at taking human life. We serve the nations of which we are citizens by saving life, not taking it.[5] So, thanking the young recruiter for his invitation, I walked back to the hotel.

That afternoon, Dad left the hotel and went house hunting. Later, when he returned, he said his search was unproductive. Next morning, December 11, he again went in search of an apartment to rent, while Mom, Charlie, and I sat around the radio listening to the news. One of the startling reports that came over the airwaves was that the British battleships H.M.S. *Repulse* and *Prince of Wales* had been torpedoed and sunk by Japanese planes off the coast of Malaya. A mother and daughter, both of whom spoke perfect English and were guests at the hotel, seemed quietly jubilant when the bulletin was broadcast. Mom said later that she believed they were Nazi sympathizers. Whoever they were, they were not interned in our camp.

That afternoon Dad again went house hunting. This time I went with him. As we walked down Session Road, the air-raid alarm at the ice plant suddenly blared forth. We heard approaching planes and sought cover in a doorway almost directly across from the Chinese Bakery & Grocery Store, where we had purchased the chipped beef the day before. A middle-aged man in civilian clothes, rather tall for a Filipino, took cover with us. He was carrying a Springfield rifle.

All eyes and ears focused on three enemy planes that circled the city. The aircraft then headed back in the direction from whence they had come. They dropped no bombs. The all clear sounded, and we assumed the raid must be over. Suddenly the planes circled back. This time they unloaded their missiles before the air-raid alarm could warn people. Someone yelled that their target was the ice plant, where the air-raid siren was located. As the planes flew north again, the man with the rifle darted out onto the sidewalk. Pointing his gun up at the planes, he squeezed off a couple of rounds, and then dashed back to the safety of the doorway. Other armed civilians did the same, but all these "marksmen" missed their target.

On Friday, December 12, Dad finally found an upstairs apartment for rent. It was located at No. 3 Legarda Road and was owned by a gracious Filipino family named Santos. We could rent the apartment, but first they wanted to fix it up. We could move in on Monday. Dad signed a contract with Mr. Santos.

Meanwhile, we were concerned about our baggage left in Manila. One of our missionary friends, who remained in the capital, promised to see that our things were shipped to us. But would our goods be lost en route? We certainly hoped not. Dad said that if our things came through, the living

The Santoses' house on No. 3 Legarda Road, where the Mansells lived in the upstairs apartment. Photo taken Feb. 1991.

room at the head of the stairs on the second floor of our apartment could easily accommodate all thirty-seven pieces of baggage.

That afternoon I went to Loakan Road, where the missionaries were staying. Ralph gave me a guided tour of the place and showed me the bomb damage and the place where Mr. Rivera had been killed and the restroom where the maid had been wounded. I also saw a truck pass by with ten or twelve Japanese men under guard on their way to internment in Camp John Hay.

On Saturday morning, December 13, the Seventh-day Adventists gathered at the home of Mrs. Longway. This was the shrapnel-riddled house on Loakan Road, near the entrance to Camp John Hay, through which Ralph had taken me on a guided tour the previous day. Mrs. Longway lived in the front of the building with Ralph and David. The China Division female secretaries occupied the rear of the house. The Longway apartment had sustained relatively little damage compared to the rest of the building, so Mrs. Longway invited us to meet in her upstairs living room for Sabbath School and preaching service.

Whoever organized the Sabbath School program for that day must have had war on his or her mind. The leader had chosen for the opening hymn, "Sound the Battle Cry, Lo! The Foe Is Nigh!"[6] We had hardly begun singing when the air-raid alarm sounded. The "foe" was "nigher" than we expected. Everything stopped. There was no panic. We all walked calmly down the stairs and across the grassy circle in front of Camp John Hay, and waited in the woods for the "all clear." When it sounded, we returned to the Longway apartment and resumed Sabbath School. We were no sooner comfortably settled, when a second air-raid warning wailed. We repeated our exit procedure. Again we could hear planes, but none came close.

By the third air-raid alarm, we were getting used to the exit drills. This time, however, the planes were closer. I had just reached the edge of Military Circle, when suddenly someone (I think it was Ralph) yelled, *"Bombs!"* We all dropped to the ground. Ralph told me later that he looked up and saw what appeared to be grains of sand falling out of the belly of the aircraft.

The bombers were directly overhead when they unloaded. The trajectory of these bombs should have told us that these aerial missiles would land far beyond us and in Camp John Hay, but we weren't taking any chances and hugged the ground. Seconds later we heard the bombs explode about a mile away. This was followed by plumes of brownish gray smoke that billowed up beyond the tree line in the military post.

When the all clear sounded, we dashed for cover in the wooded ravine on the far side of Military Circle. We all agreed that the better part of wisdom was to stay in the woods for the rest of the church services. However, no more planes appeared that day.

About noon our family returned to Washington Hotel. After lunch Dad and Charlie and I walked to Otek Street, where the Wittschiebes, the Knights, the Dinsbiers, and Miss Thora Thomsen, our Danish nurse, lived. We boys, together with Helen Wittschiebe, Billy Knight, and our dads, went for a Sabbath afternoon walk through the lower part of town and through Burnham Park. On the way we inspected the city's makeshift air-raid shelters—just in case we ever needed to use them. These subterranean places of refuge consisted of large concrete ducts five or six feet in diameter. They lay under the streets in the downtown section of the city. They were storm drains designed to carry off excess rainwater that fell during the typhoon season. Entrances had been dug down to these conduits.

After inspecting these hastily improvised shelters, we walked over to beautiful Burnham Park. At the far end were two concentric cement circles. In the center was a bandstand. The circles were used for roller-skating. Four connecting concrete entrances led from the outer circle to the inner circle. Around the outer circle were park benches on which people could sit and watch the skaters, or sit and listen while a band played. After spending a couple of hours familiarizing ourselves with this section of the city, Dad and Charlie and I returned to our hotel. The others went to their house on Otek Street.

Monday morning, December 15, our family went to the public market at the foot of Session Road, not far from the improvised air-raid shelters, and purchased black crepe paper to make blackout shades for the windows and lights of our apartment. We also purchased some lightweight blankets, because we had been told that during the winter months it got chilly at night. Although Luzon is considered tropical, Baguio, situated in a bowl-like depression almost a mile above sea level, can get uncomfortably cold at night in December and January.

Most of our idle hours while we waited to move into the Santoses' apartment were spent sitting in the hotel lobby listening to the war news. The situation was getting worse by the hour. A newscaster on Manila radio named Don Bell (Ralph told me later that his real name was Clarence Beliel) reported that the Japanese had landed at Aparri, Vigan, and Legazpi— the first two on the north and west coasts of Luzon, the latter at the southeastern extremity of the island.

We moved into the Santoses' apartment Monday afternoon. After lugging our suitcases upstairs, Mom put us boys to work making blackout shades. About 1:00 P.M. nine enemy planes flew over and dropped leaflets. They urged the Filipinos to "throw off the yoke of American colonial oppression." The appeal did not achieve the desired result. We were glad that the Filipinos were our friends.

As the days passed, events seemed to move ever more quickly. On the afternoon of December 16, we heard a truck stop in front of our apartment. We went down to investigate and saw that it was loaded with our belongings. Although the truck brought fewer than half of our pieces of baggage, what it brought was the fifteen largest crates. We helped the men off-load these items and lug them upstairs. Dad paid the driver well, and the man promised to deliver the remaining twenty-two pieces the next day.

After storing our things in the upstairs living room, we immediately opened the boxes containing cooking utensils, dishes, and flatware, so Mom could begin setting up housekeeping. Almost at once she discovered that many of the things she needed most were in the boxes that were not delivered, but we thanked God for what we got and prayed that the rest of our goods would arrive as promised.

Next morning we were pleasantly surprised when the truck drove up with the remaining twenty-two boxes, trunks, and crates. Not a thing was missing. Again we thanked God; this time, because we had lost nothing. It was only later that we learned how really fortunate we were. At that very time Japanese transports were headed south toward Lingayen Gulf. Had our goods been delayed just five days, we would have lost them all. We were blessed in another way too, although we didn't realize it at the time. When the Japanese took Baguio, the houses of Americans residing in the city were looted, but because our things were stored in the home of a Filipino family, and the Japanese were eager to win the Filipinos over to their cause, our things were not touched. In the end, of course, we lost everything, including many irreplaceable mementos. But while we were interned Mr. Santos was able to send some of our most needed items into camp.

Months later, when most Filipinos had failed to cooperate in establishing Japan's Greater East Asia Co-prosperity Sphere (Ralph called it the "Co-poverty Sphere"), they were badly treated. This was especially true of Filipino soldiers and civilians who fought against Japan. But even so, Filipino houses were seldom looted.

Among the things contained in our baggage were 50,000 sulfa pills of various kinds, which the White Memorial Hospital in Los Angeles had given Dad for mission use in Africa. These drugs were the antibiotics of the early 1940s. After we were interned, Mr. Santos sent the bulk of these life-saving medicines to us, and Dad, in turn, donated them to our hospital.

In her book, *Worth the Price,* Mary Ogle says:

> Brother Mansell . . . [was] taking a large quantity of medicines and supplies to one of our hospitals in Africa. We felt that God . . . had a hand in the preservation of those medical supplies and in enabling Elder Mansell to get them into camp. The sulfa drugs were very new at that time, and . . . [our] doctors . . . were very thankful to have the good supply of these and other medicines that Elder Mansell turned over to them.[7]

These pills saved many lives and were greatly appreciated by the internees.

On Sabbath, December 20, we decided not to take any chances on having our services interrupted by air raids, so this time we gathered for

Sabbath School and church in the wooded ravine across from Military Circle. No planes came near Baguio that day. After church we returned to our apartment and ate lunch. In the afternoon Dad and Charlie went for a walk while Mom and I stayed home and read.

On Sunday the 21st, we heard muffled explosions and went outside to investigate. Looking toward the northwest we saw a plume of grayish black smoke mushrooming up over the treetops. Mr. Santos said it came from the destruction of oil tanks at Poro, down on Lingayen Gulf. He said this was done to keep them from falling into enemy hands.

As we watched the smoke billow up, Mom spoke to Dad in Portuguese and used the word *inimigos*—enemies. Mr. Santos, who spoke Spanish, took exception to Mom's remark because he thought she was saying that his countrymen were *enimigos* (the same word in Spanish), and blaming them for sabotaging the oil supplies. Mom explained that she was referring to the Japanese, not the Filipinos. The explanation calmed the troubled waters.

That night, after Mom and Charlie and I had gone to bed, Mr. Santos invited Dad to come downstairs to listen to the news on his radio. Apparently he wanted to make amends for misunderstanding Mom's remark. About midnight an alarming news flash came over the airwaves—the Japanese were landing on Lingayen Gulf, and it was reported that one spearhead was moving toward Baguio! Dad came upstairs immediately and woke us up.

"The Japs are coming up the hill," he announced quietly but urgently. "Boys, take the gun and ammunition and run up the road and get rid of them."

Charlie and I dressed hurriedly, grabbed the ordnance, and ran up Legarda Road about half a mile. We dumped the stuff in some tall grass under a bush and covered it with leaves.[8] On the way back, we spotted a bonfire blazing away in a backyard. People were standing around it. We shouted for them to douse the flame. They immediately extinguished the blaze. As Charlie and I hurried back to our apartment, we speculated: Were these people "fifth columnists" trying to signal the Japanese who were coming up the hill?

On the afternoon of the 22nd, Dad and I attended a meeting of American citizens in the annex of Rev. Carl Eschbach's United Church of Christ. The church was situated near the public market. The purpose of the meeting was to discuss what measures to take in light of the Japanese landings on the coast earlier that day. After this was discussed at length, the question came up: Why were the radio news reports from Manila so different from eyewitness accounts of what was going on down on the coast?

In an effort to give the benefit of the doubt to whoever was broadcasting the rosy but inaccurate newscasts, Dr. Lloyd Cunningham, who had a speech impediment, stammered, "It's l-l-l-like P-p-p-postum, there's a r-r-r-reason."[9] It became evident that the American military didn't want civilian morale to sink any lower than it had already sunk. During this meeting I learned that truth is the first casualty in wartime.

When the chairman asked for volunteers to serve as air-raid look-outs on Mt. Santo Tomás, Dad and I offered to serve on Christmas Day.[10] The mountain, 7,200 feet above sea level and several miles west of Baguio, overlooked Lingayen Gulf. From there, spotters could see enemy bombers heading toward Baguio several minutes before they reached the city and telephone the information to the air-raid warden, who could then give the people time to take cover. The spotters also had a ringside view of the landings.

The day after the Japanese landed on Lingayen Gulf, Baguio's mayor and the City Council fled. After initially frustrating efforts were made to get permission from military headquarters on Bataan to authorize Col. Horan to put the former mayor, Eusebius Julius ("E. J.") Halsema, in charge of the city, authorization from General Jonathan Wainwright was finally received to do just that. Thus, on December 24, the colonel put Halsema in charge of Baguio and named several prominent citizens to assist him in maintaining order and keeping the city's services functioning. This arrangement lasted only a couple of days, after which the civil authorities resumed their posts and arranged for the city to be handed over "peaceably" to the Japanese.[11] Among those named to assist Halsema were Elmer Herold and John Woodson, who were subsequently interned with us.[12]

As for Col. Horan, he beat a hasty retreat from the doomed city,[13] and reportedly never assisted in any way the armed forces of the United States and the Philippines battling on Bataan and Corregidor. He was later captured and survived the war.[14] When he deserted Baguio, the Japanese internees were left "for 36 hours without food, light, or water."[15] Acting Mayor Halsema and Mr. Herold visited the "Jap prisoners at [Camp] John Hay to see if they had enough food." When they learned that they did not, they sought and got authorization to feed them. During the ensuing transition,

Halsema and Herold were given letters by a local Japanese civilian, Mr. Henry Hayakawa, stating that they had lived up to International Law and had helped feed the civilian Japanese POWs.[16] I am sure that these humanitarian acts mitigated the cruel treatment for which our captors were renowned for meting out to defeated enemies. Most of us internees were unaware of these deeds of mercy, and as a result many of us did not appreciate what the Halsemas, and especially the Herolds, did on our behalf.

On December 23, Mr. Santos told Dad that he and his family were evacuating Baguio and hinted that we should do likewise. Although he didn't say so, we got the impression he was afraid that if the Japanese found Americans living in his house when they entered the city, they would ransack it, and I'm sure they would have if they had found us living there. However, our problem was that, whereas the Santoses had friends outside the city who could take them in, we were in a strange country. What should we do? Where could we go? We didn't know, but we could pray, and we did pray.

We were unaware at the time, but the day before, on December 22, the leaders of the SDA missionaries in Baguio had decided that, when the Japanese took the city, it would be safer if we were all together in one place rather than scattered. When, on the 23rd, they invited our family to move in with the fifty-two[17] other Adventists who had congregated at the five bungalows just off Navy Road that were owned by the Church,[18] we saw in this invitation an answer to our prayers and moved in the same day. Except for suitcases and a few things we thought essential, we left everything in the Santoses' apartment.

During the week after moving to the cottages, but before the Japanese took Baguio, we teenagers and older children kept ourselves busy digging a trench in front of the cottages, in which we could take shelter in case of an air raid[19]—and we listened to the news. However, most of the time we played a tag game called "Beckons Wanted." Little did we consider that while we were having fun, fewer than twenty miles away, men were dying by the thousands.

A few months later, Capt. Edgar ("Ed") Dale, a wounded American Army officer who was in the thick of the battle down on the coast, gave me a firsthand account of the fighting that took place on his part of the front.[20]

On April 27, 1942, a few days before they were transferred to infamous Cabanatuan POW Camp,[21] Capt. Dale told me what happened when the

Japanese landed on the beaches in the early morning hours of December 21. His outfit, the 71st Infantry Philippine Army under Major Donald Bonnett,[22] composed of Filipino soldiers led by American officers, was ordered to hold the ground in front of the town of Bauang.[23] He said that when the Japanese came ashore, they looked like a swarm of ants coming out of a disturbed anthill. As they advanced inland, the machine gunners and riflemen of Dale's regiment mowed them down until their machine guns turned red-hot and became useless. When the enemy threatened to overrun their positions, they were forced to withdraw and fell back in good order, regrouping just east of Bauang.

That night, when casualties were counted, it was found that his outfit had lost some 700 men killed, wounded, or missing. Fresh reinforcements arrived during the night. Dale said that the next morning the American and Philippine forces counterattacked and drove the Japanese back to their bridgehead, but they could not dislodge them. Bauang, he said, was a surrealistic scene from hell. The Japanese had shot or bayoneted every living thing in sight—people, horses, carabaos, dogs, cats, and chickens.

Unable to hold the Japanese back in its part of the front, Dale's outfit was forced to again fall back through Bauang. That night his commanding officer ordered him to go up Naguilian Road to Baguio and fetch any reinforcements and ammunition he could find. When he arrived in the city, he learned that Col. Horan and the forces under him had withdrawn without a fight and dumped truckloads of ordnance into a ravine outside the city.

As Dale returned to the coast in his jeep to report on what he had found, he saw a platoon of soldiers coming up the road. He was not sure whether they were friend or foe until they began shooting at him. Although wounded several times in the chest, arms, and left hand, the bullets hit no vital spot, and he was able to turn his jeep around. However, by the time he reversed course, the index and middle fingers of his left hand had been almost shot away. He tumbled out of his jeep and flopped into the ditch beside the road, feigning death. His only weapons were his service revolver, a few bullets, and several hand grenades.[24]

As the enemy platoon closed to within a stone's throw of his jeep, they violated a cardinal rule of combat. Thinking Dale dead, they bunched up. Pulling the pin from a grenade and counting the seconds before it would blow up, Dale waited until the last moment, and then hurled it with his good hand into the midst of the enemy soldiers. The grenade exploded, killing several of the Japanese outright, mortally wounding others, and stunning the rest. Before they had time to recover, he threw several more grenades. Dale then got back into his jeep and drove to Baguio. By the time he reached the city he had lost so much blood he could no longer stand and had to be carried on a stretcher to Notre Dame Hospital, where Dr. Dana W. Nance, the chief physician, administered blood transfusions and removed the useless remnants of fingers, extracted bullets from his arms and chest, and patched him up as best he could.

Later, when Dale and his fellow officers were brought to our POW camp, they were kept in solitary confinement in a storeroom next to the dining room of the men's barracks. A Japanese sentry was posted outside the door of their cell to ensure that no one communicated with them. However, when it was safe to do so, our cooks quietly bored a small hole through the wall that separated the dining hall from the storeroom. Through that hole they threaded an enema tube. Then they filled the enema bag with liquefied food[25] and fed it to the prisoners. The Japanese never suspected what our cooks were up to.

By December 25 the news from KZRH and other Manila radio stations reported that the Japanese were driving toward the capital and General MacArthur's forces were retreating into the Bataan Peninsula. Christmas was anything but merry that year. We all knew we faced a grave situation, possibly death. On December 26 Mom wrote realistically, yet hopefully, in her diary, "We count that we are already interned by the Japanese. We hear they have landed at seven points. From 2 to 3 A.M. we listened to 16 loud detonations. We hope for the best." And we prayed.[26]

On Saturday, December 27, all of us SDA missionaries gathered for church services under the pine trees at the far end of the cottages, which were situated next to a Constabulary Cavalry Camp. Elder Frost preached a heartening sermon based on Psalm 20:7. "Some trust in chariots, and some in horses: but we will remember the name of the Lord our God."[27] When lunchtime came, none of us had much appetite. A prayer meeting was held in the afternoon and continued off and on until sundown. From time to time, when there was a break in the service, Frank Knight, designated our contact man, called City Hall to find out what was going on and what we could expect.

We were naturally concerned about the attitude of the local Japanese civilians but much more worried about the attitude of the Japanese military. Our missionaries from China knew, firsthand, how the Japanese Army had treated Chinese civilians in Nanking and other places. Would we be treated any different? The prospects were chilling. City Hall could say only that the local Japanese assured them that they wished to "avoid bloodshed." This was encouraging, but could we be sure that the Japanese military would feel the same way? City Hall, of course, didn't know. We were told that preparations were afoot to send a delegation under a white flag to meet the enemy, who was reported coming up Naguilian Road.

That evening Wendell Wilcox and I were assigned the job of staying awake to notify our leaders when the Japanese arrived at our compound. We were stationed in the garage at the entrance to the row of bungalows where we were staying. Except for the children, few, if any, of the adults slept, and most slept in their clothes. Wendell and I were given folding cots on which to lie, if we needed to rest, but we were not to sleep, and neither of us slept a wink that night.

At 11:00 P.M. the Japanese arrived at Brent School. The school was an Episcopalian institution for American and other ex-patriate children. We heard cheers of *"Banzai! Banzai! Banzai!"* coming from downtown Baguio a mile away.[28] We guessed they were the shouts of Japanese civilians and local citizens welcoming the conquerors into town. To Wendell and me it sounded like the bell of doom. What would tomorrow bring? No one could say for sure. The fear and tension that gripped everyone was almost palpable. I prayed silently that God would protect us.

---

[1]Americans contemptuously called this insignia of the rising sun on a white background "the fried egg." These planes, the famous "Zeros," were actually superior to American planes for many months.

[2]*Diary* (1942, reconstituted) by Halsema, p. [3]. Used by permission. (Hereafter designated Halsema, 1942 diary.)

[3]Ethel Thomas Herold, *Ethel's Diary* (Typed transcript dated Feb. 10, 1949: Copyright 2002 by Eleanor Elizabeth Heimke), p. 5, Dec. 8, 1941: "Mr. Rivera, my neighbor a few hundred feet away, [was] beheaded by a piece of shrapnel." (Hereafter designated Herold.)

[4]I didn't know it then, but the Philippine Army was not taking in American citizens. Apparently the young recruiter didn't know this either.

[5]The noninvolvement of Seventh-day Adventists in the military (see John 18:44) and political affairs of nations, while at the same time supporting our governments as the best of citizens (see Matthew 22:21), may account for the fact that none of us who were interned in Baguio or Manila were given the third degree by the *Kenpeitai*, the infamous Japanese Secret Police.

[6]Mary S. Ogle, *Worth the Price* (Washington, D.C.: Review and Herald, 1958), p. 137.

[7]Ibid., p, 254. Natalie C. Crouter, *Forbidden Diary* (New York: Burt Franklin, 1980), p. 127. Jan. 26, 1942: "We are all grateful to the Mansells for their communal spirit in giving hundreds [actually about 35,000] of sulfa tablets to camp which had been intended for mission use in the heart of Africa." Used by permission.

[8]A few months later, while temporarily released, we checked on our "cache" and found that someone had found it and appropriated it.

[9]In those days, cans of Postum (a coffee substitute) bore the logo, "There's a reason."

[10]Because the Japanese broke out of their bridgehead more quickly than expected, by the time Christmas rolled around, Japanese advance units were threatening to cut off access to Mt. Santo Tomás, and Dad and I could no longer go as spotters. After we were interned, Woody Bartges, who also attended this meeting and served on the mountain as a spotter on December 23, told me he had counted over eighty enemy transports in the gulf disgorging troops onto the beaches.

[11]Betty Halsema Foley, *Keepsake* (Scottsdale, Ariz.: Paper & Ink, 2001), p. 179. The message reads: "Baguio, Philippines/ December 24, 1941/ Mr. E. J. Halsema/ Baguio/ You are hereby directed to organize a city government with J. J. Murphy, E. W. Herold, Emil Speth, John Woodson and N. Villanueva as assistant./ You will reorganize the City Utilities, telephone service and arrange for reopening the stores, You are in full and complete charge of all local affairs in Baguio and are given free hand as to methods. Results are wanted./ In case of Military evacuation you will arrange for the peaceable occupation by the Japanese and continue in charge under their jurisdiction./ John P. Horan/ Lt. Col, 43rd Inf./ Comdr. USAFFE Mt. Prov."

[12]Herold, p. 15, Dec. 23, 1944. "Col. Horan deserted. City officials all gone." Halsema, 1942 diary, p. [11], December 26, 1941, says: "After [Mayor] Valderrosa and other missing city officials . . . reappeared to help volunteers arrest looters, and the telephone exchange and electrical plants again were adequately manned, Dad gave him a letter stating: 'no further action by myself and others in trying to restore normal conditions seems necessary', but he warned that unless some of the abundant stock of food in the city were made available, hunger might develop."

[13]Some in our internment camp referred to him contemptuously as "the colonel who ran" (Foley, p. 182).

[14]Foley, p. 182.

[15]Herold, p. 20, Dec. 23, 1941.

[16]Ibid., pp. 14, 15, Dec. 23, 24, 1941. James J. Halsema, the mayor's son, questions Ethel Herold's statement that his father visited the Japanese internees and received a letter from one of their leaders stating that he had lived up to international law.

[17]Among those who crowded into those cottages were the following families and unattached persons. Our leaders, Elders Frost and Hilliard, who had no dependents; the Knights, consisting of Frank, June, and son Billy; the Wittschiebes—Charles, Violet ("Doll"), Helen and Jeannine; the Dinsbiers—Ralph, Anna, Eleanor and Freddy; our family—Ernest, Edith, Donald, and Charles; and the Davises, an elderly couple who were teachers. There were a number of wives whose husbands had remained in Manila or were elsewhere. These included Mrs. Inez Longway and her sons, Ralph and David; Mrs. Mary Guthrie, Richard and Romilda; Mrs. Retha Eldridge, Norma and Larry; Mrs. Dena Hammil and Roger; Mrs. Maude Urquhart and Stanley; Dr. Vera Honor, Dorothy and Herbert; Mrs. Rosamunde Leland and Shirley; Mrs. Althea R. Dyer and June; Mrs. Hazel Wilcox, her son Wendell, and her invalid mother, Mrs. Cora Lyle; Mrs. E. W. Bahr and her son Karl; Bert and Marjorie Parsons and Joy, Anne Marie, and Petrea (Bert was not an SDA but his wife and daughters were). There were also the following single or unattached women: Minnie H. Crysler, Mary ("Mother") Blake, Bessie Mount, Rachel G. Landrum, Mildred R. Dumas, Mary S. Ogle, and Thora Thomsen, our Danish SDA nurse who moved in with us for safety reasons. That

made a grand total of fifty-five persons. Fifty of these were interned, five were not. Mrs. Wilcox and her invalid mother; Mrs. Bahr, Karl, and Miss Thomsen, whose nations were not at war with Japan, were not interned. Wolfe Ismond, an SDA businessman, did not move to Navy Road. When Wolfe is included, it makes fifty-one SDAs who were interned. Nineteen of these persons were either released or transferred to Manila, leaving thirty-two in camp at the time of liberation. The SDAs were by far the largest denominational group in camp, even after their number was reduced by transfers.

[18]Before the war these cottages served as places to stay for vacationing missionaries.

[19]Wendell L. Wilcox, unpublished memoirs, p. 11: "There was really no shelter to hide in when the bombers came over. Because of this, it was decided to dig a trench so . . . we could . . . keep away from . . . shrapnel caused by exploding bombs. Several of us young fellows got busy and dug this trench." Used by permission. (Hereafter designated W. Wilcox.)

[20]He and two other wounded American Army men, Lt. Paul Bach and Sgt. Edward ("Ed") Cook, were brought to Camp John Hay from Notre Dame Hospital on January 27. They remained with us for three months until the Japanese transferred them to Cabanatuan POW camp.

[21]J. Halsema email attachment, Sept. 14, 2002, to D. Mansell, p. [1].

[22]Ibid.

[23]Ibid.

[24]Dale told me that his fellow officers kidded him about carrying around so many grenades, but he believed they saved his life.

[25]Crouter, p. 33, Mar. 29, 1942: "When the three American soldiers were locked up and received no coffee, some of our men fed it to them through a small hole in the wall, with a small tube and an enema bag."

[26]E. Mansell, p. 8.

[27]W. Wilcox, p. 11. Hazel Wilcox with Ruth Wheeler, *Angels Over Manila* (Nampa, Idaho: Pacific Press, 1980), p. 15: "Elder S. L. Frost brought comforting words to our distressed souls that never-to-be-forgotten morning . . . [from] Psalm 20:7."

[28]Foley, p. 186. Esther Yerger Hamilton, *Ambassador in Bonds!* (East Stroudsburg, Penn.: Pine Brook Club, 1946), p. 27: "Soon we heard shouts of triumph and ran to the windows to watch. Down the winding road they came, first children waving flags and shouting. Behind them walked the men, followed by several truckloads of dirty, tired looking soldiers in full battle regalia."

Crouter, p. 11: "In the evening we heard a tremendous roar from many throats in the valley back of Brent [School] and feared rioters coming our way. We listened, frightened, then heard faint 'Banzai!' on the wind. It was the Japanese soldiers releasing their interned civilians in the school on Trinidad Road. What fierce joy it was."

W. Wilcox, p. 11: "We could hear, 'Banzai! Banzai!' . . . The enemy had taken Baguio! Our blood ran cold as we thought about what would happen very soon. That night many prayers ascended to God. There was nothing we could do but trust our Heavenly Father to care for and protect us."

CHAPTER

6

First Encounters
With the Enemy

On December 28, half an hour before daylight, Wendell and I were standing in front of the garage where we had been stationed the night before. We noticed two cars moving slowly along Navy Road about 150 yards below us. At the point where the road branched and came up toward the cottages, the first car headed up to where we were standing. The second car continued up Navy Road for a couple of hundred yards, then turned left and came up another road, which was also at a right angle to Navy Road, and stopped near the far end of the row of cottages. We were flanked at both ends. There was no escape. Our hearts were pounding. This was the moment of truth.

Wendell and I could see that the men in the first car looked Japanese. As soon as we were sure, we walked with deliberate haste toward the cottages where our leaders, elders Frost and Hilliard, and Frank Knight were staying. By the time we got there, we could see that they had already been told about the arrival of the Japanese. When our men came out, they headed toward the second car at the far end of the bungalows. Wendell and I went with them to meet the Japanese. Before we reached the car, three armed men exited from the vehicle. Glancing back, I saw that three more Japanese men from the first car were coming up behind us. In the dim predawn light, we thought at first they were Japanese soldiers. I now realized they were armed Japanese civilians. One of them was carrying an antiquated rifle that looked longer than he was tall. (The apparent enormous size of this firearm was probably created by my agitated mental state.) Only one of the Japanese men spoke English.

Aside from carrying their intimidating weapons, our captors acted peaceably. They were polite, but serious. The one who spoke English asked whether we had any guns or weapons of any kind. Our leaders assured him that we were missionaries, that we had no weapons, and that we didn't believe in violence. The Japanese interpreter told our men to tell our group to get ready to go to Brent School to register. He assured us that we didn't need to take anything because we would be "back home by lunch time."[1] To say we were relieved is an understatement. It seemed that we would be prisoners but would be held under house arrest.

Our leaders, knowing firsthand about the "tender mercies"[2] of the Japanese military, especially the *Kenpeitai*,[3] quietly passed the word for us to take everything our captors would allow us to take. Anything we left behind would almost certainly be looted. Better to take what we could, and risk losing it at Brent, than leaving it here and almost certainly having it robbed.

Most of the people in our group walked to Brent School, but the Japanese allowed the owners of cars to use their vehicles to transport our belongings.[4] I was one of those designated to move our baggage from the bungalows to the cars. We began cramming as many of our things into the cars as they would hold. The Japanese didn't object. The drivers made several trips.

When our captors were shown Mrs. Lyle, Wendell Wilcox's grandmother, who was bedridden with arthritis, they agreed that she could stay, and allowed her daughter, Mrs. Hazel Wilcox, to remain with her. But Wendell was required go to Brent to register with the rest of us.

Mrs. Bahr and her son Karl identified themselves as German citizens and were allowed to stay. Thora Thomsen identified herself as a Danish citizen and was not required to go to Brent. Denmark was under German occupation, and Germany and Japan were Axis partners, hence Japan considered Denmark part of Germany.

The drivers of the cars made several trips from Navy Road to Brent School, ferrying older passengers and luggage. I spent most of the morning loading baggage into the cars. When everyone and their belongings had left for Brent, I hopped into Elder Frost's car. As he drove off, I rolled down the window and, turning to Karl, said with a tinge of envy, "You lucky German."

When Elder Frost went up the driveway to the Brent School administration building, I saw a Japanese fighting man for the first time. He was extremely short and was standing, legs apart, on a grassy mound at a point where the road into Brent forked and circled the administration building. The soldier's khaki uniform was disheveled and ill fitting. He was holding his bayoneted rifle in front of him horizontally with both hands. I will never forget the barbaric, almost demonic, look on his face as our eyes met. If he meant to intimidate me, he did. Later, I was told that the soldiers at Brent were volunteer suicide squad men. True or not, I had no doubt that this soldier would just as soon as not run me through with his bayonet.

Elder Frost parked his car on the road between the administration building and what I later learned was Toddlers Dormitory. We got out, the owners of the last load of baggage claimed their belongings, and Elder Frost dutifully handed the keys of his car to a Japanese civilian, who was waiting to receive them with outstretched palm. The man took the keys without so much as a thank you.[5] After motioning us to join the line that was entering the rear door of the administration building, the car's new "owner" drove off.

Looking around, I spotted Mom, Dad, and Charlie. They were already in line waiting to register. When our family reached the door, I noticed a Japanese soldier (I think he was a sergeant) sitting behind a desk. Seated next to him was a Japanese civilian writing down information given by the people in front of him. The civilian was hunched over a pad of paper, meticulously listing each item expropriated, and the soldier beside him was making notations in Japanese characters. To my left, on the floor, lay a pile of forbidden items more than three feet high—weapons of all kinds, ammunition, cameras, and radios. After registering, Dad laid his offering on the altar—our precious Rolleiflex camera,[6] Dad's tiny jackknife, which he always carried around with him, and our brand-new Hallicrafter radio. When my turn came, I held out my empty hands and showed them I had nothing to contribute.

Sitting in a chair a couple of yards almost directly to my left, was a rather plump, white-haired, elderly Caucasian man with a florid, moon-shaped face,[7] somewhat resembling Col. Sanders of Kentucky Fried Chicken fame. I didn't know him, but I believe he may have been the Baguio police chief, J. J. Keith. He had what I interpreted to be a smirk on his face. I suspected him of being a Nazi sympathizer. If he were Baguio's police chief and a member of the delegation that risked their lives when they went under a white flag to meet the Japanese on Naguilian Road, I might have regarded him with greater Christian charity.

After registering, we passed the pile of surrendered items and followed the crowd down the hall that opened onto a porch. Standing on the verandah in front of the door was a Japanese soldier holding a bayoneted rifle. He was directing "traffic"—men and boys to his left, women and children to his right. Dad, Charlie, and I turned to our right. We said, "See you later," to Mom and entered a room where some men, strangers to us then, were sitting around on tables and chairs.

Most of the SDA teenagers had registered before we did and had found places to sit. We had to stand. I found a place with a closed window at my back. The talk among the men was subdued, punctuated now and then by a streak of black humor. Among those in the room whom I distinctly remember, and afterwards came to know well, were Charles Burgess, Fabian Ream, and Sid Burnett.

The room was filling up rapidly. I never liked the smell of burning tobacco, and since I couldn't open the window behind me, I went out onto the porch for some fresh air. Noticing that the women and children were being sent to the school library, I got an idea. Why not sneak over there when the soldier wasn't looking? Going back to the door of the room where the men were gathering, I gestured for the SDA boys to come out onto the porch. We huddled and I suggested that, when the soldier was busy, we slip behind him and go to the library. There we could at least spend our time looking at magazines or reading books until we were allowed to go home. Our group consisted of Ralph; his brother David; Wendell Wilcox; Stanley Urquhart; Richard Guthrie; my brother, Charles; and me.

We waited until the soldier's attention was focused on a sizable group of people coming down the hall, and then made our move. Unfortunately, the guard saw us out of the corner of his eye and waved us back with his rifle. We stepped back and bided our time. After a little while, Mrs. Retha Eldridge, who had been a missionary in Japan and spoke Japanese, walked up to the soldier, bowed Japanese style, and began conversing with him in his language. While his attention was divided between talking and trying to direct traffic, we quietly slipped around behind him, unnoticed, and joined a group of women and children who were heading to the library. Neither the soldier nor Mrs. Eldridge was aware of what we did. We spent the next couple of hours reading or looking at books and magazines.

An order came for everyone in the library to line up on the road outside the administration building—not to be released to go home, but to move over to Toddlers Dormitory. While the women and children began forming a column on the road, we teenagers tried to get back to the men's side, but the soldier would have none of it. He pointed with his bayonet for us to get in line. Being eighteen and the oldest of the teenagers, I was embarrassed, but there was nothing I could do about it. We were marched with the women and kids to Toddlers Dormitory. The upper floor of the building served as the sleeping quarters of the younger Brent students. On the floor below was the kitchen and "refectory." For some reason the women internees felt reassured by our presence. I can't imagine why. There wasn't a thing we could have done to protect them.

Don Marshall, an Australian Brent School student, was included among the women and children and us boys. He stood out because his feet were painted with gentian violet and he was hobbling around on crutches. In one hand he clutched a box labeled "Navy Chess." I asked him what was the matter with his feet, and he told me that he had a bad case of athlete's foot.

When we got over to Toddlers Dormitory, Bessie Mae Crimm, a short, plump young woman in a nurse's uniform, put us boys to work moving tables together to make room on top as well as underneath for in-comers. This done, we helped the women put mattresses and bedding on top of the tables. Mom had brought a corn-shuck tick when we moved to Navy Road, to use as a mattress in case there was a shortage at the bungalows. We boys put her tick on a couple of tables, climbed up onto it and began playing a card game called Lindy, similar to Touring. We had eaten nothing since early morning and were hungry. Playing this game helped keep our minds off our growling stomachs.

After a while, Miss Crim located a primus stove, a large cooking pot, and rice,[8] which she began to cook. The smell of just plain boiled rice sharpened our appetites. We fervently hoped she would offer us a bowl of what Ralph called "the crutch of life." We were offered none. There was barely enough to feed the younger children.

Because nothing more was said about being released after we registered, I began to suspect that we were not going to be allowed to go home by lunchtime as promised. So, before it got dark, I began looking out the windows, especially those directly behind Toddlers Dormitory, and studied the possibility of escaping. It was obvious that the Japanese were not firmly in control of Baguio. I also noticed that all the Japanese men, both military and civilian, were staying in or hanging around the administration building and concluded that, if I waited until after dark, I could climb out a back window on the second floor and drop to the ground unobserved. We were bedded down near an open window and, with a little luck, escape was definitely possible.

As night came on, the latecomers crawled under the tables and bedded down. On the floor next to our pad were an English mother, Iris Herklots, and her three children—Peter, Jeremy, and Stella. The head of the family, Professor Geoffrey A. C. Herklots, we learned, was in Hong Kong. The British crown colony surrendered December 24, and Mrs. Herklots had received no word from her husband since that date. The uncertainty of whether he was dead or alive worried her.[9] Mom did what she could to reassure her and helped by entertaining her children with stories.

After Charlie and the others were asleep, I whispered to Mom that I was thinking of escaping. It would be a cinch. All I had to do was to climb out the window, drop to the ground, sneak out of town, and join the people who were hiding in the mountains. My plan seemed so simple and easy to execute.

Mom listened, but when I finished, her response was direct and sharp. "Don't do it!" she whispered. "If they catch you, or if someone betrays you, the Japs will kill you. Even if you managed to elude the Japs, where would you go? You don't know the mountains around here."

Mom was right, and I knew it, so I gave up the idea—for the time being. Her dissuasion probably saved my life. This was the first, but not the last time Mom kept me from doing something that could have ended in tragedy.

With us in Toddlers Dormitory was a group of high-society women who kept apart from the common herd. They made it quite obvious that they were not about to lower their dignity by bedding down with the hoi polloi. Instead, they sat in chairs, smoking and talking among themselves in Castilian Spanish and stilted English. The rest of us threw pride to the wind and slept in our clothes. Next morning these women had vanished. They may have been the wives of diplomats, or they may have been citizens of nonbelligerent countries and had been released. I simply do not know.

UNDER THE SHADOW OF THE RISING SUN

Waves of hunger wakened me several times during the night. I think it must have been two or three in the morning when I awoke to the roar of a truck motor and the glare of headlights shining in through the front windows of the dormitory. Someone said it was a car bringing the Japanese officer who was going to decide our fate. It was beginning to look more and more as if the assurances the Japanese civilians had given us the day before, that we would be "home by lunch time," were nothing but a pack of lies. These promises were probably made so that we would be delivered to the Japanese military without resistance.

---

[1]Herold, p. 17, Dec. 28, 1941.

[2]Proverbs 12:10.

[3]Similar to the German Gestapo, the *Kenpeitai* were the Japanese intelligence police. They were feared by the people conquered by Japan as well as the Japanese themselves.

[4]W. Wilcox, p. 12: "Few [of us] could ride to Brent School, due to the lack of transportation, and so most of us had to walk, carrying our things."

[5]Ogle, pp. 152, 153: "Several trips were made with each of those cars to haul us and our baggage to Brent School. There were fifty-six of us, including children. When we were all there they [the Japanese] said to the men, 'Your keys, please,' and that was the last they ever saw of their cars."

[6]The Japanese apparently did not want us to have a pictorial record of our experience.

[7]Foley, p. 186.

[8]Iris Herklots, unpublished diary, p. 6: "Mrs. Hayes had a bag of rice and we managed to get that cooked, and went to bed pretty hungry; the [Toddlers Dormitory] room was pretty packed." A typewritten copy of pages 4 through 7 was sent to me on Sept. 28, 1989. (Hereafter designated Herklots.)

[9]Herklots, p. 5: "So many worries keep crowding into my mind, what is Geoffrey doing, even if he is alive[;] when my money is finished[,] what shall I do? There is much talk of the P.I. being given up. Then how are we to live? All this goes back and forth through my brain until I am nearly frantic[,] but all the time I am thinking of Geoffrey's Mother and what she must be feeling now with no news of him. God send us both courage for we sorely need it now."

CHAPTER

7

Prisoners of the Imperial Japanese Army

It was still early morning when I joined a long line of people going to "breakfast." When my turn came to be served, Doug Tyson, a local businessman, handed me a ham sandwich the size of my thumbnail (no exaggeration) and a mug with a small amount of watered-down coffee. I drank the "coffee." Having never eaten swine's flesh, the smell of pork in the sandwich turned my stomach. When I could do so discreetly, I threw the bit of ham into the bushes and ate the smidgen of bread, but the reek of ham clinging to the bread was so strong that I could hardly down it.

About 10:00 A.M. someone announced that the officer had arrived who was to decide our fate. Everyone was ordered to go to the tennis court, located a couple of hundred feet below Toddlers Dormitory. I was one of the first to enter the enclosure. When I saw Japanese soldiers setting up machine guns[1] and taking up positions outside, the thought crossed my mind that our captors might be contemplating a massacre. I decided that if I were going to die, I was going to be the last to go. So, I took a position as close to the middle of the court as I could. The problem was that others had the same idea. Thus, as more and more people crowded into the court, I got pushed around to somewhere considerably off center. After everyone was in, we waited and wondered what was going to happen to us.

At last, someone came down and passed the word that the officer was on his way. Others had already met Mukaibo, but this was the first time our SDA group had seen or heard of him. Soon I caught sight of the man as he walked down the steps and into the tennis court. He was so short that those of us who were farther back could neither see nor hear him. Someone (I think it was Frank Knight) scrounged around and found a table for him to stand on. Everyone fell silent as the officer mounted his podium and began to speak. His voice was high-pitched, he spoke in accented English—and he had difficulty pronouncing the sound of "el."

The first words I heard come out of his mouth seared their way into my consciousness: "You ah now prisoners of de Imperiar Japanese Ahmy."[2] (Loud and prolonged applause from the prisoners. We were all enormously relieved. At least they weren't going to shoot us—right away.) After a bit the officer's speech assumed a threatening tone. "Ifu you have gun, and ifu you do not surrenda immediaterry, you wirr be kirred." He emphasized his threat by saying that if a weapon was found among us, five men and five women "must be shot." Our group as a whole would be held responsible for the actions of the individual who broke the rules. The officer paused to let his words sink in—or perhaps he thought someone would come forward and hand over a weapon. He repeated his threat. Silence. I remember thinking, *I hope some stupid idiot doesn't put us at risk.*

The officer continued, "De Amerrican Ahmy is very cruerr. Dey made Japanese cibirrian [civilians] mahch to prison camp. De Amerrican Ahmy did not give de Japanese cibirrian food, but de Japanese Ahmy is not so cruerr. So rrong as you ah undah de Japanese Ahmy you sharr have food." (Vigorous applause. I was famished. They were going to feed us!)

Later we were told that the officer, Major Nagahide Mukaibo,[3] was attached to the Religious Section of the Japanese Army.[4] He was apparently a Methodist minister and a professor at Aoyama Gakuin University in Japan.[5] Whatever the case, his English was heavily accented. Just as he had difficulty pronouncing certain sounds in our language, we undoubtedly would have difficulty pronouncing certain sounds in his language. This was bound to make communication difficult.

The officer continued. Just as the American Army made the Japanese walk to prison camp, so we must walk to prison camp—but he didn't say where. So, we weren't going to be released and allowed to go home, as we had been promised. Mukaibo ordered us to form up in several groups on the road leading out from Brent School. Children were to be separated from their parents and lined up in one group. Only the old and infirm would ride. His directions were confusing at best. I heard that the men were to be in one group and that they were to gather by the administration building. At last my humiliation at being with the women and children would be over. When Mukaibo finished his speech, we streamed out of the tennis court. I joined the men who were gathering on the road between Toddlers Dormitory and the administration building.

While we waited for the command that would tell us to begin walking, I noticed a young man in his late twenties standing next to me with a couple of days' growth of reddish whiskers. His teeth were chattering as if he were cold. I could see that he was terribly worried about something. I introduced myself. He told me his name was Rolland Flory. He was a second-generation missionary to China. As we conversed, the reason for his anxiety became clear. His pregnant wife was at Notre Dame Hospital. He didn't know what had happened to her since he had turned himself in. They were expecting their first child in three months. He wondered if his wife was safe. Was she being molested?[6] He had grown up in China and was well aware of the barbarities committed by the Japanese military on the Chinese. I tried to reassure him that everything was going to be all right, but I knew that my words sounded hollow.

As we talked, some of our men, assisted by Japanese civilians, were loading several trucks with heavy items that were piled up on the lawn. I frankly doubted that their owners would ever see them again. Those of us who didn't trust the Japanese and chose to carry our belongings hoped our destination was not far away, like the Pines Hotel, for instance. Foolish thought!

Finally, around noon, the order came down to begin walking—but where? We began moving, but by the time we reached the Brent School entrance we were a confused mass of humanity. The men could walk faster than the women and children who were ahead of us. Mukaibo shouted commands and countermands. Futile efforts were made to straighten out the 600[7] of us, but it was hopeless. Finally the Japanese stationed soldiers around us at intervals. By the direction they were herding us, some of the Baguio residents guessed that we were going to Camp John Hay. They were right.[8]

Those of us who spurned the chance to load our heavier items on the trucks soon found that our loads were getting heavier and heavier and the walk was getting longer and longer. Many began discarding things as we trudged along. Some of the Filipinos along the way ran out from their houses to help women and older people with their loads, but they were waved away by bayonet-wielding guards. But not all the soldiers were so heartless. A few actually helped carry some of the loads. Here and there Filipinos standing on porches along the way wept silently as we passed. This show of compassion probably surprised and galled the Japanese bigwigs, who were convinced the Filipinos looked on them as liberators from the yoke of American colonial oppression.

Our family tried to stay together as best we could. After a while we crossed Military Circle at the entrance to Camp John Hay. This was where we had thrown ourselves to the ground the Sabbath the Japanese planes dropped bombs on that army post. I had Mom's corn-shuck tick filled with odds and ends slung over my back. As I trudged along, I must have looked like Santa Claus on Christmas Eve on his way to deliver presents. After a while I wished I had Santa's sleigh and reindeer to help carry the load.

As we came to Military Circle, instead of seeing "Camp John Hay" painted on the arch over the entrance, I imagined I saw Dante's famous line inscribed over the gate of hell: "All hope abandon, ye who enter here." Sure, I thought, our immediate future might be "hell," but there was something our captors couldn't take away from us—hope, hope that in the very near future the armed forces of the mighty United States would hurl the Japanese invaders into the China Sea.

Up the road a few hundred yards, we passed a squad of Japanese soldiers loading a truck with artillery shells taken from a bunker on the left side of the road. They ignored us, and we returned the favor. The road we were on meandered and seemed interminable. Up ahead where it curved to the right, I could see fellow internees struggling along with their luggage. Near the end of our trek we passed what someone said was the Officer's Club. From the debris scattered about, it was plain the place had been ransacked.

Except for the "ham" sandwich I'd been given that morning, I had eaten nothing and drunk little water in the past thirty-six hours. A few yards up ahead, where the road ascended steeply, I began to black out and had to sit down on the side of the road for a few moments. While I rested, Charlie tied Mom's tick to a pole, and when my head cleared, we put the pole on our shoulders and continued walking up the hill.

When we reached the top, we stood on a plateau. Someone said this was the parade ground of Scout Hill.[9] A couple of hundred yards ahead was a double tennis court, and just beyond it and to the left was a string of three barracks, painted dark green, with galvanized iron roofs. The barracks were lined up approximately north to south. They were all the same size. The northernmost barracks was later measured to be "about 36 by 184 feet."[10] They were built to billet 150 Philippine Scouts.[11] Into it the Japanese expected to pack some 600 men, women, and children. One thing was obvious—privacy, which we Westerners prized so much, would be out of the question.

A chicken-wire fence about eight feet high with several strands of barbed wire around it, surrounded[12] the barracks intended to house us. Close to the gate that exited from the tennis court, the fence was attached to the ten-foot-high tennis court fence. The other end of the fence marked the north boundary of our compound and was secured to the southwest corner of the tennis court.

Charlie and I walked into the enclosure through a second gate, that opened into the court from the parade ground, and dropped our loads. A soldier gave our baggage a cursory examination and waved us on. Ralph, Wendell, and Stanley were waiting near the gate that led to the barracks. We joined them and followed the crowd heading down the cement sidewalk that ran between the front of the barracks and the fence. Halfway down the sidewalk were steps that went up onto a porch. This porch, or verandah, extended almost the whole length of the barracks. We stepped up onto it and walked through a wide entrance into the barracks.

By the time we got into our new living quarters, the north end was packed with people who had gotten there first. We glanced around and quickly discovered why no one wanted to be in the south end—the galvanized iron roof in the southeast corner was peppered with shrapnel holes—the result of a Japanese bomb dropped the first day of the war. In spite of these holes, the south end was filling up rapidly. We had to act quickly. Charlie spotted an unclaimed space to the right of the center section, about a third of the way down the south half of the barracks that had no holes in the roof. There we spread out our blankets wide enough to accommodate the five of us.[13] Because the central part of our pad had four thicknesses of blanket, those of us who would bed down on the outer edges would have only two. Although the Philippines is considered tropical, Baguio, which is more than 4,000 feet above sea level, gets chilly at night during the winter months. We were soon to find out just how cold it could get, when it came time to retire for the night.

We had barely staked out our claim of floor space when I was startled by a high-pitched voice shouting less than five feet behind me, "Mistah Herrerrd! Mistah Herrerrd!"

It was Major Mukaibo.[14] This was the first time I had gotten a good look at the man. He was about my height (five feet seven), maybe a little shorter. He was dressed in a natty Japanese Army officer's uniform and wore black-rimmed glasses. His milk-white teeth contrasted sharply with his black Hitleresque mustache. Until the crowd quieted down, he kept calling out, "Mistah Herrerrd! Mistah Herrerrd!" What followed was a comedy of errors.

Frank Knight, who was standing on the other side of the officer, understood him to be calling for Mr. Hilliard. Knight called Hilliard over and presented him to Mukaibo. A stiff, saccharine smile spread over Mukaibo's face. Grasping Hilliard's right hand with both of his, he showered him with praise.

"Sank you, Mistah Herrerrd, sank you for your kindness herping [helping] de Japanese cibirrians," he eulogized.

Mr. Hilliard looked puzzled. He believed Christians should love their enemies, but it was obvious he couldn't think of a thing he'd ever done for the Japanese over in China that called forth this kind of adulation. "There must be a mistake," he finally blurted out.

Mukaibo, apparently mistaking Hilliard's protestation for self-effacing humility, brushed aside his disclaimer and continued his flowery encomium.

Finally, Walter ("Wally") Moore, manager of the People's Bank & Trust Co., divined that Mukaibo must be calling for Mr. Herold, who had gone out of his way to render humanitarian assistance to the Japanese internees in the early days of the war. "He's calling for Mr. Herold," Wally shouted. Accompanying Mr. Herold, he presented him to Mukaibo.

Elmer Herold was the manager of Heald Lumber Company and the leading employer of Japanese laborers in the Baguio area.[15] During the few days that the Japanese civilians were interned, he brought them food and supplied other necessities. Many of these prisoners had worked as Mr.

Herold's lumbermen before the war.[16] Mukaibo shook Mr. Herold's hand warmly and repeated his words of praise and gratitude—and ended naming him liaison man between us and our commandant, Nakamura-San, formerly a carpenter at Antamok Gold Mine. Because Wally Moore presented Mr. Herold to Mukaibo, he was apparently named assistant liaison. Thus, we were fortunate in having two go-betweens to represent us to the Japanese and vice versa.

We were fortunate in another way too. On December 24, 1941, Acting Mayor Halsema got headmaster Arthur Richardson's permission to use Brent School as a gathering place for Allied nationals. The same afternoon Halsema called a "meeting of the community." At this meeting Carl Eschbach, pastor of the United Brethren Church, was elected chairman of a committee to superintend the process of gathering us soon-to-be civilian prisoners of war at Brent School. Halsema and Richard H. Walker, a dentist, were elected members of this committee.[17] We who benefited from the foresight and leadership of these men could count ourselves fortunate to have had them to guide us through the perilous transition from free persons to civilian POWs.

We were fortunate in other ways too. According to Betsy Herold Heimke, Carl Eschbach appointed her mother, Ethel Herold, to the job of organizing the women to clean the barracks that had been left in a filthy condition by its former occupants. Ethel, a capable, take-charge kind of person,[18] accepted the daunting task reluctantly.[19] We were a mixed multitude of confused prisoners. In retrospect, we can be thankful that she brought a measure of order out of chaos, although at the time we didn't appreciate her efforts.

Because of the humanitarian aid Mr. Herold gave the Japanese internees, he was allowed to live with his wife during the whole time we were interned. This was a privilege that other couples envied. Because the Herolds' decisions at times were viewed as high-handed,[20] there were those who criticized them—and some of this criticism may have been deserved.[21] But when all is said and done, the leadership roles of the Herolds mitigated the harsh treatment for which the Japanese military was infamous.[22] We should have been grateful for what the Herolds did, but many of us were not.

When Mukaibo's speech was over, someone suggested that we teenage boys go to the tennis court and help lug in the baggage that was still out there. While one of us stayed by to guard our pad, the rest of us went out to see what we could do to assist. Our men were unloading several trucks and carrying the stuff into the tennis court for inspection. When we got there, someone told us to tote the boxes of food to the storeroom near the mess hall and pile the other things on the floor in the middle of the barracks for their owners to claim.

There seemed to be an unspoken understanding that all foodstuffs were now the common property of the camp as a whole. We teenagers hadn't had a good meal since early the day before, and we were starving. While carrying a cardboard box full of boxes of cereal to the kitchen, Charlie "liberated" a box of Rye Krisps and shared them with the rest of our gang. We were so thirsty that the wafers felt like sawdust in our mouths. We simply had to have a drink. We slaked our thirst with water that dribbled from a faucet in the kitchen. Only then were we able to swallow the Rye Krisps.

I knew that this food was stolen, but salved my conscience with the scriptural injunction, "Thou shalt not muzzle the ox that treadeth out the corn."[23] I had begun to learn the art of taking things that didn't belong to me.

---

[1]Hamilton, p. 34: "Several machine guns had been set up on the grounds round us and plenty of guards with fixed bayonets on their guns kept a sharp lookout. Then he announced that we were now in the hands of the Imperial Japanese Army."

[2]These are the first words I remember Mukaibo saying. Others who have written about the speech give somewhat different versions of it, for example:

Hamilton, "[Mukaibo] announced that we were now in the hands of the Imperial Japanese Army." Ibid. "[H]e made it very plain that if anyone had firearms of any kind and did not surrender them at that very moment, he would be shot."

Hamilton's version is closest to what I remember Mukaibo saying, when he began his speech in the Brent School tennis court.

Halsema, 1942 diary, p. [12]: " 'From now on, you are under the protection of the Imperial Japanese Army. You must obey its commands. All guns must be surrendered at once, orr you weer be kirrud!' His accent was thick with misplaced consonants but his menace was clear."

Fern Harrington Miles, *Captive Community* (Jefferson City, Tenn.: Mossy Creek Press, 1987), p. 26: " 'I wish to inform you that you are now under the Imperial Army of Japan. You can no longer look to your motherland for help, Japan will provide food for you and a place to live. We will not mistreat you as long as you obey orders. If you do not obey, we will shoot you.' "

Foley, p. 189: "You are our enemy. You will *[he pronounced wirr]* do what we tell you to do."

R. Renton Hind, *Spirits Unbroken* (San Francisco: John Howell, 1946), p. 16: " 'Ifu you have [guns] and do notta giva them up immediaterry or ifu you notta obey the orders of the

Japanese Miritary you wirra (will) be kirrud (killed)!' were his final words."

W. Wilcox, p. 6: "[If anyone escapes,] 'he must be shot.' "

Crouter, p. 12: "They called us all into the tennis court and told us that if we did what we were told that the Japanese soldier was kind. We must give up all guns or tell where they were hidden. . . . Mukibo, a Harvard graduate, with perfect English [?!] and cold, suave manner was in charge." I believe Crouter errs when she says Mukaibo spoke "perfect English."

My memory is that, while Mukaibo's English left much to be desired, it was understandable, if we listened carefully—and we were listening.

The disparities between the different versions of Mukaibo's speech are probably due to fear and apprehension, as well as trying to summarize what he said.

[3]Virtually everyone who has written an account of our internment spells his surname Mukibo, which we pronounced something like McKaibo. I understand that Mukaibo is the correct transliteration of his surname. See next endnote.

[4]Herold, p. 17, Dec. 29, 1941: "Musa Mukaibo [*sic*] (Harvard graduate who was sent there 7 years by the Methodists–at the same time he was doing espionage work for Japan, for a year he rubbed that in to Elmer) . . . [he] had the manner of a two-legged rattle snake."

[5]Halsema, email to Donald E. Mansell, Sept. 17, 2002: "Mukaibo studied at Boston University under Methodist sponsorship and obtained two theological degrees. He did not attend Harvard. Upon his return to Japan he became a professor at a Methodist university."

Herold, p. 17, Dec. 29, 1941, Ethel calls him, "Musa Mukaibo."

Halsema email to Donald E. Mansell, dated May 12, 2002, in which Halsema quotes from *The Philippines Under Japanese Occupation: Policy and Reaction,* by Ikebata & Jose (Manila: Ateneo de Manila Univ. Press, 1992). Chapter 7: "A. Mukaibo, Nagahide, age 37, a graduate of Boston University and a professor at Aoyama Gakuin University." Apparently he held the " 'assimilated' rank" of major and "came to the Philippines on the same vessel that brought Gen. [Masaharu] Homma, landing on Dec. 24, 1941."

On the basis of these facts I spell the "Major's" name Mukaibo, not Mukibo, from here on. Where his name, or nickname, "Musa" came from, I do not know.

[6]He need not have worried. His wife did not deliver until April 3, 1942, when James Arthur Flory made his appearance.

[7]Those who marched to Camp John Hay numbered close to 600. Eventually our numbers stabilized at a little less than 500 as people were released or were transferred elsewhere.

[8]Halsema, diary 1942, p. [130], Dec. 29, 1941: "Dad [former mayor E. J. Halsema] never told me his thoughts as he tramped on familiar asphalt, but they must have been bitter. He was one of the first to appreciate that our destiny would be the damaged barracks on Scout Hill [in Camp John Hay] where the Japanese civilian men had been kept, and not the hoped-for Officer's Mess and officer's cottages."

[9]See endnote 8. In 1991 I checked the distance by odometer from Brent School to the barracks on Scout Hill. It was almost exactly two miles, but on an empty stomach, thirsty, and carrying a heavy load, it seemed much farther.

[10]Miles, p. 30.

[11]Col. John Olson in an email to James Halsema, (copy sent to me is dated Sept. 19, 2002) is definitive: "[The] 43rd Infantry (P[hilippine] S[couts]): Companys: A & B, Camp John Hay/ Authorized: 150 Actual: 149/ Source: Authorized and Actual Enlisted Strength, Philippine Department, September 30, 1941."

[12]Herold, p. 28, Feb. 6, 1942; p. 30, Feb. 27, 1942, speaks of a "barbed wire fence." Herklots, p. 6: "We were put in barracks here with barbed wire all around, the same place that the Japanese

men were interned in." Miles, p. 27, states that it was "a nine-foot high chicken wire fence." Both statements are correct. The fence consisted of two widths of chicken wire reinforced with strands of barbed wire around the bottom. The fence around the tennis court was about ten feet high.

[13]David Longway and Richard Guthrie went to be with their mothers in another part of the barracks.

[14]Hind, p. 20: "We . . . assembled in No. 1 Barracks where Mukaibo gave us another talk."

[15]James J. Halsema email to Donald E. Mansell, May 12, 2002.

[16]E. Mansell, p. 20: Mr. "Harold [i.e., Mr. Herold] was telling us how two of the local guards had been his carpenters." It is regrettable that the American military authorities in charge of the Japanese civilian POWs in Camp John Hay did not live up to the Geneva Convention regarding the treatment of prisoners of war. See Hind, p. 18, and Herold, pp. 17, 20. As a signatory to this convention, American officers were honor bound to treat POWs humanely. Japan was not a signatory to this convention.

When Gen. Wainwright surrendered the forces under his command to Gen. Masaharu Homma, he asked the victor if his soldiers could expect to be treated humanely. Homma replied tersely, "We are not barbarians." However, the barbaric way he allowed his soldiers to treat the Filipino and American prisoners of war gave the lie to his statement. At the end of the war he was captured, tried, convicted, and shot.

[17]Halsema, 1942, p. [11], Dec. 23, 1942.

[18]Foley, p. 199, "Despite criticism, determined and capable Ethel Herold remained a strong force throughout the three years [of internment]." See Charles E. Wittschiebe's remarkable analysis of Ethel Herold's handwriting in chapter 16, endnote 20.

[19]Betsy Herold Heimke, email Aug. 26, 2002, to Donald E. Mansell: "I . . . believe it was Carl [Eschbach] who nominated Ethel [Herold] to get things organized. I can recall her mentioning that several times. At first she declined, using her assistance to Dad [Elmer Herold] as an excuse. His [Eschbach's] response, 'Well, Ethel, if you want to show yourself . . . a PATRIOT, you will take charge of the women.' " (Hereafter B. Heimke.)

Others have said it was Father Arthur H. Richardson who nominated her to this position, but I believe it was more likely Carl Eschbach, chairman of the three-man ad hoc committee elected at Brent School, who nominated her to the job.

[20]Herold, p. 33, Mar. 1, 1942: "they call me a dictator; so for Jean [i.e. Eugene] Hungerford's little 1-page news sheet, I wrote this about me (anonymous[ly]):

There once was a woman dictator
Who tried to be just and not cater;
But from morning till night
She did argue and fight,
And oh, how the people did hate her."

Ibid., p. 40, Apr. 19, 1942: "This business of slave-driving was not meant for me."

[21]Foley, describes Mrs. Herold as "capable," (p. 199), "a take-charge kind of person who immediately started assigning jobs" (p. 193).

Crouter describes her (she calls her "Enid") as "severe, dogmatic, takes no criticism or suggestions, is high handed," p. 27.

Miles, p. 43, states that "The women . . . resented the way Mrs. Herold 'bossed' them around."

Ogle, pp. 179, 180, says: "The woman in charge of the commissary, who was asking the missionaries to turn in their food [when they were re-interned], spotted this can of cherries and said she would take it for the children's diet. After a few days . . . I made bold to go to the kitchen and asked for it [back], but was informed that the cherries could be used in Jell-O for the children, and its return was refused. It was not long after this . . . that a cherry pie was given as a prize at a bridge party." Mrs. Herold appears to be giving her version of what happened, when she speaks on p. 29 of her diary (Feb. 9, 1942) of a "bridge" game and "a can of spoiling cherries" made into a "cherry pie." Miles, p. 42, may be referring to the same incident, when she says: "One night . . . I heard laughter and conversation in the kitchen. Curious . . . I peeked through a crack in the door, [and] I saw four or five people happily devouring a cherry pie."

[22]James J. Halsema email to Donald E. Mansell, May 6, 2002, gives it as his opinion that the "basic reason the Japanese did not act worse than they did . . . [was because] Santo Tomás camp was organized by a committee of Manila Americans on the basis of months of preparation." This may be true, but it is my belief that the better than usual treatment the Japanese military showed us was the *direct* result of the humanitarian aid Mr. Herold gave them. I base this belief on "Ethel's Diary," p. 15, Dec. 25, 1941, which states that Acting Mayor "Halsema saw [the] Baguio Jap prisoners and got two letters, one for us [the other presumably for the mayor], saying we had lived up to International Law and had helped feed [the] Jap [civilian] prisoners of war."

[23]1 Corinthians 9:9.

CHAPTER
8

The
Prisoners

Even before we SDA boys had finished carrying the boxes and cartons of foodstuffs to the storeroom in the north barracks, Ethel Herold, wife of liaison man Elmer Herold, had taken over as kitchen queen. At the same time Oleg ("Alex") Kaluzhny, a White Russian[1] from Shanghai, took over as chief cook and made Paul Trimble, an Australian, his assistant.[2]

As manager of the Pines Hotel, Kaluzhny was in on the ground floor when the internees-to-be had formed an ad hoc organization at Brent School. That Kaluzhny was a good cook cannot be denied,[3] but many felt that the friends he chose as his assistants knew nothing about the culinary art.[4] Many of these were individuals who took advantage of their friendship and used it at the expense of the rest of us. However, not all Kaluzhny's nominees for kitchen help were of this stripe. To his credit, Doug Tyson, after serving as one of the cooks for one month, resigned from the "kitchen gang" in disgust, because there was "too much graft there."[5]

It seems that in every situation involving survival, there are people who manage by hook or crook (mostly crook) to worm their way to the top of the food chain. They are the so-called survivors. In our camp these people belonged to the "kitchen clique" and the "hospital help."[6] Many of these individuals were distinguished from the rest of us by their extra padding.[7]

But then the question is Would we have conducted ourselves differently, had we been in their position?

The average adult male needs between 2,500 and 3,000 calories of food per day to maintain good physical health. Because of our lack of nourishment during our thirty-seven months of duress, food was, naturally, our chief concern. These thirty-seven months can be roughly divided into five periods: (1) The first week, during which it was estimated our food consumption was about 600 calories per person per day;[8] (2) the next five months, when our daily intake ranged between 1,800 to 2,000 calories per day[9] (supplemented in some measure by food packages sent in by relatives or friends on the outside);[10] (3) the next two years, when our rations averaged between 1,800 to 2,500 calories a day (including food packages sent in); (4) the next nine months, when our average ration (not counting food saved up for a rainy day) went down to between 800 to 1,000 calories (but punctuated now and then by a good meal); and (5) the last few weeks, when our average food consumption, including food saved up for emergencies, fell to about 800 calories a day.

The matter of pork became a problem for the Adventists as soon as we were interned. The issue boiled down to majority rule versus minority rights. Early on, Elder Frost approached Mrs. Herold privately and asked her if it would be possible for the SDAs to be served some other protein than pork. She said No, explaining that she couldn't play favorites. We could understand that. Then he asked her if we could cook our ration of vegetables ourselves, whenever pork was to be mixed with the food. Again she said No[11] and suggested that Elder Frost grant us a "special dispensation." Apparently she thought that our scruples against eating pork were a matter of preference, not principle.[12]

Back in those days, Catholics could be granted a special dispensation by their priests to eat meat (e.g., beef or pork) instead of fish on Friday. Why couldn't SDAs do the same regarding pork? After all, this was an emergency. Elder Frost tried to explain that it was not a matter of "dispensation," but a biblical prohibition, as well as a health principle.[13] He pointed out that it was a generally acknowledged fact that eating pork was less healthful than eating beef. But she was adamant. When she insisted we eat what the others in camp ate, we had no choice but to pick the pork out of the food and eat what was left—or go hungry.[14] Kaluzhny, who purchased our food at the Baguio market, was equally intransigent. To her credit, Mrs.

Herold did occasionally relent and substitute something in place of pork—to the displeasure of many of the pork eaters.[15]

After the first few months, and during the greater part of our internment, the pork problem persisted, particularly when food bags from the outside were stopped. At such times we had to revert to going without, or picking the pork out of the food. Most SDAs simply didn't take their ration of food when it had pork mixed with it. This, of course, increased the rations of those who ate pork—and sometimes it seemed to some of us that pork was put in the food on purpose. And yet, I believe that good came out of our nonconsumption of pork. Our health on the whole was probably better than that of our pork-eating friends.

It was not until August 5, 1944, when Doctor Marshall Welles, a Presbyterian missionary-physician, became a member of the Camp Committee, that the pork problem was solved. My diary for that date reads that "Doc Marshall Welles, in charge of health on the Camp Committee, asked us SDAs if we would prefer to receive our allotment of vegetables separate from the rest of the camp so we could cook our food without pork. We jumped at the chance."[16] We SDAs appreciated the Christian consideration he showed us. The food thus prepared tasted much better than the food served in the mess hall. We got the balance of our food, which had no pork, in the dining room with the rest of the internees.

The internees in our camp were predominantly Americans. The next largest group was citizens of the British Commonwealth, including nine Canadians. The rest were a mélange of various nationalities. As I mentioned before, the number of internees in our camp averaged about five hundred.

Of the internment camps the Japanese established in the occupied countries, ours was deemed by them to be the best administered.[17] There were several reasons for this: (1) The camp population seldom exceeded 500, and was therefore more manageable; (2) unlike some camps we had the good fortune of having Carl Eschbach, former mayor Halsema, and Richard Walker see us through the dangerous transition from free persons to civilian POWs; (3) we had Mr. Herold, who, because of the humanitarian aid he rendered to the Japanese civilian internees, tempered the harsh treatment our captors usually meted out to POWs; (4) we had Mrs. Herold, a capable, take-charge kind of person, who organized a chaotic mass of prisoners at the very beginning of our duress; (5) we had public-spirited individuals, who played lesser roles and never got credit for it, but who helped make the camp run smoothly and prepared the way for a democratically elected Camp Committee on February 4, 1942; (6) also important was the fact that a large percentage of adults in camp were college graduates; (7) most of the commandants assigned to camp were reasonable men (but there were exceptions); (8) on June 16, 1942, thirty-seven Anglican missionaries and their families were brought down from Sagada in northern Luzon. Among this group was Nellie McKim, the daughter of an Anglican bishop in Japan. She was born and reared in that country, and had been educated at the Peeress' School. She spoke impeccable, high-class Japanese,[18] understood Japanese customs and ways of thinking—and, above all, she was a consummate diplomat. When she became the unofficial translator for our Camp Committee, she was able to couch exchanges between the Camp Commandant and the Camp Committee, and vice versa, in such a way as to smooth over disagreements.

The rest of us weren't exactly paragons of virtue. There were among us self-serving individuals who took advantage of their position to "help themselves" at the expense of the rest of us. But when all is said and done, it would probably be fair to say that the majority of us lay somewhere between the selfless humanitarians and the egotists.

Of the 500 individuals in our camp, roughly 60 percent were nonmissionaries, and 40 percent missionaries. The SDAs, who at first numbered fifty-one, constituted about 10 percent of the camp population. We were the largest single group. Even after April 14, 1942, when nineteen of our number transferred to Manila or elsewhere, we continued to be the largest missionary group. Yet, our influence on camp life was minimal. This was probably due to the fact that we tended to remain aloof from camp politics. Our leaders never suggested to us a slate of candidates, nor did they ever encourage us to vote as a block.

There were twenty-two denominational groups in our camp. With so many different beliefs and practices, one might expect that there would be heated theological discussions. These, however, were rare. For several months in 1944 leading members of these church groups expounded their beliefs and practices on Sunday afternoons in a public forum without stirring up debates. Those who attended these sessions listened respectfully, and if a person had a question, he inquired about it privately and quietly. Missionaries were at liberty to proselytize, if they wished, and some tried—without much success. Only a very few changed denominational affiliation or abandoned religion altogether.

Before the American/Philippine Army pulled out of Baguio, Dr. Dana W. Nance was given the key to the Camp John Hay medical supplies. Before the city fell, he carted these medicines and surgical instruments to Notre Dame Hospital. When he turned himself in to the Japanese on January 1, 1942 (four days after the rest of us were taken prisoners), he brought with him many of these supplies.[19] We were extremely grateful for these things. They saved many lives—but they also gave Nance tremendous political clout. The Japanese, at Nance's suggestion, made one of the houses across the parade ground from the barracks into a hospital, and he seemed to be the natural choice to head it. On February 3, 1942, when we had our first camp election, Nance, not having been on the ground floor when the ad hoc committee was organized at Brent School, was not chosen a member of the Camp Committee. However, by February 23 he had virtually become a member due to his being the head of our hospital staff, and he had begun throwing his weight around.[20] From then on and until he left for Los Baños Internment Camp, he played a dominant role in camp affairs.[21]

Nance, an alpha-type person, was a truly controversial figure.[22] He was either loved, hated, or feared by many in camp—but not by all.[23] Dr. Beulah Allen, an excellent physician who put the welfare of others above her own, refused to kowtow to him.[24] So he didn't always get his way.

Nance was about five-feet ten-inches tall and powerfully built. He was the son of missionaries to China, grew up in that country, and understood the Oriental mind and ways very well. His knowledge and skill as a physician added to his influence, both with the internees and with the Japanese.[25] How much religion rubbed off onto him from his parents in his youth is a question, but there can be no doubt that he was autocratic, self-serving, and took full advantage of his positions. And he loved his liquor.[26]

But Dr. Nance had good qualities in spite of his weaknesses. He was a good doctor—when sober. It was he who convinced the Japanese to let us buy meat and vegetables for camp with our own money.[27] It was he who sneaked a radio into camp,[28] although, understandably, only a very few internees were in his news loop. On the other hand, he had his favorites, especially among the hospital workers, and he dispensed favors to those who cooperated with him. As the camp's chief physician, he could come and go almost at will, and thus found ways to import alcohol into camp, ostensibly for medicinal purposes, but largely to satisfy his craving for "fire-water," which he shared with his tippling friends.[29]

As with most of us, there was a good side as well as a not-so-good side to this man.[30]

On January 19, 1942, Mrs. Herold reported in her diary:

> Mukaibo came to me with that d—— smirk on his little old straight mouth and said they needed waitresses down at the Pines Hotel for the Jap officers. (Oh God, the blow has come.) I said, "We have much work to do here."
>
> "But we need waitresses and we want young ones."
>
> "Yes, I know, but there are many children to be taken care of and much washing to do."
>
> "They will have their food there, and may stay all night,"—trying to OIL his proposition.
>
> "Many of our people are sick and the children are such a lot of work for everybody." I was so scared inside that I could hardly think—but children are supposed to be a Jap weakness.
>
> "You will cooperate; we want young waitresses, and you know what I mean by young."
>
> "Oh, yes, we are very anxious to cooperate, but without any conveniences, the work here is not ever done," which was indeed true.
>
> He left me with the parting shot, "You will cooperate."
>
> I dashed to find Elmer as fast as I could, to tell him that the Japs had come for the girls. (There are about 6 Brent girls with us with-out parents, who are a constant anxiety to us. . . .) I told him [that] the excuse I put up was too much WORK. We had to think fast and get our puny forces organized. He called the Men's Committee and they said they would put up the argument of too much work—and then, after that, I guess it would be chaos—as after all, the Japs have the guns.
>
> We tried to keep this quiet, but [a thing] such as that spread like wildfire through the women's barracks. . . . I immediately called all the girls together and called [a] spade a d—— old shovel—the Japs had asked for them as waitresses at Pines Hotel—which meant only one thing. My excuse for their not going was that we have too

much work. "So, girls, get yourselves organized; each one of you be taking care of a child every minute of the day; don't dare put on any more lipstick; make yourselves look like ugly married women."[31]

Fortunately, Mukaibo didn't push his proposition any further.

During the first months in camp there were feelings of animosity against the missionaries. This was true of the Herolds, who were frequently outspoken in their antipathy.[32] But they were not alone by any means. Maybe the hostility was deserved. Perhaps we missionaries went around with what was perceived as a holier-than-thou[33] attitude. But, whatever the reason, as time went on, we all became more tolerant, and, as we came to know one another better, these hostile sentiments decreased until they virtually disappeared. Incidents like Mukaibo's "proposition" bound us together. The truth is that, after living so closely for thirty-seven months, most of us actually came to like one another. In some ways we became like one big family. This is shown by the fact that through the years those of us who survive try to attend every reunion we possibly can and enjoy renewing friendships, looking at pictures of children and grandchildren, and reminiscing about old times—even after sixty years.[34] There are exceptions, of course.

During the first twenty months of our internment, some members of the Camp Committee tended to take advantage of their position. But, in the course of time, as we were all reduced to a similar level of poverty, being a member of the Camp Committee became less and less of a political plum. Thus, it is not surprising that the best Camp Committee governed us during the last seventeen months of our duress. The Rev. Carl Eschbach, a fine Christian gentleman, was its chairman.[35] He was universally loved and respected. The same could be said of most of the other members of that Camp Committee.[36] One member, Dr. Augustus ("Gus") Skerl, an avowed atheist, acted more like a Christian than many of us who professed Christianity.

---

[1]Miles, p. 74: "Oleg Alex Kaluzhny . . . was born in Siberia, the son of White Russians. When the communists took over, his family fled to Shanghai. Later Alex went to Hong Kong where he became a British citizen. After training as a chef, he came to the Philippines where he managed the Pines Hotel"; cf. Foley, 194.

[2]Herold, p. 27, Feb. 1, 1942: "Trimble and Alex get a marvelous squeeze by being allowed to go to market." Ibid., p. 51, June 30, 1942: "Alex goes to market regularly and brings back good things for himself."

[3]E. Mansell, *A Participant,* p. 4: "Our men [under Alex Kaluzhny . . . and some of his friends] hustled up a hot drink by candle light for our weary souls. They were grand." Foley, p. 194: "He had little to work with but managed to make our food as varied and palatable as possible."

[4]Crouter, p. 20, Feb. 11, 1942: "The Inside Kitchen Group will never live down the pies, coffee, pancakes, and extras, more particularly the attitude and atmosphere that developed, glowering everyone away from the kitchen"; p. 27: "When 'shifts' had been instituted in the kitchen, the new assistants were all 'friends' of the group and no 'hold' was relaxed."

Miles, p. 42, "Internees accused the cooks of not only eating all they wanted but also preparing desserts and other extras for themselves. Yet they had the audacity to serve us 'garbage stew.' "

Hind, p. 36, "There were many items not in sufficient quantity for use in the preparation of a meal for all internees and these were reserved for the convalescents, children, or—to the disgust of many—for the private use of the kitchen staff."

Herold, p. 31, Feb. 23, 1942: "We hear [that] the men [working in the kitchen] are stealing too much chow"; p. 44, May 4, 1942: "There have always been complaints that the men in their kitchen swipe [the] good food." Ibid., p. 63, Nov. 26, 1942: "People yell about Alex swiping food; well, everyone in the kitchen does that."

Ralph E. Longway, unpublished diary, p. [242], Oct. 20, 1944: "At C[amp] J[ohn] H[ay], all us young fellows half died for lack of food, while those excuses for men [the cooks] were gorging themselves behind closed doors on 'peaches & cream,' meat, bread & milk that should have gone to the starving & sick babies!" Ibid,. pp. [131, 132], June 14, 1944: "[The] cooks [were] caught last night frying up camp pork steaks. All the cooks will be out soon. Too much of this . . . thievery, everyone sick to the belly." (Hereafter designated Longway.)

[5]Herold, p. 27, Feb. 1, 1942: "Dugg [Doug] Tyson handed in his [cook's] cap and apron and resigned from [the] men's kitchen [gang]; too much graft there."

[6]Longway, p. [237], Oct. 15, 1944: "That hospital gang of all gangs is rotten to the core & still no[t] one of them . . . [is] losing [weight like the rest of us]. They were the ones who ate beef and pork when we . . . [slaughtered] them. They were the ones who hauled off the sugar, who ate up the camp chow & lived apart from the common rabble & still do!"

[7]Bill Portrude, the only internee from our camp to be repatriated (he left Camp Holmes on Sept. 20, 1943), was Kaluzhny's friend from Shanghai days. He became a member of the "kitchen clique" and some internees enjoyed twisting his name, behind his back, of course, and associating it with his protruding paunch.

[8]Miles, p. 37: "We averaged only five hundred calories of food per day."

[9]Crouter, p. 53, June 2, 1942; Hind, p. 23.

[10]W. Wilcox, p. 14: "A few days [after the Allied missionaries were re-interned on January 30, 1942, we missionaries still on the outside in Baguio found that] . . . we could send food in to the camp to our people via the camp truck that came to market each day to buy food for the internees. Since peanuts grew profusely in the mountains around where we lived, they were not only easily obtainable, but were also inexpensive. We bought these by the gunnysackful, shelled them, roasted and ground them into peanut butter, and sent containers of this commodity into camp. Each morning Karl Bahr, Miss [Thora] Thomsen, and . . . [Wendell Wilcox] would take everything we could down to the market and meet the camp truck as they gathered supplies for the internees. This extra food was a great blessing to those who were on a very limited diet."

[11]Herold, pp. 72, 73, July 30 and Aug. 10, 1944.

[12]Ibid., p. 24, Jan. 21, 1942: "Pork [was put in the stew] by mistake in the Adventist chow; what a fuss, I quoted Mr. [Frederick] Griggs [President of the Far Eastern and China Divisions, 1931-1938], saying he ate anything [when invited to eat at her table] rather than embarrass his hostess; well, this is war." Often the "mistake" appeared to some of us to be deliberate.

[13]The reason SDAs abstain from pork is basically threefold: (1) Scientific studies show that a meat diet is less healthful than the vegetarian diet God prescribed for man in the beginning (Genesis 1:29); (2) the fact that swine's flesh decays much more quickly than the flesh of "clean" animals, argues strongly for the fact that it is unhealthful; and (3) swine's flesh is expressly forbidden under the Mosaic dietary laws. Thus, while clean meats are permissible, abstention from swine's flesh is more than a good idea, it is a divine precept. But there are additional reasons.

In Old Testament times there were four kinds of laws: (1) The *ceremonial laws,* which were "a shadow of things to come" and ended when type met antitype at the Cross (see Colossians 2:14-17); (2) the *civil laws* (e.g., Exodus 21, 22), which were binding under the theocracy, but ended when the Jews rejected Christ as the Messiah (John 18:36 and 19:15); (3) the *Ten Commandment law,* which God Himself wrote (Exodus 31:18; 32:18, etc.), which remains binding so long as man is man; and (4) similarly, the Old Testament *dietary laws,* which, unlike the ceremonial and civil laws, continue binding so long as man is man. The Creator knew (and prescribed) a diet that was best for man's well-being, and that is the reason He gave us the dentition of herbivores, not of carnivores.

[14]Miles, p. 71: "On June 9 [1942] I woke up with an excruciating pain in my stomach about one o'clock in the morning. At least half the women in our barracks lay writhing in pain . . . , some screaming for death to release them from their agony. Only the vegetarian Seventh Day Adventists were not affected. Like angels of mercy they went up and down the aisle giving us hot ginger tea to help dissipate the abdominal gas. . . . The doctors diagnosed it as ptomaine poisoning from eating tainted meat." Referring to the same incident, Ogle, p. 211, says, "When it was learned that not a single Seventh-day Adventist had joined the midnight procession [to the toilet], it gave the sick ones something to think about, and some of them declared they would never eat pork again."

To the best of my knowledge none of those who abstained from eating pork, Adventist or not, ever had these boils or stomach upsets from eating wormy or tainted pork. Perhaps there is a grain of truth to Exodus 15:26.

[15]Herold, p. 23, Jan. 18, 1942: "[The] Adventists got some of the cheese that is left—darn them"; Ibid., p. 29, Feb. 14, 1942: The Adventists had "salmon loaf."

[16]D. Mansell, p. 35, Aug. 5, 1944. On January 15, 2002, I spoke to Dr. Marshall Welles and said Elder Samuel Frost had told me that he (Dr. Welles) was the one who persuaded the Camp Committee to go along with the idea of letting us Adventists have our vegetables separate from the rest of the camp and allow us to cook them ourselves. He said he did not remember initiating this proposal, but was in favor of it. Dr. Welles was ninety-four years old when I had this phone conversation with him and later visited him and his wife. His mind was amazingly sharp and clear. He was one of the men I most admired in camp. Helen Wells, his wife, passed away on August 29, while this book was being written. She enjoyed hearing Dr. Wells read the early draft of the manuscript.

[17]Herold, p. 40, Apr. 15, 1942: "[A] Jap Gen. inspected us and says we [are] the best camp in all the P[hilippines] I[slands] and [the] China coast."

[18]Foley, p. 208.

[19]Ibid, p. 195: "Permission and transportation eventually were authorized for Dr. Nance to go to his former hospital [Notre Dame] to get needed supplies."

[20]Herold, p. [31], (Feb. 23, 1942).

[21]Ibid., p. 62, Nov. 15: "Nance . . . is usurping all kinds of authority around here."

[22]Crouter, p. 88, Sept. 1, 1942: "The men talk over Dr. Dean's [i.e., Dana Nance's] value to camp, how he was not only useful as a surgeon but that he got things done because he is a go-getter, has drive, power, and daring, which inspire confidence. Like others, he has made errors and [has indulged in] petty graft at the hospital. . . . It is too bad that errors of this sort accompany outstanding service, but it often happens and one cannot blink."

[23]Herold, p. 33, Mar. 4, 1942; Crouter, pp. 88 and 217, 218.

[24]Miles, p. 96; Herold, p. 35, Mar. 12, 1942.

[25]Foley, p. 193: "Dr Dana Nance, a bold, dynamic man who was head of Notre Dame Hospital and medical director for Benguet Consolidated Mining Corp."; ibid., p. 199: "Among the first [to step forward to a position of leadership] was Dr. Dana Nance. . . . Recently arrived from a medical practice in Shanghai, he was the son of China missionaries and was born in China. He was a big, forceful man who moved and spoke with an authority that influenced even the Japanese"; p. 216 speaks of "Dr. Nance's surgical skill."

[26]Herold, p. 26, Jan. 30, 1942: "Dr. Nance [is] a disgrace, came staggering drunk into [the] women's dining room and kitchen; I walked with him to hold him along and pretended to be laughing. . . . [Paul] Trimble tried to help us women make Nance stay in the kitchen, but no[,] he had to go back through the . . . [dining] room again. I walked arm and arm with him and pretended to joke, he went back by way of the men's barracks and, I hope, to sleep."

This same day, January 30, 1942, I saw Nance "under the influence" near the entrance to the tennis court at Camp John Hay, so intoxicated he could hardly stand. He was playing with little Karen Walker. This was the day we missionaries were let out for a day, then re-interned.

Herold, p. 33, Mar. 4, 1942: Our captors called "Nance . . . the drunken doctor."

Crouter, p. 168: "At Camp John Hay . . . Dean [i.e., Dana Nance] kept supplies under his bed, alcohol was used in vast quantity for drinks with many cans of fruit juice."

Herold, p. 65, Jan. 1, 1943: "I forgot to tell about catching N[ance] with fruit juice under his leather coat–taking it from the commissary of the women's barracks at [Camp] John Hay; when questioned, [he] said he was taking it to the hospital. But actually it went with hospital alcohol to make drinks for some of the thirsty ones."

Hind, p. 79: "Occasionally a birthday party, where liquor enlivened the affair, developed into a noisy gathering from which two or three would wander and disport themselves to the amusement or disgust of the rest of us."

Halsema, p. [18], Jan. 30, 1942: "Dana Nance, staggering drunk wandered into the women's dining room and kitchen. Ethel took him by the arm and pretended to be laughing as she tried to steer him back to the kitchen. He gets his alcohol on his trips to Notre Dame."

[27]Miles, p. 41.

[28]Foley, p. 199: "Nance, returning from one of his trips to get medical supplies from his hospital, brought in a radio and got it through the incoming package inspection by handing it to the . . . Japanese soldier who had accompanied him on that trip. The guard automatically accepted the parcel thrust into his arms and carried it passed the gate into the compound, where Dana relieved him of it before he had a chance to question its contents."

[29]Hind, pp. 79, 80. Crouter, p. 67. E. Herold, 32, (Feb. 28, 1942); ibid., p. 53, July 18, 1942.

[30]Miles, pp. 82, 83, "Dr. Nance . . . usually brusque in the way he barked orders and expected instant obedience, was also a man of compassion."

[31]Herold, p. 23, Jan. 19. Slightly edited, by D. E. Mansell.

[32]Ibid, p. [86], Mar. 23, 1944: "How the missionaries flaunt around in borrowed finery . . . these damned missionaries are having a swell time, their salaries going on meantime."

Crouter, p. 37, Apr. 11, 1942: "Arthur [Elmer Herold] blew up on religion again."

Miles, p. 44: "Evidently my Sunday clothes irked her [Mrs. Herold] because she thought I had dressed up to get out of work. I also sensed that she disliked missionaries in general."

[33]See Isaiah 65:5.

[34]The 57th Manila Liberation Reunion met in San Antonio, Texas, from January 31 to February 3, 2002, and I attended. During the past 60 years since internment there have been several large reunions, and many, many mini reunions. The fiftieth reunion, which I also attended, was held in 1991 in Baguio.

[35]Crouter, p. 417, Nov. 30, 1944: "Carl [Eschbach] has kept aloof from graft, with no breath of scandal or suspicion, in his position [as chairman of the Camp Committee]. It is an integrity which no other chairman has achieved in here. Some of them [have been] kept in position by those they shared [their graft] with. The constant reelection of Carl is our great claim to democracy."

Three Year Picnic, by Evelyn Whitfield (Corvallis, Ore.: Premiere Editions International, 1999), p. 207: "Carl Eschbach was a minister of the United Brethren Church in Baguio. He had been reelected, almost unopposed, to the last Committee, for the internees realized that he was the outstanding citizen of the Camp, and was regarded as our best hope during the final months. Tall, slender, blonde, with courage and humor to match his intelligence, he seemed to know no fear, and time and again he literally snatched a burning branch from the fire of Japanese wrath to avoid disaster to the Camp. He was just, honorable, and sweet, slow to anger but firm in his convictions, with the saving grace of a marvelous sense of the ridiculous. His sense of humor certainly was the preserver of all who had to deal directly with our hosts."

[36]Whitfield, p. 193: "They attained their position because they were so outstanding. They had to be that, to be chosen in secret ballot by a critical, familiar electorate."

CHAPTER
9

Camp John Hay Concentration Camp

At the beginning of our internment, our inadequate diet of 600 calories a day[1] was due to two causes: Mukaibo's failure to keep his promise that "so rrong as you ah under de Japanese ahmy you sharr have food,"[2] and our uncertainty as to how long the food supply we had brought in would last. This compelled us to ration our food as sparingly as possible. It was estimated that we only had enough food for three or four weeks at most.[3] Our diet improved considerably after the Japanese allowed us to buy meat and vegetables with our own money.

The rear of the barracks into which we were put was connected in back by a covered porch, which in turn was attached to a smaller building that housed a kitchen, a pantry, a mess hall, a storeroom, and a bathroom. On our first night in camp our cooks made a hot drink for us. About 10:00 P.M. someone (I think it was George Bell) shouted, "Come and get it!" We lined up outside the mess hall door. The cooks poured me half a mugful of the stuff. I was so thirsty I swallowed it in one gulp. It was supposed to be coffee, but it left a bad taste in my mouth and did nothing to slake my thirst or fill the void in the pit of my stomach.[4]

After drinking the stinky potion, we boys went to bed in our clothes. As the oldest, Charlie and I took the outside positions. These, as I have mentioned, had only two thicknesses of blankets under us, and two over us. The others in the middle had twice as many thicknesses over and under them. During the night cold air continually seeped up through the half-inch-wide cracks between the floorboards. Charlie and I didn't get much sleep that night. I got up as soon as it began to get light and walked around to get my blood circulating. Later that day we got a couple of extra blankets from our parents (the ones we had bought at the Baguio market), and the next night we slept more comfortably.

Everyone was thirsty, stinky, and starved, when we got up the second morning as prisoners. At 10:30 A.M. someone with a British accent and a foghorn voice, hollered, "Breakfast is suhved." It was Ernest ("Col.") Kingcome, a retired businessman from Cebu.[5] We lined up outside the mess hall door. Breakfast was served in five relays[6] of about a hundred each. We were allowed into the dining room until the tables were full.

Breakfast that morning consisted of a small bowl of oatmeal, a hot biscuit, a mug of coffee, and a smidgen of scrambled bacon and eggs. By the time my turn came to eat, the cooks had thankfully run out of bacon.

The server at my table was a skinny, angular-featured, medium-tall young man in his twenties. Someone said he was Rufus Gray, a Baptist missionary to China.[7] I remember him well because he picked up a couple of grains of rice that had fallen on the tray as he was bringing breakfast to our table and ate them. It was only a couple of grains, but I resented the fact that he got more than I did. I'm sure I would have felt differently if I had known what would happen to him at the hands of the terrible *Kenpeitai.*

The water system at Camp John Hay was damaged when the Japanese bombed the post on the first day of the war. This meant that, after whatever water was left in the water tank and pipes had been drained out, we had no drinking water, no bath water, and no water with which to flush the toilets.

The bathroom of our barracks was built for soldiers, not a mixed multitude. Open in front, it allowed for virtually no privacy. Down the middle, as one entered, was a long washstand with a sink and several spigots on each side of it. The toilet stalls had no doors.[8] On the opposite wall were several urinals. The showers at the far end were wide open. For Western women used to caring for their bodily needs in private, the accommodations must have been extremely distasteful. But, in spite of these unpleasant conditions, our womenfolk as a whole managed to find humor in their predicament. When one woman complained that she couldn't find a single, solitary, secluded spot in camp where she could enjoy a moment of privacy, another woman quipped, "If you want privacy, shut your eyes."[9]

Without water to flush the toilets, the commodes filled up almost to overflowing within a few hours after we arrived in camp. The next morning former mayor Halsema, realizing that this unsanitary situation posed a serious health problem, asked the Japanese for a shovel with which to dig a slit trench for a latrine. They refused. So he made a makeshift shovel by attaching a piece of galvanized iron roofing to a piece of pipe and began digging in the southwest corner of our compound. Only then did our hosts relent and give him a couple of real shovels. Several volunteers assisted him in excavating the trench.[10]

Some unnamed, ingenious soul hammered loose a shelf on the front porch, used to hold fire buckets, and made a "two-holer" for the latrine. The shelf was nailed to a couple of crates[11] and placed over the trench. A wooden framework was built around it, and sheets of old galvanized iron[12] were nailed to the back and sides. It faced out toward the southwest corner of the fence. It was open in front—at least on the men's side. The partition between the male and female sections was made from a dirty Brent School sheet.[13] To keep flies from breeding, we were instructed to dump a shovelful of earth into the pit after each use. One-hour intervals were assigned to each of the sexes. When their respective times arrived, "Col." Kingcome, the self-anointed Camp Crier, would announce, "Men's tuhn" or "Women's tuhn."[14] He continued making these hourly announcements even after the water system had been repaired. He was a colorful character.

To humiliate us, the Japanese placed a couple of overstuffed chairs just outside the corner of the fence facing the latrine. There those Peeping Toms would sit and watch the movements going on inside the outhouse. I'm sure they knew we didn't like it. I went to this facility only once to answer a call of nature—and, not surprising, nothing happened. I walked away in disgust. I don't know how our women coped with this voyeurism until water was restored to the camp.

On New Year's Day 1942, three cases of dysentery showed up. These were undoubtedly caused by flies that came from the overflowing commodes and perhaps the latrine. One of the three was our friend and pad mate, Stanley, another was Preston ("Pop") Funkhouser, who by coincidence, slept head-to-head opposite Stanley. The third victim was a child,[15] three-year-old Malcolm Watson.[16] All three dysenterics were taken to Notre Dame Hospital for treatment. This, and other intestinal maladies, eventually afflicted 80 percent of the campers.[17] It was usually accompanied by grunts and groans of all sorts. Because of our diet, and the often less than ideal sanitary conditions, dysentery and other intestinal ailments afflicted us internees throughout the entire period of our duress.

The *Camp John Hay Daily News,* founded and produced by James J. ("Jim") Halsema, was first issued on January 5.[18] Early on, it published the following limerick submitted by "Gus" Skerl, our camp geologist, which accurately described these afflictions, with a touch of humor:

> I slept near five hundred and three,
> It was just as I thought it would be;
> His rumblings abdominal
> Were simply phenomenal,
> But everyone blamed it on me.[19]

We suffered terribly from dehydration for the first several days. I have never been so thirsty in my life. Virtually everyone who has published an account of our internment experience mentions the awful thirst we endured during the first three or four days in camp.[20] Until the water system was repaired, our hosts hauled in a few tanks[21] of water once a day.[22] When we complained that we weren't getting anywhere near enough, the Japanese, who had been interned in the same barracks, replied that they went without water for several days (actually only thirty-six hours[23]) and we would have to go without it too.[24] They now had the upper hand, and it was payback time with a vengeance. Most of this water was doled out a cup per person the first day, and two cups per person the second day.[25] People were offering $5.00 for a glass of water, and that was when $5.00 was worth a lot more than it is today. There were no takers.

Meanwhile, Mr. Herold, accompanied by a Japanese soldier, went in a truck that had been assigned to our camp and got a pump and parts from a couple of gold mines in the Baguio area. He brought these back to camp.[26]

He, together with Ray Hale and Phil Markert, our camp electricians, worked on the pump for four days before it was back in working order.

Near sundown on December 31 they tested the pump. Water gushed from a fire hydrant just outside the fence in front of the barracks, but we were not permitted to get any, even for our most urgent needs.[27] It was not until the morning of January 2 that work on the pump was completed. I remember seeing Markert returning to camp, wearing Bermuda shorts, carrying a pipe wrench in his hand, and announcing that we would soon have all the water we needed. This was the best news we'd heard since being taken prisoners, but it was too late to avert the dysentery outbreak.

When dysentery broke out, in spite of our best efforts to prevent it, the Japanese ordered all internees inoculated against cholera, typhoid, and dysentery. When I heard that we were to be vaccinated with triple vaccine, I thought we were supposed to get three separate shots. It was only after I had received my second shot and was looking for the third, that I discovered I had already been given twice as much vaccine as I was supposed to get.

It wasn't long before I began to feel the effects of the double dose. I developed a fever. The muscles of my upper arms ached, and at night I was unable to sleep. After a few days the pain began to subside. One of the benefits I gained from this experience was to listen more carefully to instructions. Another plus may have been that I never came down with any of the intestinal maladies that afflicted us during the entire thirty-seven months of internment.

Babies wait for no man—or woman. There were sixteen pregnant women when we were interned,[28] and all these gave birth to babies in 1942. However, Janice Allaine Taylor, who was born on Christmas Day, 1941, jumped the gun on the others. The first baby born after we were in camp was Sara Ann Mather, the daughter of Dr. and Mrs. Bruce Mather. She was delivered at Notre Dame Hospital, and made her appearance on New Year's Day, 1942. The second child was Carole Louise Angeny. She was born on January 19. I remember that the morning after her arrival her missionary father was kidded about the custom of passing out cigars for such occasions. The next birth gave some of the Camp John Hay inmates a little midnight excitement.

Isabel Scott's third child [Richard H.] gave notice of his imminent arrival in the middle of the night of January 14. Nakamura was alerted. He phoned his military superior to request transportation and was refused. "Let the woman wait till morning," said the Major. Nakamura was frantic. "That @#$%! major know plenty army. No know how baby come," he exclaimed. . . . The baby was coming despite the military. Permission and transportation eventually were authorized for Dr. Nance to go to his former hospital to get needed supplies. A metal cot was found for Isabel. The elderly deaf couple now occupying the room in which . . . [Rupert and Betty Folly] had slept was aroused and moved temporarily into the main barracks. Being deaf they found it hard to understand what was happening to them in the middle of the night. A drawer from the kitchen table was emptied of utensils to become a bed for the baby. A tea strainer substituted for an ether mask. He was delivered. He was given . . . [the name of Richard Hawkins Scott], but to the internees, he was forever John Hay Scott, a symbol of a challenge met and overcome.[29]

For the next couple of weeks things quieted down, so far as new births were concerned, but about twelve o'clock on the night of February 14 Jesse Junkin began having labor pains, and at 5:30 in the morning William ("Billy") Junkin III made his appearance. The next day, February 16, Peter Collyer was born. The following day, when Herbert Honor, Jr., one of the Adventist youngsters, heard that Ann Catherine Rynd had been born in our hospital across the parade ground, he informed his mother that "they had a new baby on the men's side last night."[30] Three weeks later on March 22 another child was added to the growing list of newborns, Charles Hughes ("Chucky") Harrison.

Our family had no idea, when we were on the *Grant*, that Sara Bartges was expecting. She remained slim and petite, even after we were interned. Her baby, Woodrow Allen Bartges, Jr., was born on March 28, and tragically, lived only a few hours. This was the first death in camp.

About a week later, on April 3, Rolland ("Rolly") Flory, the man who was so concerned about his expectant wife and their unborn child as we waited to walk to prison camp, became the father of a healthy boy, James A. ("Jimmy") Flory. Jimmy was born while his father was in the hands of *Kenpeitai* inquisitors. On April 10, a week after Jimmy was born, Mila Mount gave birth to Patricia Gene ("Patty").

Terrence Holmes ("Terry") Kneebone, who arrived on May 1, was the first child born after we moved to Camp Holmes. Four weeks later, on May 28, Robert Ernest ("Bobby") Tangen made his appearance. Betty Halsema Foley, daughter of former mayor Halsema, gave birth to Michael Merrick Foley at 8:00 A.M. on June 15.[31]

A week later, on June 22, Harry L. Turner was born, while his father was a POW in Cabanatuan. His father never got to know him. He lost his life in November 1944, when an American submarine sank the "hell ship" on which he was traveling to Japan. Henderson Rey Allen was born by cesarean section at Notre Dame Hospital on July 4, 1942.[32] Anna Rae Dirks was born on September 1, 1942. This completed the crop of babies conceived before internment.

One baby, Richard Lloyd Hale, was "born out of due time."[33] Three other children, Ronald Richard ("Ronnie") Barz, Linda Moule, and Garnet Green Morris III, were born out in the hills to couples who turned themselves in to the Japanese after the rest of us had been in camp for some time.

During the week that we men lived in the same barracks with the women and children, we were "favored" each night with a serenade of crying infants. It even bothered the women who didn't have babies to care for.[34] During that week seventy-five-year-old Mr. Watson threw a shoe at Dicky Welles, when he persisted in crying all night.[35] And, of course, the crying bothered us teenagers. (Now that we have grown up, married, and have children and grandchildren of our own, our attitude toward mothers with crying infants has greatly improved.)

On Thursday evening, January 1, 1942, I heard Wendell crying quietly. He wouldn't tell me what the trouble was, but I suspected he was worried about his mother and grandmother, who were living with little help off Navy Road. Next morning he came running into the barracks, out of breath. He was obviously excited, but said nothing. He began rolling up his blankets with his belongings in great haste. I asked him why he was in such a hurry. He never answered.

When he finished packing, he dashed out of the barracks with his little bundle. I followed him to the sidewalk in front of our barracks, and the mystery was solved. Outside stood Thora Thomsen. She had evidently persuaded the Japanese military to release my friend on humanitarian grounds. I can still see Wendell and Thora trudging across the parade ground, with

Wendell carrying his small parcel of belongings on his shoulder.[36] How I envied him.

During the idle hours of our first days in camp, we SDA boys and other teenagers with whom we became acquainted, such as Don Marshall and Bertrand ("Sonny") Woodson, and to a lesser extent, Dick Patterson, spent many hours sitting on our pad playing games such as Lindy, Navy Chess (a game similar to Stratego, which Marshall brought in with him), and watching card tricks. Most of the adults, when they weren't occupied on work details, spent their time reading their Bibles (if they were missionaries) or playing cards (if they weren't).

Charlie was more gifted in social skills than I. He made friends easily with the girls and found a special friend in Mary Catherine ("Kay") Bell, a lovely student from Brent School. She was the daughter of George and Faye Bell. Before the war, her father was a mill superintendent at Demonstration Mine. Besides Kay, the Bells had a small son, David.

After Kay became better acquainted with us, she told Charlie that when she first saw us, we were lugging Mom's corn-shuck tick suspended on a pole on our shoulders and wearing those very short navy blue pants with narrow white stripes down the sides. She was carrying a pet canary in a birdcage. Until Charlie told Kay otherwise, she thought we were wearing those shorts because the Japanese had taken us prisoner so suddenly that we'd been caught with our pants down, and she felt sorry for us.

Charlie and Kay's friendship blossomed into romance, and two years later they were married—the second of two such unions in camp. On November 29, 2002, they celebrated their 58th wedding anniversary.

---

[1]Hind, p. 23.

[2]E. Mansell, *A Participant*, p. 4.

[3]Ibid.

[4]Wilcox, p. 12: "When some water was brought into camp, it was all made into coffee, because most people were dying for their caffeine. Since this was the only thing there was to drink, I tried to drink some of it, but could not stomach it, and so swallowed only a mouthful or two."

[5]Foley, p. 193.

[6]Herold, p. 18, Dec. 30, 1941.

[7]Miles, p. 13.

[8]Ibid., p. 30, says, "Two or three Japanese were putting up a partition in front of the stools on the far side." This may be true, but if there were such a partition, I didn't take advantage of it, and this is probably the reason I don't remember it.

[9]E. Mansell, p. 9, Jan. 1, 1942; Foley, p. 207.

[10]Foley, p. 193. Cf., Herold, p. 18, Dec. 30, 1941.

[11]Foley, p. 193.

[12]Miles, p. 34.

[13]Herold, p. 18, Dec. 30, 1942.

[14]Foley, p. 193.

[15]Miles, p. 35.

[16]Herklots, p. 7: "Jan 1st 1942. . . . Dysentery has started among the children . . . Jan. 2nd Mrs. [Kathleen] Watson's little boy of 3 who is in our 'square' was taken off with dysentery to the hospital."

[17]Foley, p. 193.

[18]E. Mansell, pp. 25, 26, says that "The *Camp John Hay [Daily] News* . . . [was] 46 days old," by that date, hence that sheet apparently began publication on or about January 5, 1942. James Julius ("Jim") Halsema, son of the acting mayor, was its publisher. The *News* was posted on a bulletin board near the kitchen and read by those interested in camp happenings.

[19]Skerl disclaimed authorship.

[20]Miles, pp. 34, 35; Foley, p. 192; Hind, p. 31; E. Mansell, p. 8; Crouter, p. 12, Dec. 29, 30, 31, 1942; Ogle, pp. 157, 158.

[21]Crouter, p. 12, Dec. 30, 1941.

[22]Herold, p. 18, Dec. 31, 1941.

[23]Ibid, p. 20, Jan. 6, 1942.

[24]Crouter, p. 12, Dec. 29, 1942; Foley, p. 192.

[25]Ogle, pp. 157, 158.

[26]Herold, p. 18, Dec. 30, 1941.

[27]Ibid., p. 18, Dec. 31, 1942: "About dark the water gushed from the yellow hydrant out front; oh . . . to see WATER again. But it gushed only a minute or two. [It] did not come in the pipes in . . . [our barracks. It came] too late to catch [it] from [the] open hydrant, and no one [was given] permission to go there anyway."

[28]Foley, pp. 194, 195. Foley says twenty women were pregnant; actually the number was sixteen.

[29]Ibid., pp. 194, 195.

[30]E. Mansell, p. 38.

[31]Foley, p. 209.

[32]Henderson's brother, Lee Allen, in an email dated May 5, 2002, says: "[My mother] had my brother delivered by C section on July 4th against the wishes of the Japanese. We have always celebrated the birth as an act of defiance and celebration of our faith in our country. My brother was born 17 days after my father [Major Allen] died at Cabanatuan." See chapter 8, endnote 21.

[33]1 Corinthians 15:8. Crouter, p. 293, Feb. 24, 1944: "Mela [Mount] gave a baby shower for Ray [Hale]'s wife who delivers in May. There were twenty guests, a crib basket and a layette. It is best summed up in Mrs. [Dorothy F.] Greer's verse with her gift.

Roses are red, violets are blue,

It can't happen here

But it happened to you."

[34]E. Mansell, *A Participant*, p. 6: "Today [Jan. 3, 1942] is the thirteenth day [of our internment] but [we] are all good sports, even the 101 children [under age 21]. Nobody knows how many of that number are babies. [It] seems to me [that] all of them are [babies] judging by the bawling. Wow!"

[35]Halsema, 1942, p. 18, Jan. 31, 1942: "The [James J.] Watsons are back in the store room with two mothers and their newborns. He's a 75 year old retired sugar miller and she is a 72 year old Irishwoman. Both swear at the crying of babies and he threw a shoe at the Welles infant [Dickie] when it persisted in crying all night." I remember Robert ("Bob") Wells as a model youngster—polite and thoughtful of others.

[36]W. Wilcox, p. 12: "[On the sixth day of our internment there was an announcement over the loud speaker system, which] . . . at first I could not understand. They kept shouting, 'Wilcot, Wilcot, come to the front office.' I decided I had better go and find out whether they were calling for me. Upon reaching the office I asked if they wanted me for something, and that I was Wendell Wilcox. They told me yes, I was the one they wanted. They had a piece of paper in their hands and as they shoved it toward me they pointed to the front gate and said, 'Go, Go!' You can be sure I didn't need a second invitation. I ran back to my living area, grabbed my things and headed for the gate. There by the gate was Miss Thora Thomsen, a Danish nurse who was connected with the China Division office. . . .

"This was Friday, January 2, 1942. Miss Thomsen had decided that she was going down to the Japanese office in Baguio that morning and try to get me out of the internment camp, since I was just 14 years of age at that time. She announced her plans to Mother, who had decided to fast and pray on that day for my release from camp. As soon as she got the permit for my release from Dr. Mokibo [i.e., Mukaibo], she went immediately to Camp John Hay, so it was late Friday afternoon when I walked out of that internment camp, a free person."

H. Wilcox, p. 20: "Dr. Mokibo [i.e., Mukaibo] had given Miss Thomsen a pass to enter the camp [i.e., Camp John Hay] and also a note of release for Wendell." (Hereafter H. Wilcox.)

CHAPTER

10

The First Months Under the Japanese

On January 4, 1942, a week after we were taken prisoner, all males[1] over the age of thirteen moved to the second of the three barracks at Camp John Hay. This new barracks became known as Barracks Number Two, or the Men's Barracks. The building into which we were first put became known as Barracks Number One, or the Women's Barracks. Four days later, on January 8, "the first contingent of 462 Chinese"[2] took over the third barracks. This building became known as the Chinese Barracks. We were strictly forbidden to contact the Chinese, but someone must have talked with them because we knew the exact number of Chinese internees.

In the same way that a chicken-wire fence surrounded the Women's Barracks, reinforced with strands of barbed wire, so were the Men's Barracks and the Chinese Barracks. A gap about fifteen or twenty feet wide separated the compounds. At the point where the sidewalk passed from the Women's to the Men's Barracks, our men built two gates in the fences. These gates were kept closed and padlocked, and were opened only by Mr. Herold when the Japanese permitted. The structure where the soldiers stood guard was a shack built on the parade ground a few feet beyond the sidewalk between Barracks One and Two. During the day Mr. Herold often sat with Nakamura in front of the guardhouse discussing camp problems. Being liaison-man was no easy job. It meant being on call to deal with practically any and every problem that arose, day or night. During the first week it meant being routed out of bed at night at least once every hour to take roll call. While on these nocturnal checkups the accompanying soldier would stomp through the barracks waking up everyone who was sleeping.[3] At first, the Japanese were paranoid. They seemed to be afraid that we, who had surrendered to be interned, might escape, but as time went on they became less suspicious.

The Women's Barracks was greatly relieved of congestion when the men moved to Barracks Number Two. For a couple of days after the move, we continued to eat our meals at the mess hall of the Women's Barracks. During this transition, the major portion of the camp's foodstuffs was lugged to the pantry of the Men's Barracks and placed "under guard."[4] After the kitchen in the Men's Barracks was scrubbed clean, the "kitchen clique" took over the job of cooking for the whole camp.[5] For some time after that, much of the chow for the women and children was hauled by the men to Barracks One in large aluminum vessels.

Now that the men and women were living in separate quarters, the Japanese forbade all communication between the sexes, except for one hour on Sunday evening between six and seven. These sixty minutes became known as "Commingling[6] Time."[7] To announce its beginning, Mr. Herold blew a whistle. To make sure that there was no contact between the sexes, two lines were painted on the tennis court eight feet apart, one red, and the other white. The men had to sit or stand behind the red line, the women behind the white line.[8] When Commingling Time was over, Mr. Herold would blow his whistle and everyone returned to his or her barracks. At the distance of eight feet, private conversations between husbands and wives, or boyfriends and girlfriends, were virtually impossible. But people soon found ways to get around this regulation.

During the first week in camp, when everyone lived in the same barracks, our men put up clotheslines on the south end of the women's compound, and when we men moved to Barracks Number Two, we erected similar clotheslines on the north end of our compound. By standing back from the fence among the sheets, husbands and wives, and boyfriends and girlfriends, could communicate across the fences by signs or short sentences, even when the guards were less than fifty feet away.

Another way we got around the no-commingling rule was during afternoon volleyball games on the tennis court. By the time the Japanese allowed us to play that game, we were buying meat and vegetables with our own money, and thus we had a bit more energy to expend. Teams adopted such names as the Sky Pilots, the Circuit Riders, the Businessmen, the Hamatures,[9] and the Juniors. While the people cheered on their favorite team, the nonparticipants, who were supposed to maintain a discrete distance from members of the opposite sex, found ways to discreetly get around the segregation regulation.

There was yet another way we got around the no-commingling rule. The men were required to attend roll call on the tennis court at seven each morning. On the way there, they had to pass in front of the Women's Barracks and, as they walked by, the women would be on the porch, and notes and brief messages would be exchanged between husbands and wives, and boyfriends and girlfriends.

Every morning before roll call, all the teenage boys were required to sweep the tennis court.[10] The cleanup detail worked under the supervision of William ("Col.") Dosser. Due to the limited supply of brooms, Colonel Dosser would hand each of us a small tree branch stripped of leaves with which to sweep. The job was nothing but busywork. There wasn't much to sweep up, for only rarely did a leaf flutter over the fence and into the court. To our considerable relief, this chore was abandoned after a few weeks.

When the men entered the tennis court for roll call, they would line up alphabetically in columns four across and face toward the entrance to the enclosure that led to the barracks. At seven sharp, Nakamura-San, our commandant, accompanied by Mr. Herold and one of the soldiers, would arrive to call the roll. When these "officials" entered the tennis court, they would stand in the corner of the enclosure near the gate leading out to Barracks One.

"Ky o ts'kê! [Attention!]" Mr. Herold would call out, and we would come to attention.

"Keirei! [Salute!]" Mr. Herold would command. We had to bow, Japanese-style, from the waist. A simple nod was not good enough and could invite a slap.

"Heitai san ohayo gozaimas' [Good morning, honorable soldier]," we were supposed to say. Some profane campers muttered uncomplimentary remarks about our hosts and their mothers—under their breath, of course.

Nakamura, wearing black riding boots,[11] a suntan uniform, and helmet, and accompanied by Mr. Herold and the "honorable soldier," would

A typical Japanese soldier sketched by the author in 1942.

come down the left side of the columns and call our names from a roster held in his hand. Our commandant had difficulty pronouncing our names, but we had no difficulty understanding the blasphemous language[12] that accompanied his "name-calling."

"*Hai!* [Yes, or present!]" we had to shout as soon as our name was mispronounced.

After everyone was accounted for, Nakamura, Mr. Herold, and the soldier would return to their position near the gate.

"*Yasumê!* [At ease!]" Mr. Herold would command. We would relax. Then he would make the day's announcements.

"*Wakarê!* [Dismissed!]" Mr. Herold would finally order, when he finished.

After the "officials" left the tennis court, those who wished could stay and do calisthenics, led by Sid Burnett. At 8:30 everyone lined up for breakfast, the men at the door of their mess hall, the women and children at their dining-room door.

Breakfast was served at nine, and varied little throughout the entire period of our internment. It usually consisted of boiled rice (later on, cornmeal mush), which we sweetened with syrup made from *panocha* (raw cane sugar diluted with water), a banana, and coffee or a mug of hot water for those who didn't drink coffee. When coffee could no longer be obtained at the Baguio market, the grounds were steeped repeatedly until they had no more caffeine in them. This dilute drink was called "submarine coffee." Later, when real coffee completely disappeared, we drank ersatz "coffee" made from roasted rice or corn.

Lunch was served at noon, and consisted of a *cincomas*,[13] or a banana, or, on rare occasions during the early months, a small bun called a *pan de sal.*

Dinner, served at four, was the main meal of the day. After the Japanese allowed us to buy meat and vegetables, this meal usually consisted of a helping of vegetable stew made either with beef or pork, boiled rice, and a piece of fruit, or a *camote*.[14] During the first weeks, and until the occupation *peso* lost much of its value, it cost 100 Philippine *pesos* (equivalent to

US$50) a day to feed the entire camp. In other words, our meals cost about ten cents per person per day—not much, even when money was worth a lot more than it is today.

We maintained our health fairly well on these rations, but they were never enough to gain any weight, unless, of course, you belonged to the "kitchen clique." Since I wasn't part of this gang, I lost fourteen pounds after a few weeks in internment camp.[15]

As soon as the Japanese permitted work groups to do jobs outside our compounds, our carpenters made a wagon to haul garbage to an incinerator within Camp John Hay. This wagon was ingeniously constructed by our carpenters from two artillery caissons.[16] These two-wheeled carriages were attached to a platform about four by eight feet long, made of inch-thick boards, around which sideboards were nailed. A tongue was attached to the forward caisson, which swiveled so that the wagon could be steered. The brake was a six-foot long, inch-and-a-half diameter piece of iron pipe hinged to the rear of the wagon. Wire cables attached from the lower end of the pipe to brake shoes that were fitted over the rear wheels enabled the garbage gang to control the wagon while going downhill. One man stood on the wagon to brake it, two men steered it, and eight men pulling on ropes attached to the sides of the wagon provided the motive power. Garbage from the camp was collected in eight garbage cans. These were loaded onto the wagon every few days. The refuse was hauled to an incinerator, located about a mile from our barracks. Gene Kneebone was head of the "garbage gang" for many months.

Whenever the garbage crew went out to dispose of the trash, a soldier accompanied them, and they did more than just haul garbage. Sometimes, when the guard permitted, the wagon was used to bring loot into camp from various places in the army post.[17] This loot consisted of mattresses, mosquito nets, and whatever the crew thought might be useful in making life behind barbed wire more comfortable. Those who took part in these forays were known as "lootenants"[18] or, if they happened to be gentlemen-of-the-cloth, they were called "the looting parsons."[19] This latter term was quite appropriate. One day, when these "ministers of the gospel" returned from a raid on the Baguio Country Club, they brought back a load of monk's cloth.[20]

It seems as if everyone in the Men's Barracks wanted to belong to the garbage gang. The reason? One could enjoy an hour or two of freedom outside the confines of our compound. But, above all, it offered an opportunity to loot. The problem was that some of the guards wouldn't let us take property they deemed not ours. So, first we tested them, and, if they didn't care, we appropriated anything we could find that we considered useful.

The guards who wouldn't let us loot apparently assumed that anything that formerly belonged to America or Americans was now the property of the Imperial Japanese Army.[21] We took a very different view of the matter. We regarded that the things we took were United States property, and rationalized that, in the absence of our government, "we the people of the United States" had a perfect right to them, if we could get away with it.

Through the diligent efforts of our "lootenants," everyone in camp had a mattress and a mosquito net by January 11, 1942.[22] These creature comforts went a long way toward making life in camp bearable. Before we got them, it was difficult to sleep at night because of the cold and the bloodthirsty mosquitoes that kept us awake much of the night. To get any sleep at all we covered ourselves completely with our bedclothes, except for our noses, but, even then, the bloody critters would manage to find our blowholes.

Another much-sought-after work detail was the "garden gang." Like the garbage detail, membership in this work group was not permanent. Our garden plot was a former flower garden located a few hundred yards down the hill from the northwest corner of the Women's Barracks. It was surrounded by pine trees and thick underbrush. This work detail began to break ground on February 8.[23] Clayton O. Douglas, a former teacher at the Trinidad Agricultural School, headed it up.[24] Most of the workers were teenagers, including me. Under Mr. Douglas's supervision we spaded up the soil and planted sweet potatoes and other vegetable crops.

A Japanese soldier always accompanied us on these excursions. Occasionally, the guard would "recline" on the job, and when he did, we took full advantage of these rest periods. One or two of us would sneak off and do a little private looting. This was dangerous. If a looter was caught, he risked a severe beating. If he returned undetected, and with loot, the booty was shared with those who continued to work and acted as cover for him.

On one occasion, when I went with the garbage gang to the incinerator, the guard accompanying us didn't object if we went into the houses along the way and looted. The abandoned house I went into that day had already been thoroughly ransacked, but I did find a telephone that hadn't been disturbed. I ripped it off the wall and dropped it in a garbage can. Although the guard turned a blind eye to my act, I knew that the sergeant took a dim view of such activity. So, after we were back in our compound, I reached into the garbage can and retrieved it. After cleaning it up, I turned it over to one of the men who knew how to make radios. I don't know if any of the parts were ever used for that purpose, but I know I never got a scrap of news for my efforts. To get real news one had to belong to the radio loop, a very small and tight-knit group. Most of us never knew on a regular basis what was truly going on in the outside world. Listening to Allied radio broadcasts was an offense punishable by death,[25] and few of us wanted to take that risk.

On another occasion, when I went with the garbage gang to dispose of our trash, the guard accompanying us was very kind, but would not allow us to go into abandoned houses and loot. He spoke some English. On the day I refer to, after we had burned the garbage and were almost back to camp, he motioned us to sit down on an embankment under the shade of a large tree behind the Women's Barracks. While we sat there, he stood on the road and plied us with questions. I was sitting at one end of the group, and he directed his first question at me.

"Are you married?"

I said, "No."

Turning to Wolf Ismond, who was next to me, he asked the same question. Mr. Ismond said he was married and had two children. His family lived in Vancouver, British Columbia. The soldier continued putting the same question to others.

When the guard finished, Mr. Ismond asked, "Are you married?"

He replied, "Yes."

"Do you have a picture of your wife?" He did. He took out his wallet and opened it. We crowded around to see. Inside was a small photograph of a beautiful young Japanese woman.

"She work in the *moshi moshi*[26] in Tokyo," he told us.

"Do you have any children?" we wanted to know. He did. Again he flipped open his wallet and showed us the pictures of two darling little Japanese girls. He said they were three and four years old. Pressing the open wallet to his chest, he sighed, "War no good." We agreed.

We sat down once more under the tree, and he continued plying us with questions.

"Who to blame for the war?" he asked.

Silence. We weren't falling into that trap.

"I know," he grinned, "you think Japan at fault."

Again, silence.

"Look," he said, "it take two to make fight. Both Japan and America to blame."

"Yes! Yes!" we agreed. Then he led us back to our barracks.

We agreed among ourselves that this soldier was most unusual.

One day, my best friend, Ralph, and I and Richard Guthrie signed up to go on the garden detail. The same soldier, who was so different from the other soldiers, was sent along to guard us. Some twenty-five or thirty other teenagers, mostly students from Brent School, were on the garden detail that day. When we reached the garden plot, but before we began to work, I started plying this friendly guard with questions.

"How do you say, 'What is this' in Japanese?" I asked.

"*Corê wa nandes' ka,*" he replied.

"How do you say, 'What is that'?"

"*Sorê wa nandes' ka.*"

"*Corê wa nandes' ka?*" I asked, pointing to my hair.

"*Sorê kami,*" he answered. I got a little bolder.

"*Corê wa nandes' ka?*" I asked, pointing to his bayonet.

"*Corê quen.*" The word *quen* sounded like the Portuguese word *quem* (who). I continued asking questions.

"*Sorê wa nandes' ka?*" I asked, pointing to the pouch full of bullets on his belt.

"*Corê tama iri.*"

"*Sorê wa nandes' ka?*" I queried, pointing to a bullet.

"*Corê tepo no tama.*"

When the impromptu Japanese language class was over, we teenagers went to work. The guard sat down on an embankment under a tree a hundred feet above us. We hadn't worked five minutes, when I whispered to Ralph and Richard, "Let's go exploring." We whispered our intentions to the others, and they agreed to cover for us.

When the guard wasn't looking, we slipped off into the underbrush. A couple of hundred yards beyond the garden we found two pup tentlike shelters made of gasoline tins that had been opened, flattened, and bent in the shape of an inverted *V.* Under the "tents" were two unopened army footlockers.

We pried the locks open with a hoe. Inside were someone's precious belongings. Thirteen-year-old Richard spotted an electric flatiron and grabbed it.

"Richard," I remonstrated piously, "it's wrong to take what doesn't belong to you."

Richard obediently returned the iron to its place—and the moment he did, I took possession of it. Richard was a good sport about it and didn't protest.[27] After we had appropriated several other useful items, we hid our loot in the underbrush near the gate and went back to work. The guard didn't notice our absence. When it was time to return to our barracks, we picked up our loot and managed to keep it out of sight until we reached the gate into our compound. By going in as a group we managed not to get caught and divvied up the loot. At my first opportunity I gave the iron to Mom, and she shared it with the other women in camp.

The next time Ralph and I went on the garden detail, the same friendly guard accompanied us. Richard wasn't with us that day. Ralph and I decided to sneak off again, if the circumstances permitted. Imagine our chagrin when we arrived at the tin pup tents and discovered that someone had "stolen" our loot—all of it! There wasn't a thing left except the empty footlockers. We were incensed. We picked up the footlockers and lugged them cautiously through the woods and behind the guard to a spot near the entrance to the garden. There we deposited them in the bushes and went back to work. Again the soldier didn't notice our absence.

When it was time to return to our barracks, the guard ordered us to line up on the path going up the hill to our compound. Ralph and I took our time in obeying his order. We wanted to be sure we were the last ones in line.

"*Kyo ts' kê!*" We snapped to attention. Then, "*Susumê!* [March!]" The soldier had no sooner turned his back than Ralph and I dashed back, grabbed the footlockers by their handles, slung them over our backs, and waddled back to our places in line. We hoped that we could reach our compound and get the empty trunks inside the same way we had gotten in other loot.

We hadn't gone thirty paces when the guard looked back and spotted us.

"*Tomaru!* [Halt!]," he ordered. The whole parade came to a stop, and he came back to where we were standing. I feared I was going to get a beating.

"Your trunks?" the soldier demanded. He was serious.

"We found them," I answered lamely.

"No! Your trunks?" he persisted.

"No," we confessed, sheepishly.

"You take back," he ordered.

To take them back to where we found them would have held up the line for too long, and we had no desire to attract any more attention to ourselves than was already focused on us. So, we just hurried back to the entrance to the garden and hid them in the underbrush. Our idea was to retrieve them next time we went to the garden. But next time we went, someone had "stolen" our loot.

The lesson this soldier taught us that day didn't sink in immediately, but it started a train of thinking that led to a higher ethical standard than I then possessed. I also learned from this experience that not all Japanese soldiers were brutes. I wondered whether this soldier had ever been in America, had learned some English while there, and had become a Christian. I wish I had asked him, but after the trunk episode, I was too ashamed to inquire. But Buddhist or Shintoist—or atheist for that matter—this man was a better Christian than I professed to be.

Sixty years later, while researching for this book, I learned that Mrs. Herold recorded in her diary for April 9, 1941 (the very time when the footlocker episode took place), that "one of . . . [the Japanese] Sgts. [sic] is not too bad. His sister was a singer in the MIKADO in the States. He thinks it['s] too bad about the war."[28] The very next day, April 10, when our captors nailed up a sign announcing the surrender of Bataan, "The good corporal [sic] pointed to the sign and shook his head [in disapproval]."[29] He obviously did not hate America and Americans. I have every reason to believe that it was this soldier who pointed me to a higher ethical standard.

When Japanese soldiers came to our camp fresh from fighting on Bataan, they were usually hostile[30] and we stayed away from them as much as possible. These men had seen buddies killed, and they probably looked on us as ready to kill them, given the chance. These guards enforced the rules rigorously. We felt that many of the regulations they imposed on us were for the purpose of humiliating us and showing us who was boss. For instance, one of the rules, which didn't affect me because I didn't smoke, required all smokers to carry around a little tin can in which to flick their tobacco ashes.[31] Smoking at night was limited to certain areas outside the barracks.[32] Only at these designated places could smokers "imbibe the weed"[33] at night.

Any smoker caught breaking these rules could expect to be slapped, and some, in fact, had their face smacked.[34]

But it wasn't long before we learned how to humanize the "brutes."[35] In most cases these men had wives and children in Japan, and we learned that Japanese soldiers loved children. They seemed especially fascinated by the little towheads. It was common to see a soldier passing out candy or cookies and making over the younger children. It was comical to watch a dozen little kids trailing behind one of the guards—reminiscent of the legend of the Pied Piper of Hamelin.[36]

From becoming friends of the children, it was but a step to becoming friends of the parents, and before long, those hostile men, who at first acted like beasts, became more human.[37] This, however, was not true of all of them. There were those who continued to exhibit hostility and never changed—and the same was true of some internees who forever hated the Japanese. The soldiers who never changed showed their contempt for us by tromping through the barracks at all hours of the night. The *clomp, clomp, clomp* of their boots would waken everybody, and they seemed not to care.

One night in February 1942 I was awakened by someone pulling at the covers of my pad. There had been some thievery going on among the internees,[38] and I assumed that one of them was trying to rob me. Although I had very little of which to be dispossessed, I eased myself stealthily to a sitting position and cocked my arm ready to let the would-be thief have a fistful in the face. It was so dark that all I could make out was a crouching figure.

When I moved slightly, I heard, *"Orai, orai,"* spoken in a low whisper. This was not one of us! His speech betrayed him. It must be one of our guards. Apparently he was trying to say, "All right, all right." *What's all right?* I sneered to myself.

I decided the better part of wisdom was not to hit him. Then he did something that took me by surprise. He pulled the covers up over me and patted me.[39] *"Oyasumi,"* he whispered. *What does that mean?* I wondered. (I didn't know then that the word meant "Goodnight.") I was still suspicious. What was this character up to? I decided to keep an eye on him. He moved to another pad without making a sound. Either he was shoeless, or more probably was wearing the two-toed rubber sneakers *(tabi?)* the soldiers sometimes wore when off duty.

I was still unconvinced that his intentions were honorable, so I continued to watch him. I saw him slink over to another pad and gently pull the covers up over another internee who had gotten uncovered. This time he was more careful, or at least more successful. But he didn't stop there. I watched him covering up other people until he disappeared from view.

How I had misjudged this man! *What an example,* I thought. Here was an enemy soldier acting like a Christian ought to act. Had our roles been reversed, would I have treated him as he had treated me? I thought about this a long time.

On January 10, A. H. Nagatomi,[40] a local Japanese businessman, showed up with a dozen friends. He announced that we must hand over all our valuables—cash, uncashed checks, stock certificates, and so forth.[41] We could keep 100 *pesos.* We assumed that these gentlemen were acting under orders from the Japanese military, and perhaps Nakamura thought so too.

Whatever the case, Nagatomi and company began the collection in the Men's Barracks. He had his henchmen set up a table in the center section of our living quarters, near the entrance. Two chairs were placed behind the table. He and one of his cohorts were the picture of authority as they stood behind the table and ordered the men in the south half of the barracks to go to the tennis court. After they exited, he ordered the men in the north half of the barracks to line up single file and fork over all their valuables, minus the "generous sum" of 100 *pesos.* Then, he and his assistant sat down at the table to "take up the offering."

I lived on the north end of the barracks close to the entrance, so I was among the first to "pass under the rod."[42] The men ahead of me were taken by surprise and were fleeced right and left. While Nagatomi raked the money into a paper bag, his sidekick wrote a receipt for the valuables confiscated and insultingly handed it to the victim. When my turn came, I turned my pockets inside out to show I had nothing to contribute. I was only eighteen and probably didn't look too prosperous anyway. Nagatomi waved me on. As I walked out the barracks entrance, I looked to my left and saw Nagatomi's bandits systematically ransacking our pads. It raised my dander. This was highway robbery pure and simple. I began to worry about what would happen when they plundered the south end of the barracks, where Dad had his pad. He was the one who always carried the family purse. I needn't have worried.

Because the Japanese were a male-dominated society, Dad guessed correctly that if they relieved us of our cash, they would begin with the men. So, before we were interned, he had put all our valuables in Mom's hands.

When the men on Dad's end of the barracks went to the tennis court, the women, of course, wanted to know what was going on over in our barracks. The men said they were being fleeced,[43] and many of them were able to slip their valuables to their wives.

When Dad told Mom what was happening, she immediately went to her pad, rolled up our paper money into a tight wad, and wrapped a wire around it. She hung it in a crack between the boards in the floor, near a pier that supported the building, and covered it with her corn-shuck tick. Other women hid their cash in similar ways. Some of them were ingenious in the way they hid their valuables.[44] One, for instance, afraid that Nagatomi and company would take her diamond ring, removed it, put it in a wad of chewing gum and kept it in her mouth. Another hid her gold bracelet in a sanitary napkin.[45] Because the women had been forewarned, Nagatomi garnered few valuables from them. He got far more from the men on the north end of the Men's Barracks. But not all the men on that end lost everything.

One man, who saw what was coming, claimed he had to answer an urgent call of nature. He was allowed to go to the toilet unaccompanied. The Japanese apparently had too many other prisoners to look after to send someone with him. When the wily guy got to the bathroom, he climbed up on the commode and tossed a wad of bills in the water tank above the toilet, then returned to his place in the barracks. After Nagatomi and his henchmen left, this man retrieved his cash, a few bills at a time, and for weeks afterwards surreptitiously dried a few of them while sitting in the tennis court.[46]

After Nagatomi and company departed, our leaders complained to the Japanese authorities that we no longer could buy meat and vegetables to supplement our diet. This was not entirely true. Although the robbers "sequestered"[47] more than 5,000 *pesos,*[48] we were not as destitute as we pretended to be.

It appears that when the Japanese military learned that Nagatomi had robbed us, and that we could no longer buy food with our own money, they took a dim view of his cupidity[49] and apparently demanded he make "restitution." I say this because on the afternoon of March 16, when Dr. De Venicia, head of the Philippine Red Cross, drove into camp in a car bearing the Red Cross flag, Nagatomi, dressed in suntans and wearing jodhpurs, rode in with him on a motorcycle. The crook seemed anxious to convey the impression that he was responsible for the gifts the Red Cross representative was bringing. The vehicle was loaded with medicines, powdered milk, fruit juices, cod liver oil, and cloth. Nakamura and our "grateful" camp leaders met Nagatomi and Dr. De Venicia in the guard shack. After a long powwow, the supplies were unloaded and brought into camp, amid great fanfare.[50]

Apparently, this act of penance was not sufficient to satisfy the Japanese military. My reason for this opinion is that, a short time after our food money "ran out," Nakamura announced that the Japanese Red Cross in Tokyo had generously sent us the equivalent of 6,100 *pesos* (US$3,550)[51] with which to buy food to supplement our daily rations. I believe it would have been too much loss of face for the Japanese to admit that one of their own was a thief, so they gave it out that the funds were a gift from the Japanese Red Cross. But, whatever the truth, this was not the end of Nagatomi's fall from grace.

Months later one of our fellow internees, Joe Icard, was taken to infamous Santiago Prison in Manila for interrogation by the *Kenpeitai*. When he returned, he told me that he saw Nagatomi in shackles.[52] This may have been his punishment for plundering our valuables. If true, the Japanese had strange ways of meting out justice—without losing face.

Early on the morning of January 23 word went out that all missionaries were to go to the tennis court for an important announcement. *What is this all about? What does it mean?* we wondered. At 10:00 Mr. Herold announced that all heads of households should prepare to go to Baguio in groups of five for interrogation by the *Kenpeitai*. This sounded ominous. The Adventists were first on the list. Mom wrote cryptically in her diary: "Mrs. Eldridge [the former SDA missionary to Japan] 'went to town' first for examination. [When she returned a few hours later,] she told us she had [been given] bread and butter & a personal quiz."[53] This was strange. Stranger yet, no other missionaries were taken in for questioning the rest of that day.

The next morning only male heads of households were taken in for interrogation, beginning with the Adventists. When his name came up, Dad went, but was brought back to camp a few hours later. Apparently the documents he presented and his explanation that our family was on the way to Africa as missionaries when the war broke out, must have satisfied them.[54] So far, so good, but the SDA missionaries from China were apprehensive. Yet, they, too, were returned to camp after being questioned briefly.[55] We hoped and prayed that our other missionary friends would be treated the same way. But it was not to be. Rolland Flory, Rufus Gray, Carroll Hinderlie, Herman Larsen, and Herbert Loddigs were taken to *Kenpeitai* headquarters in Baguio and not returned to camp for varying periods of time. Poor Rufus Gray never came back.

Hinderlie and Larsen were released January 25. It was evident from their bruises that both had been manhandled. In her diary, Mom wrote: "Hinderlie, a Lutheran missionary . . . [and student at the Chinese] Language School, came back with his neck all beaten up, and he didn't want to talk about it."[56] The same was true of Larsen. On the afternoon of January 30, as these men stood in line ahead of me on the tennis court, I saw welts and dark bruises on their necks.

Loddigs and Flory were only released two-and-a-half months later on April 14, four days after Jimmy Flory was born. For a while neither man would talk about his experience publicly,[57] although privately they probably told their wives what they went through. Finally, on February 4, 1945, after the Japanese had left our compound and the American Army was knocking at the gates of Bilibid Prison, Loddigs told me and a group of internees what happened to him. He said that he was roughed up quite badly during his interrogation. When the *Kenpeitai* didn't get out of him the information they were after, they threatened to kill him. When he insisted he was innocent, they brought in a box with sand or sawdust in the bottom and made him kneel with his head bent over it. A Japanese officer drew his sword and raised it as if to behead him.

Loddigs told me that when the officer did this, he knew it was the end and he was terrified. However, after he committed himself into God's hands, all fear left him. The officer did not carry out the execution, and Loddigs was thankful for what we agreed was Divine intervention.

The case of Rufus Gray was different and tragic. Fern Harrington Miles, in her book, *Captive Community*, quotes Marion Gray, Rufus's wife, as saying: "Hayakawa [the Japanese civilian commandant of our camp at the time] told me that the Japanese first suspected Rufus was a spy while we [Southern Baptist Missionaries] were in Peking. Surveillance of Rufus's later activities confirmed their suspicion. . . . [Hayakawa] claimed that [Japanese] Peking officials had ordered Rufus to return to the United States, but he came to the Philippines instead."

Miles continues: "[One day while] in Peking . . . Rufus came back from taking pictures and said in a quivering voice, 'We've got to get out of China as soon as possible.' The photographer from National Geographic who was with him that day left immediately." The Southern Baptist missionary "group went to the Philippines soon after,"[58] but from then on Rufus must have been a marked man.

The *Kenpeitai* established its headquarters in Baguio in the former Whitmarsh Cold Stores building. Mr. Herold, who was incarcerated there for a short time in August 1942, described his cell thus: It was about eight by twelve feet, and just high enough to stand up in. The windows had wooden bars about six inches thick and one-and-a-half inches between the bars. There was a dismal electric light, a toilet, consisting of a square can in the middle of the floor, smelling to high heaven. There was a small four-inches-square window situated high up near the ceiling. The cell was empty except for the can and the prisoners. These included Mr. Herold, a Filipino, three Igorots (native tribesmen), and a worried Japanese soldier, who was reputedly condemned to death. The soldier kept walking about nervously.[59] But being in these cells was nothing compared with what the inmates endured when they were taken out for interrogation and torture.

Orientals had exquisitely cruel ways of torturing people. One of the most common was the Water Cure. In this form of torture, the victim was strapped down to a table or chair, or pinioned to the ground, and his head immobilized. If a chair was used, he would be bound to it, then the chair would be tipped on its back.[60] The victim's nose would then be held tightly. Each time he opened his mouth to take a breath, water was poured in. The victim had to swallow the water or suffocate. This procedure was continued until the stomach was full. Then, by pounding the victim's abdomen, they usually extracted the desired information—but not necessarily the truth. If what they wanted was not forthcoming, the procedure was repeated until the victim either broke down and told them what they wanted to hear, or succumbed from peritonitis, a horrible way to die.[61]

For many years it was believed that Gray died on March 15,[62] 1942,[63] from this form of torture, but information subsequently discovered by Fern Harrington Miles seems to show that he was beaten to death, probably the day he was taken in to the *Kenpeitai* headquarters.

Mrs. Miles states:

> Mr. [S. C.] Lee, one of the Chinese language school teachers, gives information about Rufus Gray's torture, as well as graphic details of his own experience. The Japanese questioned Mr. Lee about language students on four consecutive days.

Mr. Lee was paralyzed with fear the minute he entered the interrogation room the first time. Before him stood a fierce, evil-looking interrogator with a leather whip in his hand; beside the interrogator stood his interpreter, a Japanese with beady eyes and a scarred face. They pointed to a chair behind the table and Mr. Lee sat down. "Scarface" took out a long knife and started sharpening it on a whetstone. After a minute or two, without saying a word, the interrogator began whipping Mr. Lee on the face until blood ran down, blurring his vision.

Scarface asked Mr. Lee to list the names of all the students and faculty in the language school. Mr. Lee knew only the Chinese names of those who had been in his classes. Then they showed him a copy of the language school roster with names in both English and Chinese. They demanded, "Name the ringleaders of anti-Japanese spy activities in the language school."

"These students are all studying Chinese to go to China as missionaries. None of them are spies."

Unconvinced, the Japanese gave Mr. Lee the water cure. When he regained consciousness, they returned him to the interrogation room where they repeated the beatings with the same questions, receiving the same answers.

The second day, after whipping Mr. Lee, Scarface showed him the names of Rufus Gray and Herbert Loddigs. "Do you have proof that these two are not spies and leaders of anti-Japanese activities?" Once more Mr. Lee denied their accusations and reaffirmed that the students were all genuine Christians preparing to go to China as missionaries. The Japanese then left Mr. Lee alone in the room the rest of the day.

Mr. Lee dozed off to sleep and was suddenly awakened by the cries and groans of someone being whipped in the adjoining room. With each lash of the whip, the victim called on God for help. A Japanese voice snarled, "I'm going to kill you, you American spy."

Between cries, the man gasped, "I've told you . . . many times . . . I'm not a spy." This clearly was the voice of Rufus Gray.

"You're not a spy, huh? Then why did you have so many photographs of China stashed away in your house?" Each word was stressed with a lash of the whip.

"Those were pictures I took in Peking when I was studying there. That's all . . . Haven't I already explained that? Oh . . . oh!"

The beating continued but the shrill snap of the whip changed to a dull thump as if . . . [his tormentor] were using the handle of the whip. The cries and moans grew fainter and fainter until there was a thud—no doubt the sound of Rufus's body hitting the floor. This was followed by excited Japanese voices and the scuffle of feet. Suddenly the door opened. Looking surprised to see Mr. Lee there, the Japanese hurriedly escorted him down the hall to another room. Mr. Lee sensed that something was dreadfully wrong.[64]

It was tragic that this promising young missionary, with his whole life ahead of him, should have had it cut short, leaving behind a grieving wife and an infant son, but such are the horrors and injustices of war.

---

[1] For the sake of simplicity I will refer to all males in the Men's Barracks as "men," although a few of them were hardly old enough to be classed as such. These younger males were either considered too old to be in the Women's Barracks, or had no relatives in camp and were looked after by teachers from Brent School.

[2] Hind, p. 27.

[3] Herold, p. 18, Dec. 29, 1941.

[4] It was rumored that the three young men who were charged with guarding the camp's foodstuffs, acted the part of the proverbial fox that was put in the chicken coop. It is also alleged that they "signed chits" for the food they consumed. If true, I never heard that they redeemed those IOUs. See Hind, p. 36; cf. Herold, p. 19, Jan. 1, 1942.

[5] Ibid., p. 42, Apr. 26, 1942.: "The men do all the cooking now."

[6] This was an expression apparently coined by the Japanese.

[7] Foley, p. 198, says: "I don't know who first used the word *commingling*—blending together—for our Sunday night's walks with our husbands, but we knew the Japanese were dead set against the mingling of the sexes."

[8] Crouter, p. 18, Feb. 3, 1942.

[9] The SDA team was called the Hamatures because we abstained from eating swine's flesh, including ham. Some of us younger SDAs played on more than one team.

[10] E. Mansell, p. 24: "Don was out early helping . . . [sweep] the tennis court."

[11] Whitfield, p. 186: "This first wretched period was ruled by the Baguio [Japanese] military, but nominally in charge of the Camp was a man named Nakamura, immediately recognized through the masquerade [sic] of military *accouterment* as a former boss carpenter (the very one who confiscated Norman [Whitfield]'s boots, which he was still wearing."

[12] E. Mansell, p. 194: "Our commandant, Nakamura, was a civilian, a simple, uneducated carpenter with a rough voice. . . . His vocabulary was embellished with colorful profanity he had learned from his boss at Atamok Goldfield mines."

[13]A pithy tuber similar to a turnip, and called *jicama* in some Spanish-speaking countries.

[14]The Filipino word for sweet potatoes.

[15]E. Mansell, p. 16, Jan. 30, 1942: "Don says he lost 14 lbs."

[16]Halsema, diary 1942, p. [19], Feb. 7, 1942: says that it was "a discarded Army wooden flatbed wagon." If I remember correctly, Jess L. Vickers and J. Bartley ("Bart") Rice built the garbage wagon on the road behind the Men's Barracks by the shop under the mess hall.

[17]Herold, p. 23, Jan. 19, 1942: "Some of the guards are good and close their eyes to the getting of stuff."

[18]Crouter, p. 16, Jan. 28, 1942: "The lootenants told a good story of a guard wanting to get in a house to capture something they fancied. He handed his gun to one of our men to take care of, climbed in a window, gathered up the object and came out to retrieve his gun which was still there."

[19]Foley, p. 201: "Since most of the [garbage] crew were [mostly] missionaries, we dubbed them, 'the looting parsons.'"

Crouter, pp. 17, 18: "Ministers of the gospel are pulling a pushcart full of wood or mattresses or kettles. One of them wears an army hat [called a campaign hat] always jaunty above a faded blue army coat."

[20]This heavy cotton material was later cut up and sewn into *fandoshis*—loin cloths that our loggers wore while cutting down trees for firewood.

[21]Herold, p. 22, Jan. 14, 1942.

[22]Ibid., p. 22, Jan. 11, 1942.

[23]Ibid., p. 28, Feb. 8, 1942.

[24]Ibid., p. 38, Mar. 26, 1942.

[25]Thora Thomsen, our Danish SDA nurse, listened to KGEI, the American radio station in San Francisco, and was caught. In her diary for May 26, 1942 (p. 50), Mom wrote, cryptically: "A note came in to Hilliard yesterday indicating no one knows what. Miss T had some visitors. Possibly investigating." Her entry for June 16 says, "Our Sabbath or Sunday [June 13 or 14] package had Omega on it."

This was Miss Thomsen's last food package to us. Omega, the last letter of the Greek alphabet means "the end" (see Revelation 1:8).

When the SDAs were temporarily released in September 1942, Miss Thomsen told us she had had to reprimand her maid for something. To get back at Miss Thomsen, the girl betrayed her to the *Kenpeitai*. When they checked Miss Thomsen's radio, they found it dialed to KGEI. She was arrested, tried, convicted, and sentenced to Bilibid Prison in Manila. She was the only woman in a sea of male prisoners. An American naval officer, also a POW, assumed the responsibility of protecting her. She was very thankful to have him as a protector. Mom's diary (p. 56) for August 8, 1942, says: "Miss Thomsen was released the 6th [of August]." She had been in prison fifty-five days.

Longway, p. [35], Nov. 27, 1943: "[I was] amazed to see Miss Thomsen (and Mr. Bahr), who've come to visit us in camp. They tell about Manila, etc., and [her] long, scary prison term."

E. Mansell, p. 29: "[The] death penalty is now the sentence [imposed] for listening to . . . short wave [radio broadcasts from Allied stations]."

Herold, 29, Feb. 14, 1942: "Death penalty for Filipinos to listen to [U.S.] news [on the radio] in Baguio."

Miss Thomsen probably escaped this penalty because she was a Danish citizen. Germany was Japan's Axis partner, and her country was under German occupation at the time.

[26]Literally, "hello, hello." He meant the telephone exchange.

[27]In 1999, almost sixty years later, I met Richard for the first time since internment, and apologized for my rank hypocrisy. Richard had forgotten about the incident, but I hadn't.

[28]Herold, p. 40, Apr. 9, 1942.

[29]Ibid., p. 40, Apr. 10, 1942.

[30]Foley, 200: "Guards sent straight from the front lines in Bataan arrived in our camp belligerent, fired up with anti-American propaganda."

[31]Herold, p. 39, Mar. 26, 1942: "[Frank] Delahunty was slapped by a guard because he was smoking without his tin can hanging around his neck. Tonight little Mrs. Timm was also slapped."

[32]Ibid., p. 32, Feb. 27, 1942; Hind, p. 32.

[33]A favorite expression of James ("Jim") Thompson, a pipe smoker, who joked about his habit. He was a graduate of Colorado School of Mines. He taught me high school chemistry, and was one of the finest teachers I ever had.

[34]Dorothy Timm was one of the women who got slapped for smoking where she wasn't supposed to. When Floyd, her husband, heard about it, be became livid with rage. I remember seeing him standing on the porch of the Men's Barracks, yelling curses and obscenities at our guards. The soldiers either ignored him, or, more probably, didn't understand what he was saying. Cooler heads made him stop his tirade before he got all of us into trouble.

[35]Herold, p. 62, Nov. 16, 1942: "It's queer how most of these guards look like wild demons at first and always carry fixed bayonets, then, after they are here a few days, they calm down and some of them get exceedingly human, maybe it is the awful propaganda they have been fed on about us all their lives, after all we are maybe not too bad. Their first warming-up with us is always with the little children."

[36]Lee Allen, the three-year-old son of Dr. Beulah Allen, observed that our guards were free to go in and out of camp as they pleased. In her diary for January 27, 1942, page 15, my mother records that Lee was heard to say, "I'm not going to be a doctor like my mother, nor a major like my father, when I get big; I'm going to be a Jap, so I can be on the other side of the fence."

[37]Foley, p. 200: The belligerent Japanese soldiers "were corrupted soon after their arrival [in camp] by seeing our children. It ruined their enemy-fighting morale. Within a few days they put their bayoneted guns at rest on a playpen to pick up a baby or stop on their night rounds to pick up a sleeping child. The next step was to show us pictures of their own children in Japan and to relax as they recognized us as fellow human beings."

Herold, p. 20, Jan. 5, [1942]: "Jap soldiers gave candy and graham crackers to the kids."

[38]Longway, p. [38], Dec. 1, 1943: "They steal everything in here, from watches and spectacles to garbage."

[39]Crouter, p. 18, Feb. 5, 1942: "I was up at two and saw the guard covering small [sleeping] Diana."

[40]Foley, p. 196: "A. H."; Hind, p. 25. Fellow rotarian Hind gives his initials as H. A., rather than A. H.

[41]Hind, p. 26: "Stock certificates, life insurance papers, cheques, etc., were to be taken up and each of us was obliged to go to a table when cash was counted. All but a hundred pesos was placed in an envelope upon which the victim was to write his name."

[42]See Leviticus 27:32.

[43]Herold, p. 21, Jan. 10, 1942: "Even though there is supposed to be no communication between the barracks . . . [the news that we were being robbed of our valuables by "Nagatomi and his compadres"] spread like wildfire."

[44]Miles, p. 42.

[45]Ibid. Herold, p. 21, Jan. 10, 1942: "[I] sewed our traveler's cheques, Elmer's bonus check, some U.S. and P.I. bills into my brasier."

[46]Foley, pp. 196, 197.

[47]This was the term used in the *Camp John Hay News*. The word means, "to take possession of by confiscating," a euphemism the publisher apparently assumed the Japanese would not understand.

[48]Hind, p. 26, says "a conservative estimate being 5,200 pesos."

[49]Herold, p. 27, Jan. 11, 1942: "We hear that they [the Japanese military] disapprove of the Nagatomi hold up."

Foley, p. 197: *"Long afterward, we learned that the Japanese civilians had stolen our money without the knowledge or permission of the military."* (Her italics.)

[50]Crouter, p. 30, Mar. 16, 1942.

[51]Miles, p. 57: "Nakamura received sixty-one hundred pesos ($3,550) from Japan to replenish our food fund."

[52]Crouter, p. 155, Apr. 12, 1942: "The Japanese tell of Nagatomi in jail with heavy leg irons and an iron bar across his back, [and that he is] forbidden to see his wife and two children." Herold, p. 67, Jan. 28, 1943: "We hear the Japs put Nagatomi in jail in Manila for looting us at Camp John Hay."

Halsema, 1942, pp. [15, 16], Jan. 10, 1942: "As some had suspected, this action was not sanctioned by the Japanese Army and eventually Nagatomi was sent to prison, but his loot was never returned to his victims." It is my opinion that the loot was returned as a "gift" from the Japanese Red Cross, although I cannot prove it.

[53]E. Mansell, p. 14.

[54]Ernest P. Mansell, *A Missionary's Diary*, unpublished, p. 81: "When I explained to the [*Kenpeitai*] officer that I had been in the Orient but a few days before the invasion . . . he seemed satisfied. My passport substantiated my statements." (Hereafter designated P. Mansell.)

[55]E. Mansell, 15.

[56]Ibid.

[57]Foley, pp. 197, 198: "Roll[e]y, who had been born in China [29 years earlier], was a very quiet Mennonite [actually Church of the Brethren] dedicated to helping the Chinese peasants through improving their farming methods. . . . When he returned at last there was rejoicing. When questioned about torture, he undramatically described the 'water cure.' "

[58]Miles, p. 80.

[59]Herold, p. 56, Aug. 15, 1942.

[60]Hind, p. 27.

[61]Another method of torture practiced in the Far East was known as the "green death." A bamboo shoot grows at the rate of three or four inches a day. The end of the shoot is hard and sharp. A frame is built over the shoot and the victim is strapped over it in a sitting position. The shoot grows up through the victim causing peritonitis and resulting in an excruciating death.

[62]Fern Harrington Miles correction, Sept. 13, 2002: "[The Japanese] reported that Rufus died on . . . [this] date, but we all believe he died on the day he was taken in January."

[63]Miles, p. 80. It was late July before Hayakawa told Marian Gray that her husband died on March 15, 1942.

[64]Fern Harrington Miles, monograph titled *CAPTIVE COMMUNITY: What has happened since then?* Updated June 2002. Pp. 6 and 7, under the subhead, "A DESCRIPTION OF RUFUS GRAY'S TORTURE," which was found in "a Chinese book, *The Baguio Concentration Camp*, by S. C. Lee (Manila: Philippine Ling Nan Students Assn., 1946, pp. 41–73) translated into English by Miles.

CHAPTER
11

Released for
One Day

After breakfast on January 30, Mr. Herold came through our barracks and announced that all missionaries and their families must be on the tennis court at eleven o'clock.[1] When we got there, he told us we were going to be released. We were overjoyed. More than 160 qualified for this privilege. We were instructed to gather in denominational groups. Nakamura called the roll of those eligible, beginning with the Adventists. As soon as we were dismissed, we went to our respective barracks with the "glad news." Half an hour later Nakamura sent word that we were to be ready to leave at 2:00 P.M. We began packing as fast as we could. No sooner were our spaces vacated than they were taken over by our non-missionary inmates. They envied us, and expressed the hope that soon they, too, would be released. We hoped so too.

At two o'clock sharp trucks appeared on the parade ground, and we loaded our belongings onto them, climbed aboard, and, after waving goodbye to those we were leaving behind, we were on our way. Twenty minutes later we arrived at Baguio Hotel to register. A Japanese soldier seated behind a desk asked me my name. I told him. He transliterated it into hira gana syllabaries, and pronounced it Donarudo Mansero. After inquiring about my age and nationality, he inscribed this information and the fact that I was an enemy alien on a small oblong piece of cloth, handed it to me with a pin, and indicated that I was to pin it to my shirt pocket.

When everyone had been processed, Major Mukaibo said we must wear our identification tag at all times, and warned us against making any "trouble for the Imperial Japanese Army."[2] We promised, of course, that we wouldn't. Then he dismissed us. Tired and hungry, and lugging our belongings, we went our separate ways. Some had to carry their suitcases and other parcels considerable distances. Our family was fortunate. Legarda Road was only a few city blocks from Baguio Hotel.

It was sunset by the time we reached our apartment. The Santoses were surprised and delighted to see us. They said that their home had not been looted and that our things had not been touched. When we went upstairs, we found that this was true. Mom hastily prepared a delicious meal from our canned goods. We sat down and thanked God, not only for some good nutritious food but especially for being free and the fact that our goods had not been tampered with or stolen. Then, with full stomachs, and exhausted from the day's activities, we went to bed early and fell asleep.

Some missionaries were just as fortunate as we were.[3] Regrettably, others were not. Our fellow SDAs on Loakan Road found their house a shambles. Cases of food had been opened and their contents scattered all over the floor. Ralph told me later that hundreds of cans had been systematically punctured by bayonets and their contents left to rot. The locks on trunks had been pried open and boxes had been smashed and their contents lay scattered everywhere. The devastation was heart sickening. Fortunately, the vandals had not made off with their mattresses and, after cleaning them off, their owners were able to bed down for the night.[4]

At eight o'clock the next morning there was a knock at our door. Dad answered it. It was Elder Hilliard. His group on Loakan Road had received orders from the Japanese that all missionaries were to "report at Baguio Hotel at 9:00 A.M."[5] We got up immediately, washed, dressed, and ate a hurried breakfast—and wondered what this was all about. Was our release a big hoax? We hoped not.

When we reached Baguio Hotel, Major Mukaibo told us "to wait for an important announcement. It came at 1:30 P.M. We must all return to Camp John Hay, except those missionaries who had been appointed to Baguio."[6] So *this* was the big news we had been waiting to hear.

It seems that there had been a misunderstanding. The telegram from the Japanese Army's Religion Section, which said, "Release all Baguio missionaries," did not mean he should release all missionaries *in* Baguio. Rather, it meant, release all missionaries *appointed to* Baguio. To say we were disappointed is an understatement. Only a handful of missionaries qualified under these terms. Children, and even some adults, cried. I remember seeing big tears roll down the cheeks of teenager Barbara Hayes. She was standing across the room from me, next to Dr. Ralph Wells, who put an arm around her and tried to console her.

For a couple of hours it was chaos thrice confounded. Major Mukaibo and the Japanese officers argued in a language we couldn't understand. There were commands and countermands. At last the major spoke. "Everyone begin warrking to Camp John Hay." Our leaders approached the officer and protested that our suitcases and other belongings, which we had brought with us from camp, were still at our homes. How could we be expected to go back to camp without these essential items? More wrangling between Mukaibo and his fellow officers followed. After a while they relented a bit. Each household group must select one person as their representative. This person would be allowed to go to their home to gather up their things. The rest must stay and get on trucks that would arrive to pick us up. On the way back to camp, the trucks would swing by and pick up our belongings and our representatives.

Dad called a family pow-wow. We chose Mom as our representative. She would know best what to take back to camp. We would join her and help load our things onto the truck when it swung by our apartment. Mom had not finished packing when we got there, but we piled on what she had set out for us. After we got back to camp we discovered that she had "failed to include some of poor Don's and Daddy's clothes."[7]

When we reached camp and went into our barracks, we discovered that we were not the only people who were disappointed. Our fellow internees were also chagrined. Our return meant that they had no hope of being released. It also meant that they would have to give back the extra living space they had taken over in our absence. To their credit, most surrendered their newly acquired space like good sports, but some tried to hang on to as much territory as they could.[8]

Some of the returning missionaries brought back cases of food for personal use. These supplies were promptly confiscated by the Camp Committee.[9] As for our much-maligned cooks, they prepared us a snack so we didn't have to go to bed hungry.

In spite of all the negative things that have been said and written about Major Mukaibo, and he certainly could be highhanded and did many things that irritated us, I believe it must be conceded that his interpretation of the telegram from Manila, which he understood to be a blanket permission to release all missionaries in Baguio, seems to argue in favor of the fact that he expected all missionaries in Baguio to be released. To conclude otherwise would mean that he deliberately played a cruel trick on us. Perhaps he did, but I think I'd rather give him the benefit of the doubt.[10]

[1]Herold, p. 26, Jan. 30, 1942.

[2]E. Mansell, p. 17.

[3]Miles, pp. 49, 50.

[4]Ogle, pp. 173, 174.

[5]E. Mansell, p. 17.

[6]Ibid.

[7]Ibid.

[8]Halsema, p. [18], Jan. 31, 1942: "Reallocating floor space was an acrimonious affair." I must have been fortunate and had no trouble regaining my lost space.

[9]Ogle, p. 179.

[10]See chapter 9, endnote 34, for support of this conclusion.

CHAPTER
12

Life Behind Barbed Wire

During the first six weeks of internment most of us believed we would be liberated in a few weeks at most.[1] A few pessimists thought we might be in for a few months, but Daphne Bird, an English evacuee from Hong Kong, believed the war would last three years.[2] To my knowledge, no one else shared her rank pessimism (or was it realism?). But the fall of Singapore on February 15, 1942, began to alter our thinking. The next morning, before sunrise, the women were awakened by someone pounding. When they investigated, they found Nakamura and the guards nailing up a poster on a tree by the fence in front of their barracks. It read:

Singapore FELL on February 15, at 7:30 P.M.

When we men went to the tennis court for roll call that morning, those were the discouraging words that greeted us.

Each evening after supper we were allowed to listen to Tokyo Rose broadcast the latest "news" over Radio Tokyo, as we stood on the sidewalk in front of the shed where our guards stayed. These broadcasts were always introduced by a martial air, "March to the Pacific." I still remember the tune.[3] In a few rare instances, in those early days, our guards, who apparently didn't understand English, set the dial for KGEI or the BBC. On these rare occasions we were careful not to show any elation if the news was good. We discounted as propaganda and pure lies 90 percent of what Radio Tokyo reported. On the other hand, Allied news was "credible." But the news we heard, as well as news filtering in via the grapevine, was sobering. It confirmed that Singapore, "the lion of the east," had fallen, and the naval battles being fought in and around the Dutch East Indies were not re-sounding Allied victories. Slowly, we began to realize we would be prisoners far longer than we at first believed.

The day Singapore fell, we witnessed a scene of brutality we shall long remember. We had a new sergeant named Nobu. He was considerably larger and taller than the average Japanese soldier. I estimate he was close to 5 feet 10, weight about 190 lb., and was all muscle. I was on the gar-bage detail one day when he accompanied us. While we were at the incin-erator burning trash, he drew a scene freehand with nothing but a pencil and a scrap of paper. It was exquisitely beautiful. The man was a gifted artist. Bob Dyer, who could speak a little Japanese, exchanged small talk with him. He appeared to be very amiable. I believe he gave the drawing to Bob.

One evening, several days after this trip, and during the Tokyo Rose "newscast," it was whispered about that trouble was brewing. Two Chinese men had been caught looting in Camp John Hay. Nothing happened im-mediately. When the broadcast was over, Dad and I, and some of the men, went to the north end of the porch of our barracks to observe what was going to happen.

We didn't have to wait long. Soon we saw a soldier approaching the guardhouse with two rather small men in tow. They were handcuffed one to the other. These were the Chinese we'd heard about. As soon as the soldier turned them over to Sgt. Nobu, he began to beat and kick them, and do jujitsu with his hands and feet. The men fell in a heap. They rose to their knees, hands upraised, pleading for mercy. Unfazed, the brute contin-ued beating and kicking them viciously.

I must have looked away for an instant, or perhaps blinked, because I didn't see what happened next. The next image recorded in my mind is that of the two men coming down head first, one on top of the other. The image is indelibly etched in my memory. The first man hit the ground with the other on top. I heard the first man's shoulder bone snap. Harold Palmer, who was standing next to me, asked rhetorically, "Did you hear it pop?"

Not content with breaking a helpless man's shoulder, the fiend contin-ued to practice his martial "skills" on the poor wretches, while they pleaded for mercy. It was more than I wanted to witness. I went inside and didn't see the end of Nobu's sadism. This was not the only time this brute demon-strated his "tender mercies."[4]

On Sunday, March 16, some of the teenage girls and kids put on a satire of camp life titled, "Life Behind Barbed Wire." The producers were Susan Burnett and Billie Dosser. It had previously been performed in the Women's Barracks. Now it was being acted on the tennis court for everyone's enjoy-ment. The first scene portrayed nighttime in camp, with people stumbling over mattresses and sleeping people, babies bawling, depriving everyone of sleep. Next came the dining room scene with an internee sitting on a com-mode, scratching his head and reading a menu—hinting at the inadequacy of our diet. Another scene portrayed a guard insisting that an internee carry around a little can in which to deposit his tobacco ashes. Then someone portrayed Mr. Herold "calling for cups and knives and [asking] 'what is this? a clip joint or a concentration camp?' "[5] The satire's theme song was "Mañana." Later, Billie wrote the words of this song in Mom's diary.[6]

Beginning February 15 the missionaries were forbidden to hold reli-gious services. Up to that time they met quietly on a mattress or in a corner of the tennis court in small groups to hold Bible classes or prayer sessions.[7] "The Seventh Day Adventists would gather around the . . . [pad] of one of their number at sundown on Friday for a reading of the Scriptures and an impromptu discussion of theology. On Sunday morning an orthodox Prot-estant group would follow suit. At neither gathering would anyone dare suggest the singing of a hymn"[8]—for obvious reasons. After a few weeks members of the Camp Committee felt that to continue these religious gath-erings would cause trouble for the camp as a whole and they asked us to stop. From then on, and until we moved to Camp Holmes, regular reli-gious services had to be carried on as private devotions.

The one exception against group religious services at Camp John Hay was Easter Sunday. It fell on April 5 in 1942. In her diary entry for April 4, Ethel Herold wrote that: "Elmer [was] going through all sorts of red tape to get permission from Mukaibo for church services on Easter Sunday morn-ing."[9]

Apparently, we were not ordered or commanded[10] to hold an Easter Sunrise service, as some have supposed. But perhaps there may be a grain of truth in the following question: "Why would Nakamura order us to have a sunrise Easter service? Could it be, he thought this service involved worship of the rising sun? By the time we had gathered for our service, the Japanese guards had assembled near us for their worship of the rising sun."[11]

Whatever the reason, an Easter Sunrise service was held on the tennis court early on the morning of April 5. The minister in charge (I believe it was Carl Eschbach) stood on the southeast corner of the court and spoke on Christ's resurrection and the renewal of hope. Mary Dyer sang, "I Know That My Redeemer Liveth." It was an impressive and spiritually uplifting service.

That afternoon families were allowed to walk around and around together in the tennis court for an hour for the first time since being interned. We didn't know until too late that the no-commingling rule applied to unmarried couples but not to married people.[12] Everyone was in a festive mood. The women livened up the occasion by wearing all kinds of creatively designed Easter bonnets made from scraps of material, diapers, and pieces of paper made into chicks and bunny rabbits. Nakamura, "completely confused, ran about yelling, 'Wassomatta? Everybody go crazy?' "[13]

Most families and married couples without children walked together. I walked with Mom and Dad, and I believe Charlie walked with us too. One "couple" were simply boyfriend and girlfriend—Henry ("Buck") Parfet and Geraldine ("Gerry") Robinson. They were in their late teens and looked old enough to be married. None of us imagined they were doing anything wrong. As a matter of fact, they were virtually indistinguishable from other couples who were newlyweds.

I shall never forget seeing one of the guards sauntering over to where we were promenading and look intently through the fence. I don't know whether Buck and Gerry parted company when he came over, because I didn't look. To look might give them away. I do not know why they were singled out, but I have a feeling that they may have separated when the guard came over, and this tipped him off that they were unmarried. On the other hand, someone may have snitched. (We had that kind too, although they were rare.) But, whatever the reason, Buck knew he was a marked man.

When the walkabout ended, the women and children went to their barracks and we men went to ours. Buck waited until the last possible moment to come over to the men's compound. He could see, as could we, Sgt. Nobu standing in front of the guard shack located between the gates and next to the sidewalk. Nobu, feet apart and arms akimbo, had a hostile expression on his face. By now Dad and I were standing on the end of the porch of our barracks with several other men. We were waiting to see what was going to happen when Buck walked past Nobu. We didn't have long to wait.

Buck was seventeen, rather slim, and a couple of inches taller than Nobu. He walked out the gate and began to go past the sergeant. As soon as he was directly alongside Nobu, the sergeant threw a vicious punch to the left side of Buck's head, knocking him to the ground. Buck staggered to his feet, a stunned expression on his face that I'll never forget. Nobu waited until he was almost standing, then delivered another powerful blow to his face. Again Buck went down. As he struggled to get up, the sergeant struck a third vicious whack to the back of Buck's head, which sent him sprawling toward the gate.[14] Apparently satisfied with his accomplishment, Nobu let him go. Buck was lucky. We already knew the kind of damage this brute was capable of inflicting.

Buck was dazed as he walked into our compound. His left ear and nose were bleeding freely. Several of us accompanied him to our bathroom. There he washed the blood from his neck and face. He said nothing, and neither did we. After a while the bleeding slowed, and Buck went to get first aid. He was lucky Nobu didn't cause more damage than he did. Even so, the sergeant broke Buck's eardrum and his ear became infected.[15] In time it healed.

Four days after Buck's beating, Bataan fell. Next morning our guards nailed up posters in front of both barracks announcing:

Bataan Fell
finally with
Unconditional Surrender
April 9–7 P.M.
Now let us realize
"The Orient for the Orientals"

This was the sign that the "good guard"[16] shook his head at in disapproval.[17] Up to that time we had pinned our hopes of release on Bataan holding out, but news filtering into camp confirmed the worst, and we began to accept the fact that we would be prisoners longer than we at first anticipated.

On April 20, Ray Hale, who drove the camp truck to the Baguio market to purchase our food, reported that he overheard the Japanese talking about our camp moving to Camp Holmes. Before the war, this military post had been a Philippine Constabulary camp on the Mountain Trail. Later the same day we heard that Nakamura had told the garden gang to begin harvesting all the vegetables, because we were moving. The *Camp John Hay Daily News*, soon to become the *Camp Holmes Daily News*, confirmed the report. In less than a week, crews composed of our internees and the Chinese were taken by truck to Camp Holmes to clean up the place.

---

[1]Hind, p. 30: "Our release was only a matter of days or weeks. We never dreamed that it would be years before freedom would come."

[2]Foley, pp. 199, 200.

[3]In 1993 the plane on which I was traveling stopped at Narita Airport in Japan. While walking around the terminal, I noticed a group of Japanese youngsters and an older man. They were wearing small flags of Japan and Brazil on their lapels. Because I was born in Brazil and speak fluent Portuguese, I was curious and asked the man the significance of the flags. He understood no English or Portuguese and my Japanese was not good enough for intelligent conversation, so we parted. A few minutes later the man returned, this time with a young Japanese woman who spoke impeccable American English. She told me the man was the mayor of one of the cities of Japan and that he was taking a group of school children to visit some Japanese agricultural colonies in South Brazil. She was their tour guide. I told her I was born in Rio de Janeiro, spoke Portuguese, had been a civilian POW in the Philippines during the war, and had learned the martial air, "March to the Pacific." I began to hum the tune. The older man, who was about my age, picked up on the melody and we sang it through together. He, of course, sang the words, I could only hum the music. I corresponded with the young woman for several years after returning to America.

[4]Proverbs 12:10.

[5]Crouter, p. 31, Mar. 16, 1942.

[6]E. Mansell, p. 37: There's a great day coming mañana,
With a wonderful, wonderful dream,
Everybody, we're told, will be rolling in gold;
We'll be out of the doldrums mañana.
There'll be beer and pretzels mañana,
There'll be strawberries floating in cream,
With a happy refrain, with a quart of champaign,
We'll be launching a rainbow mañana.

[Chorus:]
High times, I hear the sky chimes,
So come you mourners and pick your plums,
Oh, come and pick 'em;
There's a great day coming mañana
If mañana ever comes.

[7]Foley, p. 198.

[8]Hind, p. 51.

[9]Herold, p. 39, Apr. 4, 1942. Crouter, pp. 34, 35: "An Easter service of prayer and songs, with Nakamura present, will be allowed tomorrow."

[10]Miles, p. 59, says, "Nakamura . . . *commanded* [sic] us to have an Easter sunrise service." Foley, p. 198, says, "permitted"; but on p. 202, she says, "Nakamura ordered." See footnote 9 above.

[11]Miles, p. 59.

[12]Halsema, p. [24], Apr. 5, 1942: "Elmer [Herold] didn't warn everyone but his excuse is that he didn't know about the order until ten minutes to six."

[13]Foley, p. 198.

[14]Halsema, p. [24], April 5, 1942, says that "Buck Parfet was slapped on the head and face five times for being caught walking this evening with Gerry Robinson. Dr. Nance says his eardrum is infected, although it may heal."

Herold, p. 39, Apr. 5, 1941: "Buck Parfet . . . walked with the Robinson family (chiefly Geraldine)—when he went back to the men's side, the Japs knocked him down for disobedience—fortunately Buck took it—but what a sorry ending to an otherwise good day." As I remember the incident, Nobu cuffed and punched Buck three times.

P. Mansell, p. 84, says in his diary that he went "down four times."

Halsema is probably right in saying that Buck was hit five times.

[15]Halsema, p. [24], Apr. 5, 1942. See endnote 13 above.

[16]See p. 96.

[17]See pp. 93–96

CHAPTER

13

We Move to Camp Holmes

The cleanup crew returning from cleaning out the barracks at Camp Holmes reported that the former Constabulary post was about eight miles distant from Camp John Hay.[1] They said it was located just off the Mountain Trail, which links Baguio with Bontoc, some ninety miles to the north as the crow flies, and, like Baguio, was about a mile above sea level. A relatively level area of about ten acres had been bulldozed out of the northern side of a mountain ridge that ran east and west. The camp had a magnificent view of the mountains to the north and northeast. The crew also said that they could see the China Sea twenty miles away to the northwest.

Three barracks were lined up roughly from north to south along the eastern edge of the parade ground. Near the southern end of the barracks stood two *nipa*[2] shacks lined up roughly east to west and at right angles to the barracks. A few yards south of the shacks was a steep red clay bank. A hundred and twenty yards north of the *nipa* shacks and across the parade ground was a drop-off that descended steeply for seventy feet to another ruggedly level area. Near the middle of this relatively flat area interspersed with pine trees was a sunken garden with a dry pool. This lower portion of the camp, which they dubbed Bottom Side, was bisected by an asphalt road that ran generally from east to west, and joined the main road coming into camp at its western end. On the far side of this road stood three houses spaced unevenly along its length. At the eastern end of the road was a two-story building that became our hospital. Nearby was a one-story house that became the Baby House. At the western end of the road, near where the asphalt road joined the main road coming up into camp, was a one-story building on the left painted dark green with white trim. This building became our high school for a time.

The cleanup crew reported that the mountain ridge south of camp ran roughly west and east. It rose sharply and was marked by steep limestone cliffs and thickly wooded ravines and gullies. Many of the trees were majestic pines. The crew said they found many useful things left behind by the constabulary soldiers. Among these were leather pouches that could be used to repair our worn-out shoes. There were many double bunk beds that would save on living space, and reams of military forms that could be used as scratch paper, if a school were ever started.

On the morning of April 23, at seven sharp, buses and trucks drove into Camp John Hay to pick us up. As our people passed through Baguio, Filipinos along the way waved furtively. Some even had the courage to hold up two fingers in the "V for victory" sign[3] when the Japanese weren't looking. By noon, five hundred Allied and three hundred Chinese internees, with the exception of the garbage gang, were settling into their new living quarters.[4]

Ralph and I were on the garbage crew that morning and helped pull the wagon the eight miles to our new location.[5] The last mile of our trek was almost all uphill. As we came to the fork in the road that led up into camp, I noticed two bullet-shaped cement columns a couple of feet in diameter set on either side of the entrance to the camp. The Mountain Trail veered off to the left in a rough semicircle that marked the northern and northeastern boundary of our camp.

The road up into camp was paved with asphalt. Thirty yards up this road and on the right was a warehouse or bodega, covered with corrugated galvanized iron sheeting on the roof and sides. Another twenty yards up this road, it branched off to the left past the Green high school, the Baby House, and the hospital. The main road continued up another 150 yards and leveled off where it came to the parade ground and bisected it. The area on the right was roughly twice the size as the one on the left. The far end of this main road T-ed into another road that ran parallel to the barracks and a few yards in front of them. The two barracks to the right were identical two-story buildings painted cream brown. The barracks to the left was a one-story structure

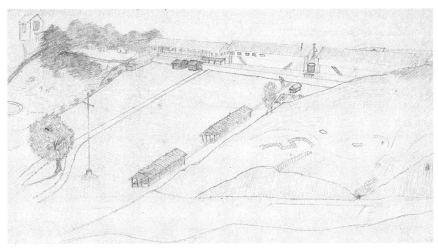

A bird's eye view of Camp Holmes drawn on January 4, 1944. The sketch is unfinished because a few days later internees were forbidden to go up on the hill.

painted dark green with white trim. It had a verandah in front. We eventually called it the Green Barracks to distinguish it from the other living quarters.

The light brown barracks on the extreme right, and closest to the base of the mountain, was assigned to the Chinese. The upper floor of the middle barracks was allotted to the women and children. The lower floor of this barracks housed the kitchen and the dining room. The Green Barracks was turned over to the men. After considerable wrangling, the Japanese let the mothers with babies have the one-story house on Bottom Side near the hospital.[6]

I noticed that beyond the *nipa* shacks the red clay bank rose sharply. In places it rose almost vertically to a height of some sixty feet, then leveled off onto a low, undulating shelf before rising steeply up the mountain ridge to the south. The western portion of the mountain was covered from bottom to top with all sorts of trees. Up this part of the mountain I could see a wide, heavily wooded gully, which we came to call The Slot. The eastern portion of the mountain ridge was considerably higher than the southern end. It was also wooded, and at the point where the cliff disappeared around a bend, I could see a rock formation that resembled the profile of an elderly Queen Victoria. We came to call this visage, "The Great Stone Face." Looking directly up the mountain from the road, parallel to the barracks, I could see a blocklike limestone formation at the top of the ridge, which Ralph later dubbed, "The Castle."

Directly to the east and on the other side of the barracks was an amphitheaterlike depression that sloped southward toward the foot of the

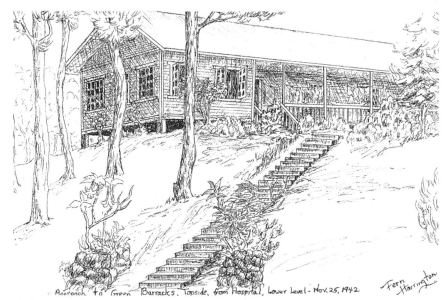

A sketch by Fern Harrington Miles of the north end of the Green Barracks and the steps leading down to Bottom Side.

mountain. It was filled with jerrybuilt shacks with rusting tin sides and roofs. Old-timers said that these hovels formerly housed the families of Constabulary officers, most of whom were Igorot natives. The northeastern and eastern sides of this area were bounded by the Mountain Trail.

At the insistence of the Japanese, our men erected a couple of fences between the Middle Barracks and the Green Barracks to separate the sexes. But, as the children played around these obstacles, they were soon demolished and never replaced.

Unlike Camp John Hay, the Camp Holmes barracks were not surrounded by a fence. Only a flimsy chicken-wire fence, hastily erected by our men, partially enclosed the camp. It was quickly apparent that Camp Holmes was going to be a much better place in which to live than Camp John Hay had been. However, we were not allowed to roam around freely on the parade ground until mid-November 1942.[7] Thus, if we had to go to the workshop for some reason, we had to secure permission, unless, of course, that was our assigned place of work.

By the time Ralph and I arrived at the Green Barracks, those who got there first had claimed all the good places. We found a rickety double-tier bunk and laid claim to it. Someone warned us that the bunks were infested with bedbugs. So, we first eradicated the pests with boiling water and, after letting the frame dry, lugged it up onto the porch and put our mattresses, sheets, blankets, and other belongings on it. From the verandah we had an open view of the parade ground and the guardhouse, a hundred yards to the west. To the left of the guardhouse, and some two hundred yards from the barracks, was the workshop.

April 29 was Emperor Hirohito's birthday. The morning was overcast. Sitting on our bunk, Ralph and I watched Doc Walker, chairman of the Camp Committee, and Jim Black, a gold miner, cut down a huge pine tree with a crosscut saw. The tree grew just below the mouth of the gully we called The Slot. When felled, the stump of the tree showed eighty-six rings.[8] After the wood was split and dried, the Japanese and our kitchen crew used it for firewood.

Because this was Emperor Hirohito's birthday, our captors allowed those who had relatives or friends on the outside to visit for a few hours in the afternoon. Lines were drawn by the Japanese with a "no-man's-land" between internees and visitors. Guards stood by to make sure that there was no close contact between the groups. However, internees were allowed to receive gifts, after they had been inspected.

Camp Holmes, now Camp Bado Dangwa, with the author and his daughter, "DeDe" Wood. "The Great Stone Face" is silhouetted against the clouds in the background.

One of our guards befriended me, probably because we were both eighteen. His name was Tatsumi. I never learned his full name. He sported a little Hitler mustache and spoke a little English. He taught me many Japanese words and phrases, and I taught him their English equivalents. It didn't take long for us to be able to communicate reasonably well. I still remember many of the Japanese words and phrases he taught me.

Late one afternoon, I believe it was May 4, it began to drizzle. Fortunately it was not accompanied by high wind, but Ralph and I realized that the porch was no place to be when the monsoon season began. The heavy rains would start in a few weeks, and we hoped to find a better location for our double-tier bunk before the wet weather set in. For several days, rumors had been floating around that the rest of the Chinese internees were going to be released. If true, we hoped to be able to find better sleeping quarters in their barracks.

Our Camp Committee put Dad in charge of the crew that cleaned the gutters around the Middle Barracks. Dad chose Ralph and David Longway, and Charlie and me as his helpers. Our job was to clean out the bones and refuse that fell into the gutters when the cooks disposed of the kitchen garbage. The kitchen was located at the south end of the Middle Barracks. The debris and wastewater that accumulated in the gutters had to be cleaned out with push brooms and a scoop every few days. We boys hated this filthy job, but someone had to do it, so, why not us?

On the morning of May 5 word spread that a Chinese man named Leung Soon had lost his mind and simply walked out of camp. The Chinese headman, Leung Nang[9] (no relation), immediately reported the missing man to the Japanese. They told the commandant that the man had been showing signs of mental illness for several days. Nakamura was upset. Nang and the rest of the Chinese became concerned that Leung's "escape" would put an end to their hope of being released.

When we first moved to Camp Holmes, the Japanese ordered our Camp Committee to appoint an Officer of the Day. This individual, we were told, would have to answer for anyone who escaped. When Leung was reported missing, Nakamura sent the following note to Lowell Harrison, our Officer of the Day for May 5:

> Harrison, O.D.
> Your *first* duty as
> Officer of the Day is to
> bring in that Chinese.
> (Signed) Nakamura.[10]

We were forbidden to communicate with the Chinese, and, if anyone did, I never knew about it. So, since we had nothing to do with this individual's "escape," we just ignored the demand. The order was not en-

The Guard House at Camp Holmes, where Leung Soon and later Frank Mount were beaten by the guards.

forced, and after a while the Japanese sent one of their soldiers to bring in the "escapee." We learned later that the soldier found him three or four miles away in Trinidad Valley. He was walking nonchalantly down the road toward his home in Baguio.

When the deranged man was brought to the guardhouse, the soldiers began beating, kicking, and knocking him to the ground. They did this again and again, seemingly oblivious to the fact that anyone who would walk out of camp, when he was on the verge of being released, could not be in his right mind. After roughing up the poor fellow for perhaps twenty minutes, the guards tied him to a tree and flogged him mercilessly.[11] From time to time they threw a bucket of water over him, apparently to revive him.

After about an hour, his tormentors untied him. The poor man tried to stand, but his legs buckled under him. "He was pulled up by his tied hands, [and] the same process [was] repeated again, beating [him] with sticks and the butt of a gun. All the guards took a turn at it. . . . [even] the little mustach[io]ed guard whom we like[d] took his turn with the rest at knocking . . . [Leung] down, [and] kicking [him] with [his] hobnail boots."[12] The little guard was my "friend," Tatsumi!

It rained that night, and Leung was left out in the downpour. Next morning I awoke about 5:15 and heard thumping sounds coming from the direction of the guardhouse. I rolled over and looked across the parade ground to see what was producing these noises. Through the twilight I saw poor Leung in a fetal position on the ground with a Japanese soldier kicking him. I watched with indignation as the soldier walked backward, then ran forward, hesitated long enough for his victim to relax, then charged again and kicked the helpless man full force in the back with his boots. This was what was producing the thudding sounds I heard. The soldier did this again and again until he tired of the sport. It was diabolical, and it roused my ire. The guard ministering these "tender mercies"? My "friend," Tatsumi!

Later that morning the sun came out. Leung, his hands still shackled, was left out in the hot sun. By now he was in a sitting position, his legs drawn up to his chest. We who saw the way the unfortunate man was being treated were outraged but powerless to do anything to help the poor wretch.

About ten o'clock Dad took us "gutter snipes" to the camp workshop to turn in some worn out push brooms and get some new ones. Before going, Dad warned us boys not to look at Leung. We looked anyway as we passed on the road within thirty feet of the poor man. His face was bloated and smeared with blood. His hands were bound, his arms and legs and back black and blue with bruises. He said nothing, but held up his hands in a pitiful gesture of "Help me." We wished we could do something to stop the sadistic brutality, but we could render no aid without bringing the wrath of the Japanese down on ourselves. Yes, there were times when our hosts acted like devils.

I must have been trying to put the horrible picture I had just witnessed out of my mind, because I was whistling when I arrived at the workshop. As I walked in, something on the floor must have attracted my attention, because I didn't see what happened next. I heard a crash behind me and Mr. Fabian Ream, the shop foreman, yelled, *"Don't you know that whistling is mental masturbation!"* I'd never heard of such a thing. I didn't even know that whistling annoyed the man. The clatter was caused by a hammer that crashed into the wall behind me. David Longway, who saw it all, told me later the hammer missed my head by inches.

I expected Dad to give Mr. Ream a tongue-lashing, but he said nothing. Dad was smaller and older than Mr. Ream, but he stood his ground and looked him straight in the eye. Mr. Ream must have realized that, intentional or not, he could have caused serious injury and, although he didn't apologize, he quietly handed Dad some new push brooms, and without a word, took the old ones in to be repaired.

Later, when I told Dad he should have given Mr. Ream a piece of his mind, he replied, "That's not the Christian way of dealing with problems.

'A soft answer turneth away wrath: but grievous words stir up anger.'[13] Violence only breeds more violence." I learned something about how to handle disagreements that day. I also learned that the Japanese were not the only ones capable of irrational behavior.

In spite of his irascibility and aversion to whistling, Mr. Ream was a good man at heart and a veritable genius at inventing and making useful things for camp.[14] For instance, he made soft soap for washing clothes by leaching potash from wood ashes and boiling it with leftover animal fat from the kitchen. When his lower plate broke, he made a partial from some old aluminum cooking pots. I remember seeing him come to breakfast one morning sporting his new "dentition." He sat down to a mug of ersatz coffee and said that he had to be careful, because aluminum transferred heat much more quickly than regular denture material. He said that the first time he took a hot drink, it burned his gums.

On May 7, a couple of days after Leung's terrible beating, Radio Tokyo reported that Corregidor had fallen, and a big poster was nailed up near our barracks proclaiming the Japanese victory.[15] Radio Tokyo triumphantly rubbed it in by announcing that Corregidor had fallen after seventy-two hours of pounding from land, sea, and air.[16] From now on, and for the next year, the war focused in Guadalcanal in the Solomon Islands and the Dutch East Indies, far to the south of us. There was nothing we could do but accept the fact that it would be a long time before we were liberated.[17] How long, we didn't know. It might be years. We resigned ourselves to making the best of the situation. From this time on and for the next year-and-a-half, our captors relaxed many of the onerous restrictions they had earlier imposed on us.

On May 13, when my "friend," Tatsumi, came to the barracks to tell me goodbye, he was all smiles and friendliness. We walked together from the Green Barracks to the place where the main road into camp ended at the road running parallel with our barracks. In his limited English, he told me he was leaving for China and hoped we could meet after the war.[18] I tried to be friendly, but I'm afraid my response was not as cordial as it should have been. This soldier, who had been so amiable to me personally, had a sadistic streak. I now realized that if he were ordered by an officer to run me through with his bayonet, he would have done so without batting an eye.[19] The Japanese soldier understood obedience to a command far better than any American soldier ever did.

During another changing of the guard some six weeks later, the departing soldiers told someone that they had had the best time of their lives while

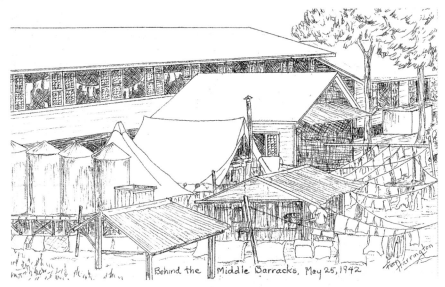

Behind the Middle Barracks, May 25, 1942

An "aerial" sketch by Fern Harrington Miles of the back of the Middle Barracks at Camp Holmes.

guarding us. It seemed a pity that our enemies should tell us this—that internees in a prison camp had given them more fun and shown more friendliness than they had ever known before. Their association with us must have lightened up the poverty and severity of their lives.[20]

If I had taken this sad fact into consideration, I might have had a better understanding of Tatsumi's behavior. I have since wondered if his demonstration of cruelty was a perverse way of trying to tell his American friends that he would never do to us what he had done to Leung.

In spite of Leung's "escape," the rest of the Chinese were released from camp between May 12 and 15. Now our hope was that with their departure the barracks they occupied would be made available to us. We were gratified when the Japanese told us a few days later that we could move into their building as soon as it was cleaned up. We swept and scrubbed it, and on May 28 the men moved from the Green Barracks to the Chinese Barracks. The same day, the unattached women moved from the Middle Barracks to the Green Barracks. This allowed the women with children in the Middle Barracks to have more room to spread out.[21]

On Sunday, May 24, the Japanese permitted two Catholic priests to conduct mass in the *nipa* shack farthest from the barracks. Soon after this, our captors allowed the Catholics to celebrate mass every Sunday at 7:30 A.M., and the Protestants were allowed to have a union service at 10:30. The Anglicans and Episcopalians, who wished to have their own worship service separately, were permitted to meet at 6:30 on Sunday mornings. Six months later the Adventists were allowed to hold services on Saturday morning—Sabbath School from 9:30 to 10:45, and preaching service from 11:00 to 12:00 noon.

Prior to receiving permission to have separate services, most Adventists attended the Protestant union service. We learned much-needed lessons in tolerance and respect for the religion and practices of other people. We might not understand the Bible in exactly the same way, but in a concentration camp, where everyone's character was revealed in the raw, one could quickly pick out the genuine Christians from those who merely professed to be Christians and came to realize that God's children are scattered in all churches.[22]

---

[1]Foley, p. 203.

[2]*Nipa* is made of palm fronds that the Filipinos used for thatching. It covered the roof and sides of the shacks.

[3]Crouter, p. 41, Apr. 23, 1942.

[4]E. Mansell, p. 46. By now many of the Chinese had been released, hence only about 300 moved to Camp Holmes.

[5]Foley, p. 203.

[6]Herold, p. 41, April 22, 1942: "After no end of coaxing by Elmer and Wally [Moore] and me, we were finally granted the use of that 'baby house.' "

[7]Ibid., p. [62], November 16, 1942.

[8]Crouter, p. 78, Aug. 3, 1942.

[9]Hind, p. 48, gives both names.

[10]Ibid.

[11]Crouter, pp. 44, 45, May 5, 1942.

[12]Ibid., p. 45.

[13]Proverbs 15:1.

[14]William R. Moule, *God's Arms Around Us* (New York: Vantage Press, 1960), p. 316: "Another godsend to the camp was Mr. Ream's [work]shop. It was about the size of an oversized woodshed. Mr. Ream had collected some crude but valuable tools and the things that were made and repaired in that little shop would surprise a magician."

[15]Herold, p. 45, May 8, 1942.

[16]Hind, p. 50.

[17]Halsema, p. 26: "We knew we would stay awhile."

[18]Crouter, p. 65, July 1, 1942.

[19]"We had few doubts that the Japanese soldier would obey his commander if he was ordered to kill the baby he had cuddled." Foley, p. 225.

[20]Ibid.

[21]Herold, p. 48, May 28.

[22]Ogle, p. 221.

CHAPTER

14

The First
Escapee

The rainy season in Luzon usually begins in July and ends in late
November. Old timers in camp could usually tell when a typhoon was
brewing. Although Noah ("Sy") Sorrell was a native of Tennessee, he had
lived so long in the Philippines that many considered him an old timer.
He was married to an Igorot woman and had two children by her, a
teenage daughter and a ten-year-old son. Sorrell was short and had an
unruly salt-and-pepper beard that swept toward the left side of his face.
His incisor teeth were gold-capped, but worn till the dentine showed,
and his mouth was constantly foul with profanity. A former navy man, he
was a southern rebel at heart, and was still fighting the Civil War. He
"chafed under the restraints enforced upon us by internment and had
often voiced the opinion that escaping from camp presented no serious
problem."[1]

Before decamping, Sorrell smuggled out a message to his wife telling her he was leaving and instructing her to go with their children to
a certain barrio off the Mountain Trail, far to the north of Camp
Holmes, where he would meet them. From his knowledge of Luzon
weather, he figured that mid-July would probably see a typhoon blow
in. The morning of July 16, 1942, dawned with the kind of overcast
sky that was almost a sure sign that a typhoon would begin within the

next twenty-four hours. Sorrell left camp shortly after roll call. Later, when he related his experience to me, he said he simply walked out of camp under cover of darkness.

Typhoon weather was definitely brewing when July 17 dawned dull and rainy, so roll call on the parade ground was dispensed with. But immediately after breakfast we were assembled in our barracks and a check was conducted under the watchful eye of the sergeant of the guard.[2] When Sorrell was discovered missing, the alarm was sounded. After a careful search, it was confirmed that he had gone AWOL.

Sorrell's escape started speculation among the internees as to what punitive action would be taken against us. After all, Mukaibo had threatened that, if anyone escaped, five men and five women would be shot. The Japanese did nothing in reprisal, however. Apparently, a single escape in six and a half months among a group of hundreds of internees guarded by a mere handful of soldiers and hemmed in by an inadequate chicken-wire fence, which only partially encircled the camp, probably satisfied the Japanese that to let well enough alone might, after all, be the best policy.[3]

On the night of October 21, 1944, Sorrell told me how he escaped and what happened after he left camp. He said that when his wife got his message she immediately contacted the guerrillas in Northern Luzon and made arrangements for Igorot *cargadores* to carry their luggage to a little valley farther north, just off the Agno River.[4]

By roll-call time on the morning of July 17, Sorrell and company were well on their way to their destination. As a Navy man, he knew how to handle weapons. Col. Parker T. Calvert, the guerrilla commander in and around the Agno River area, made him a sergeant and issued him "a Garand rifle, a Japanese rifle, a sidearm, 45,000 rounds of ammunition,[5] and six grenades."[6]

While waiting for orders to harass the Japanese, Sorrell built a little shack out of materials found locally. He planted a vegetable garden, in which he raised corn, *camotes*, and other crops. He said that the soil of his little paradise was fertile.

When the guerrillas became active in the early fall of 1942, he participated in several raids against the Japanese. These sorties goaded the enemy into action. They launched forays against the guerrillas. As a result of these raids a number of guerrillas were killed, and several were captured and publicly executed. For a few weeks the guerrillas laid low and Sorrell went back to his little valley. He stationed an Igorot sentinel at the entrance with instructions to warn him at the first sign of Japanese in the area.

He told me that some traitor disclosed his whereabouts to the Japanese and they entered the valley about sundown on November 16[7] and took him by surprise. They apparently expected resistance, because they came in firing. Unfortunately, his little paradise was surrounded by hills on three sides, and had only one way out. This sole escape route, an irrigation ditch,[8] was covered by the enemy, so he and his family took to some tall grass near his shack and hid. He said bullets whizzed four inches above their heads throughout the night. Fortunately, none of the members of his family was hit, except his daughter, who was wounded by a ricochet bullet.[9]

Sorrell said that when the Japanese entered the valley, he only had time to grab his weapons and ammunition and run with his family into the tall grass. He was later told that the Japanese fired 1,080 rounds during the night.[10] He realized he faced impossible odds and buried his weaponry in a hole he dug in the soft dirt and covered it up. Then he and his family crawled to a different part of the field.

Sorrell said that at first light the Japanese charged with fixed bayonets. He was sure this was the end. As one soldier lunged at his face, he seized the end of the weapon and drove it into the ground. Close behind the infantryman was an officer, who ordered that Sorrell be taken prisoner. He said that the soldiers beat him, his wife, and his daughter terribly, but they never laid a hand on his son. Instead, they fed him that night, while the others went without food for three days.[11]

After his capture, the Japanese loaded Sy down with as much of their equipment as he could carry, and he was taken to a field command post and handed over to a Japanese colonel. The officer asked him what part of a telegram he had received from headquarters in Baguio was true. The telegram accused Sorrell of being a guerrilla leader. In reply, Sy simply gave him his name and the date of his escape—July 16, 1942.

Sorrell said that the next thing he knew six *Kenpeitai* men pounced on him and beat him up. He claimed that he hit every spot in that interrogation room before they were through with him. But it was in Baguio that he was beaten up worst of all. He said that he and his family were jailed in the military police headquarters there.[12] After a couple of months there the Japanese brought him to Camp Holmes.

Sorrell took his punishment philosophically. I have never forgotten his words as he ended his hair-raising tale: " 'When you dance, you have to pay the fiddler.' "[13]

Soon after Sorrell's capture, Hayakawa, our new civilian commandant, let it be known that within a week Sy would be brought to Camp Holmes, tortured,[14] and publicly executed[15] as an example to us. Weeks went by and nothing happened. Thanksgiving came and went, then Christmas, and still no execution. Meanwhile, Sy and his family were held prisoners in Baguio. Finally, on January 20, 1943, his family was released from jail, and he was brought into camp and kept in the guardhouse.

I remember seeing him under guard from time to time when he was allowed to come out for exercise and fresh air. He was dressed in U.S. Army suntans, and walked or stood in front of the guardhouse with a soldier nearby. No one dared communicate with him. So far as we knew, he was going to be executed. But then, to our surprise, on January 29 he was released to join us. He didn't have much to say about his escape for quite a while.

In *Spirits Unbroken,* Renton Hind speculates that Sorrell was not executed because "General Nagasaki, a kindly old general in charge of the Baguio area—strangely enough, a Christian—took a fancy to Sorrell's ten-year-old son . . . and spared his father's life."[16]

---

[1]Hind, p. 59.

[2]Ibid.

[3]Ibid., p. 60.

[4]Ibid., p. 74.

[5]Some with military experience have pointed out that 45,000 rounds is an immense amount of ammunition. For one man to grab up and bury all the ordnance he claimed to have in one night would have been a Herculean task under ideal conditions and virtually impossible under fire. Sorrell was known to exaggerate.

[6]D. Mansell, p. 66.

[7]Hind, p. 74.

[8]Ibid.

[9]D. Mansell, p. 66.

[10]Ibid.

[11]Ibid.

[12]Hind, p. 74.

[13]Ibid., pp. 66, 67.

[14]Crouter, p. 124.

[15]Herold., p. 66, Jan. 21, 1943.

[16]Hind, p. 90.

CHAPTER
15

School Behind
Barbed Wire

Early in February 1942 the Maryknoll Sisters sent into camp books for the grade-school kids. At the same time Art Richardson, principal of Brent School, sent in a few books for the high-school students. Doug Tyson, who had resigned from the "kitchen gang" because of too much graft, was chosen our first high-school principal. Classes began on February 18. I signed up for Spanish I, with Jose Antonio ("Pepe") Icazbalceta as my teacher.

Pepe and his wife, Angelita, were survivors of the Spanish Civil War. He told us students how they had narrowly escaped death at the hands of Gen. Franco's Falangists. After they fled Spain, they went to Mexico and subsequently came to the Philippines, where apparently they had relatives. Pepe spoke Castilian Spanish and insisted we learn his pronunciation of his mother tongue. Mexican Spanish was abhorrent to him. I also signed up for a class in Bible, taught by Elder Frost, and a class in ancient history, taught by Charles Wittschiebe.

On February 22 the Japanese demanded that all schoolbooks be turned over to them to be censored. The books were never returned. Thus, our first high school died aborning. The elementary school children continued to be taught privately by women teachers until a regular school could be established, but plans for a high school had to be shelved for the present.

"Old China hands like [Dr.] Dana Nance recalled World War I and the havoc caused when German men were interned by the Japanese for four years . . . disrupting their children's education. They were determined not to let this happen to our children. There was no equipment, and for most classes there were no textbooks, but there were children and . . . many qualified teachers, [so that] classes were tutorial in size"[1]—"49 kids and 42 teachers."[2] Of the kids, twenty-three were high-school students, and of the teachers, nineteen taught high-school classes. So, about the time we moved to Camp Holmes, permission was sought from the Japanese to establish both a high school and an elementary school.

On May 26, 1942, the Japanese granted permission to open these schools—on condition that American history and geography not be taught. The reason? According to Major Mukaibo, Japan was remaking these subjects.[3] Since Japan was going to win the war, the geography of the Far East would be vastly different from what it had been before the war, and Japanese would be the lingua franca of the Greater East Asia Co-prosperity Sphere. Hence, no geography or American history, and the need to learn to speak Japanese. Although our leaders doubted his assumptions, they agreed to Mukaibo's proposal in order to get a high school started. The dark green house, a stone's throw from the place where the main road into camp branched off and went by the Baby House and the hospital, became our first high-school building. Preparations were made to begin classes in mid-June.

On June 14 we heard that a group of Anglican and Episcopalian missionaries were coming from Sagada and Bontoc, ninety miles north of Camp Holmes. We knew that several of these missionaries were teachers, so plans for opening our schools were put on hold until they arrived. On June 16, three army trucks came into camp bringing thirty-two nuns, teachers, and priests and their families. Father Vincent Gowen, an Anglican priest and an educator, was among the new arrivals. He was chosen principal of the high school. He did a remarkable job of educating us young people. "Half a century later [at the 1990 reunion], he was extolled as the most outstanding educator of anyone's memory."[4] This was true, but I would have to add that many of the other teachers were just as outstanding in their particular fields.

We got the textbooks for the allowed subjects from Brent School through the Japanese. The forbidden textbooks were smuggled in by Father

Richardson and the Maryknoll Sisters via an intermediary, and delivered to a store about a mile down the road from Camp Holmes that was run by a Filipino named Tabora. Mr. Herold, whom the Japanese trusted, simply walked down to the store on the pretext of buying food, put the books in the bottom of a pillowcase, and brought them back to camp. The Japanese never suspected a thing.[5]

About a week after school began, our teachers went to our commandant and explained that the students were six months behind in their studies and asked if the students with the greatest amount of catch-up work could be excused from taking the Japanese language class. Our hosts made an exception, probably thinking that only a few students had catch-up work. When the rest of us heard about the exemption, we decided en masse to take so many hours of class work, that we wouldn't have time to take Japanese. We had Japanese language class for only two days. Fortunately, our hosts never checked up on us or they might have closed down the school.

I have since regretted that I didn't learn to speak Japanese. I had a facility for learning languages, but because I wanted to be "patriotic," all the Japanese I ever learned were words and phrases the soldiers taught me. Instead of *nihongo*,[6] I studied three years of Spanish under Rae Hix and a year of German under Herb Loddigs. We were taught geography and American history, but American history was called biography, and my father taught geography to the elementary school children under the name of "reading."[7]

Dr. Ralph E. Longway records that "books, writing paper, ink, and other school supplies were all scarce and the classrooms Spartan to the extreme. [High] School began in the former commandant's residence [the green high school building], but once our labors rehabilitated the building, it was taken over by the new military group and we were displaced to a bare warehouse [the bodega]." He continues:

> The teachers' enthusiasm and our own interest more than made up for a lack of conventional educational tools. We internees had to rely on our own resources for everything we needed, and natural ingenuity . . . [supplied the wherewithal for] many an "impossible" necessity. We rummaged through heaps of waste, discarded files, and police records for our writing paper. Algebra problems we puzzled out on the backs of railroad forms, enlistment blanks, or corporation reports. Term papers and essays we scrawled on rain-

bow-hued kindergarten paper. When we ran out of ink, a chemist collected soot from a lamp and stirred it with some chemical that produced jet-black suspension. In need of a blackboard, our mathematics instructor daubed paint on a sheet of plywood, and when we ran out of chalk he used pieces of slaked lime. . . .

We were a seedy looking bunch of students, barefoot most of the time and shabby, but we had a great zeal for learning. We knew that knowledge was the only possession we would salvage from internment life. The dedication of our teachers and our lack of distractions and diversions gave us such a store of knowledge that in later years many of the college courses, even some of the premedical science requirements, were largely a review.[8]

Because I was a high-school student during most of our time in camp, my daily schedule usually went like this: 7:00-8:00 A.M., rise, clean up, dress, and go to breakfast; 8:00-8:15, roll call; 8:15-9:00, first study hall; 9:00 A.M.-12:45 P.M., high-school classes; 12:15-1:15, lunch; 1:15-3:00, classes; 3:00-3:30, free time; 3:30-4:30, study hall; 4:30-5:15, supper; 5:15-6:00, study or reading; 6:00-7:00, walking on the road; 7:00-7:15, evening roll call; 7:15-9:15, study, reading, or parlor games; 9:15-9:30, another walk on the road; 9:30-10:15, scrub the kitchen; 10:15-11:00, write up the day's happenings in my diary; and 11:00 P.M.-7:00 A.M., sleep.[9] Of course, on Saturdays and Sundays, or when we didn't have classes, this routine changed. On these days we either worked or attended church. Besides working as a member of the garbage crew, I sometimes worked with the wood crew rolling rounds of firewood into camp, or did other odd jobs. Other students had their own routines. These differed in one way or another from mine.

About a year and a half after our high school was established, the Japanese took over our schoolhouse for their own use and we were given the bodega near the entrance to camp. On February 4, 1944, I was sitting alone at the table in study hall in that building when our new commandant, Capt. Rokuro Tomibe,[10] walked in. I was caught by surprise and remained seated and merely nodded instead of rising and bowing[11]—and, of all things, I was studying "biography." Because I had never before met Capt. Tomibe I was sure I was going to be reprimanded for showing disrespect by not rising and bowing, but worse, he would catch me studying the forbidden subject, American history, so our high school would be closed and I would be blamed for it. I felt I had to do something. I watched Mr. Tomibe closely. Apparently, he had simply come to inspect the bodega. As he walked past the study hall table, he turned his head away from me for just an instant. At that fleeting moment I slipped the book I had been studying off the table and onto my lap, and replaced it with an American literature book, which I intended to study later. I began to peruse the literature book with great earnestness.

I acted just in time. When Capt. Tomibe turned around, he came over to the table, sat down across from me, and began a friendly conversation. He spoke some English and asked me what I was studying. I told him,

Captain Rokuro Tomibe with his family after the war. The captain was commandant of Camp Holmes Internment Camp for most of the year he was with the internees, who remember him with respect and even affection.

The words "The Ground," which Capt. Tomibe wrote on a scrap of paper the author handed him.

truthfully, "I'm studying American literature." He said he had read *The Grapes of Wrath* by John Steinbeck, and liked it. But there was another book he also liked.

"Do you know book . . ." he paused. His brow furrowed. He obviously couldn't remember the name of the book or its author. "About China," he mused. "Very good book. Author born in China." Another pause as he searched for a pencil and piece of paper. I tore off a small scrap of paper from a sheet I had with me and handed it to him with my pencil. He wrote, "The Ground," and handed it back to me.

"Do you mean *The Good Earth,* by Pearl Buck?" I ventured. I'd never read the book, but I'd heard about it.

"Yes, yes," he responded. "Very popular in Japan," he added.

As we conversed, I could feel the American history book slipping off my knees and casually reached down to keep it from falling on the floor. When it was time to go, Capt. Tomibe rose and bowed as he left. I nodded as far forward as I possibly could without standing. It wasn't a proper Japanese bow, but he didn't object, to my great relief, and left. I vowed never again to study "biography" in study hall, and I kept my word. I also kept that scrap of paper with the words "The Ground," written on it. I still have it.

In 1977, thirty-two years after liberation, Capt. Tomibe was the guest of honor at a reunion in San Francisco of former Camp Holmes internees. I showed him the scrap of paper with, "The Ground," written on it, and asked him if he remembered the incident. He couldn't remember it, but recognized his handwriting. I told him he had given me a big scare. He seemed surprised by my remark. I don't think he considered himself capable of scaring anyone.

Our high-school teachers were truly outstanding pedagogues,[12] no doubt about it. I didn't realize it at the time, but Father Gowen's classes gave me an appreciation for English and American literature I'd never had before. Years later it had an important bearing on my becoming a book editor and an author. Another teacher, Carroll Hinderlie, who taught ancient history, also had a lasting impact on my life. I could name others, such as Gene Hungerford and Harold Fildey, who were very good teachers. But James Thompson, a gruff young graduate from Colorado School of Mines who taught chemistry, was my favorite. I would have to consider him one of the finest teachers I ever had. Although I didn't pursue a career in chemistry, he sparked an interest in science that continues to this day. Whenever I open a newsmagazine, the first thing I look for is the science section.

Besides the elementary and high-school classes, there were qualified individuals in camp who taught adult classes. Sid Burnett, for instance, taught Navigation and Dead Reckoning, Roy Barton taught Philippine ethnology, and Miss McKim taught Japanese. (Capt. Tomibe frequently attended her classes and helped the students understand Japanese customs and practices. Natalie Crouter, who took this class, mentions his frequent visits in her book, *Forbidden Diary.*)

During the latter part of my senior year in high school, I took a college-level class in anatomy and physiology taught by Dr. Marshall P. Welles. I enjoyed the course immensely and thought I had found my niche in life. On September 26, 1944, I wrote in my diary: "I talked to Doc Welles about the requirements for taking the medical course. He said I had about seven years of study ahead of me."[13] Doc Welles was a fine Christian gentleman, an outstanding teacher, and he exerted a positive influence on my life.

On October 1, 1944, Nora Ream, Billie Dosser, and I graduated from Camp Holmes High School. Although my academic record was not outstanding,[14] Father Gowen must have seen something I didn't recognize in myself when he wrote the following encouraging words on my transcript: "Handicapped by lack of continuity in his earlier schooling, this student showed an admirable capacity for hard retentive study and steady improvement." Not until I graduated from seminary magna cum laude did I justify his optimistic assessment.

After liberation, when I presented my transcript, which carried, not just the names of my teachers but their degrees and the various colleges and universities they had attended, I had no problem being accepted as a freshman at Pacific Union College in Angwin, California. (Incidentally, our high-school diplomas had a symbolic "ball and chain" wrapped around them, crafted by Mr. Ream, Nora's father.) Other students who attended school in Camp Holmes also had their transcripts or credits accepted without difficulty when they enrolled in high school in the U.S. upon repatriation. Some of these students later achieved distinction in various fields. Ralph Longway, for instance, graduated as a medical doctor from the College of Medical Evangelists (now Loma Linda University) with an outstanding record.

At the 1977 reunion I took the opportunity to thank Father Gowen, Carol Hinderlie, and Jim Thompson for all the hard work they put into my education. In recent years I have expressed my appreciation to Dr. Welles about the impact he has had on my life.

---

[1]Foley, p. 208.

[2]Herold, p. 52, July 7, 1942.

[3]Halsema, 1942, p. [22], Feb. 22, 1942.

[4]Foley, p. 209.

[5]Herold, p. 44: "[We] cannot buy things at the gate, but Elmer [is] allowed to carry bags up from Tabora's store; he [is] the only one permitted to go down there." Ibid., p. 51: "[Fr.] Richardson sent books in via the camp trucks–[I'm] so glad the Japs didn't stop them; the other [forbidden] school books . . . come via Agpaoa to Tabora's and then Elmer carries them up the hill (the Japs do not inspect that)."

In an email from Betsy Herold Heimke, dated July 17, 2002, Betsy says: "I remember Dad coming up to our cubicle in the night from Tabora's [store] on the Mt. Trail and happily opening the bag for Mother and me to see. He acted like a kid who had robbed his Grandmother's house. Tabora's daughter had been a teacher and when she learned [that] a school was to be established in camp, she went to Brent and got those books." Betsy also says that the bag was a pillowcase.

[6]Japanese language.

[7]Betsy Herold Heimke in an email dated July 17, 2002, says: "In the grade school the subject 'geography' was named READING on our Report Cards, but not consistently. On my 5th grade Report Card one of the teachers who taught GEOGRAPHY was listed as 'Mr. Mansell.' That must have been your Dad." It was. He taught me geography when I was in grade school.

[8]Ralph E. Longway M.D. in the Loma Linda University *Alumni Journal,* September-October 1993, pp. 35, 36.

[9]D. Mansell, p. 40.

[10]Frances B. Cogan, *Captured: The Japanese Internment of American Civilians in the Philippines* (Athens, Ga.: University of Georgia Press, 2000), p. 113: "Tomibe, for example, was very popular with the internees; according to interviews of Baguio internees taken over thirty years later in 1977, 83 percent of those interviewed said Tomibe was 'humane' and 'an officer and a gentleman' under whose aegis the camp experienced 'a period of peace and calm' (Bloom, "Death," 81). Under Tomibe's civil hand, internees were allowed to picnic outside the camp on the surrounding hills, to take walks in and around the compound, and to hold Easter egg hunts, Christmas celebrations, and even a wedding (Tomibe, 41-43). Internees from other camps heard stories and soon envied those 500 or so at Baguio. . . .

"Tomibe also attended church services with the internees, respected their religious beliefs, gave extra food to the children, and made sure the camp residents received their Red Cross parcels without the supplies being pilfered by guards or the omnipresent *kempei-tai* (Japanese secret police), who were often guilty of using the slightest excuse to hold back or ransack parcels (Bloom, "Death," 81). . . .

"[T]he Baguio inmates remembered Tomibe so fondly and with such affection that they made him the guest of honor at the 1977 reunion in San Francisco at the Presidio; Tomibe and 135 former internees present had, apparently, a marvelous time. Notes critic Lynn Bloom, in conclusion, 'As far as can be determined, this was the only prison camp of World War II (perhaps of any war) to maintain such affectionate relations with their former captor' ("Death," 81)."

Longway, p. [36], Nov. 30, 1943: "The Japs don't slap comminglers down anymore, but they have diverse punishments. Admittedly this is heaven . . . [when compared with] Cabanatuan, but [treatment in] that [camp] is actual hell and death." Ibid., p. [47], Dec. 25, 1943: "[Since Tomibe was appointed camp commandant] we get more and more concessions. [I] rejoice to see it and am jealous of [the] happy couples."

Crouter, pp. 303, 304, Mar. 17, 1944: "Miss McKim says that Tomibe San is by far the best man we have had on the job. He is making a real attempt to understand and adjust problems, with a wider scope, vision and comprehension than others before him."

[11]It was Japanese custom for students to rise and bow when teachers entered a classroom. This is what I should have done, but I was caught off guard and merely nodded. Most Japanese would at least have reprimanded me and perhaps even slapped me. But Capt. Tomibe was made of different stuff. He was more broad-minded and tolerant of people with different customs than the majority of his compatriots. Thus, he took no umbrage because I simply nodded. We could not have asked for a more humane commandant than this gentleman. We respected him and, yes, you might even say, we loved him. See chapter 14, endnote 9.

[12]Longway, p. [205], Sept. 22, 1944: "I have obtained 3 most valuable years of schooling in here, years which cannot be improved upon."

[13]D. Mansell, p. 56, Oct. 1, 1944.

[14]J. Halsema, 1944 diary, Oct. 1, 1944: "The program was well done, its units: talks by Carl Eschbach; the graduates (competent Nora Ream, er, er, fumbling Don Mansell, Billie Dosser with real stage presence)." (Hereafter designated Halsema, 1944.) Longway, p. [217], Oct. 1, 1944: "Don . . . gave a good speech, as did Nora & Billie. All of them know what they're about. They're not gawky dumbbells." I believe Ralph was biased.

CHAPTER
16

Halcyon
Days

The year and a half from July 1, 1942, when our captors began to loosen restrictions on us at Camp Holmes, to February 1944, when some of the restrictions were reimposed, might be called our halcyon[1] days. Looking back on those nineteen months, and hopefully with greater objectivity, it must be admitted that, in spite of having our lives disrupted, living with great inconveniences, and having a proverbial Damoclean sword[2] hanging over our heads, life at Camp Holmes was not as bad as it could have been. In fact, compared with other prison camps, both civilian and military, it was not bad at all. In no way could our incarceration be compared to the horrendous conditions endured by our soldiers in O'Donnell and Cabanatuan camps, nor could our "march" from Brent School to Camp John Hay be compared to the infamous Death March from Mariveles to Capas. And yet, imprisonment in a Japanese concentration camp was certainly no picnic.

Compared with the internment camp in Manila, we had by far the better climate.[3] But, while we had that advantage, the Manila internees received more Red Cross food packages (we only got one), and they got more mail than we did.[4] According to the Japanese, social conditions in our camp were far better than those of other civilian camps, especially the camp in Manila. Ray Hale, who occasionally drove down to the Santo Tomás Internment Camp, told us that the Manila camp seemed like a restricted resort, with all sorts of vices. There were other ways in which we were better off than the camps in Manila and Los Baños. During the last months of our duress, but prior to our moving to Bilibid Prison in Manila, the internees in Santo Tomás and Los Baños suffered greater privations than we did at Camp Holmes. This was because the mountain people in the Baguio area raised an abundance of *camotes, camote cahoy,*[5] and green vegetables. Thus, we occasionally got a decent meal of fresh food, even in the worst of times.

So far as having our lives disrupted is concerned, millions of others, including citizens of neutral nations, had their lives turned upside down by the war. So, what we went through was not terribly unusual. On the other hand, I do not mean to imply that our experience is something we'd like to repeat, especially the first six months and the last year. Having one's liberties taken away and living on a starvation regimen is no fun.

During the relatively "good times," the worst part of internment camp was the boredom and frustration we experienced at not being able to get on with our lives.[6] The following verse I wrote expressed my feelings during those monotonous months:

> O this melancholy cloud
> Hangs about me like a shroud
> O'er my head,
> And I wish that I were out
> And could go the world about,
> Or be dead.
> But here we sit and sit,
> And the moments pass and flit,
> While we stay,
> And we do what we have done
> From the dawn to set of sun
> Many a day.[7]

I was not alone in expressing sentiments like these. Many others felt the same way.

After the war moved south, the Japanese lifted many of the restrictions imposed on us during our stay at Camp John Hay and even the first couple of months at Camp Holmes. As the Japanese relaxed the rules, we tested the limits of the liberties granted us as far as we dared,[8] all the while aware that what had been given could easily be taken away. However, the reimposition of restrictions was usually temporary. For example, when smuggled notes were found in packages, food bags would be interdicted for a time. And yet, except for the last year, the suspensions of food packages usually lasted only a few weeks at most.

There were several other factors that tended to increase our limited liberties. As I have mentioned, the flimsy fences erected when we moved to Camp Holmes broke down after a few days as the children played around them. By the first of May 1942 we were no longer confined to the immediate vicinity of our barracks, but could go to the hospital, the Baby House, and the high school, all on Bottom Side. By mid-November 1942 the chicken-wire fence that separated most of us from the workshop had broken down too, and we were allowed to walk freely all over the parade grounds.[9]

But perhaps the greatest factor in the enlargement of the physical limits of our camp was the felling of the trees on the slope southeast of camp near the rifle range and the workshop. Our guards needed firewood to cook their meals, and so did we, and the conifers and deciduous trees growing on the mountainside were a convenient source of fuel. A wood crew was organized to cut down these trees. A soldier always accompanied this crew to make sure no one escaped or contacted the Filipinos. But, as the men worked their way up the slope, the area increased for those who had legitimate business up on the mountain. This included those who took the food up to the wood crew and those who herded the goats. For many months this did not include the women. However, during the last months of 1943 and the first months of 1944, families and small groups that secured prior permission from Commandant Tomibe could go up on the hill and have picnics.

When we high-school students didn't have classes, or when we were on vacation, some of us were given the responsibility of taking the noon meal up to the wood crew. We were supposed to return to camp immediately after delivering the food, but often we didn't. We would sit down while the men ate their meal. When they finished and got up to go to work, we would get up with them and begin walking down toward camp. Then, as soon as they and the guard were out of sight, we would turn around and go exploring up on the mountain above the camp.

Ralph and I were two of several twosomes of high-school students who took the noon meal up to the wood crew then sneaked off and explored the mountain. We were especially interested in limestone caves that made good hiding places. Most of these were located on the higher elevations of the ridge. Whenever Ralph and I came to a rock formation that looked promising, he gave it a name. One such formation was a tunnel-like cave that went into the mountain about fifty feet then turned sharply left.[10] Ralph dubbed it "The Dog Kennel." The only time we went into this cave, I was in the lead. The farther in we went, the darker it became. When we reached a point where the cave angled sharply left, it became pitch black and we had to feel our way along.

Some forty feet beyond this angle, I felt a boulder about four feet high blocking my way. I could tell by the echo of my voice that there was more of the cave beyond. So I climbed up on the rock and was preparing to slide down the other side on my belly, when something seemed to warn me to stop. I believe it was my guardian angel. When I got back on my feet, I asked Ralph to hand me some stones. He felt around and found several small pieces of limestone and put them in my hand. I dropped one directly in front of me. At least a second elapsed before the stone clattered on the rocks below. I suddenly realized I was standing on a boulder perched on the edge of a chasm at least sixteen feet deep, probably deeper, and, for all I knew, the rock I was standing on might dislodge at any moment and take me down with it to oblivion.

I slid back down off that rock on my abdomen very carefully. Then, with Ralph in the lead, we groped our way back to where we last saw daylight. As I reflect on what could have happened, I believe God spared my life. I also believe that there is a spiritual lesson that can be drawn from this experience. As one Christian has put it, "When . . . darkness seem[s] to surround your soul, look to the place where you last saw the light."[11]

Sometime in the fall of 1942 Ralph and I decided to hide some of our mementos up on the mountain above camp. Our treasures consisted of bullets, a canteen cup, and some bandoleers and leather pouches. We sneaked away from the wood crew as we had often done before and took our souvenirs to a place that overlooked Trinidad Valley. From previous excursions, we knew the location of a large limestone outcropping that projected upward and outward some seven or eight feet at a sixty-degree angle. At the base of this formation was soft dirt. Here we dug a hole, buried our "treasures," and covered them over. Our plan was to retrieve these things after the war. However, about a year later, when the wood crew's logging operations were nearing an end and it was rumored that the loggers would be moving to a new location, Ralph and I decided to dig up our cache and bring it back to camp. When we unearthed it, the leather pouches and the bandoleers were badly deteriorated, but the metal objects—the bullets, the ammunition clips, and aluminum canteen cup—were still in good shape. We took these back to camp, and some of them survived the war.

We reburied the bandoleers and pouches and placed a slab of limestone rock over them. The slab was approximately fifteen inches long, a foot wide, and two or three inches thick. In 1991, during the fiftieth anniversary re-union of internees in Baguio, I went to Camp Holmes (by then named Camp Bado Dangwa). I climbed the mountain with sergeants Rogelio A. Ramos and P. Brioso and easily located the large limestone outcropping, under which we had buried our souvenirs half a century before.

The sergeants brought along shovels and insisted on doing the digging. So, I just pointed to the place under the rock outcropping, and they went to work. We had buried our mementos under less than a foot of earth. Now, half a century later, the soldiers dug down well over a foot before they came to the limestone slab. I took pictures of the sergeants digging. The soldiers removed the stone slab, and I looked for the things we had reburied, but these had totally disintegrated. I snapped pictures of the slab, the limestone outcropping, and the soldiers, then cracked off one end of the slab for a souvenir, so now I own "a piece of the rock."[12] I also broke off a couple of small pieces from this fragment and mailed them to my friends, Ralph Longway and Dick Patterson.

Yet another factor that contributed to our halcyon days was the fact that, because the main theater of action in the Pacific was now far to the south in the Solomon Islands, the soldiers who were stationed at our camp were far less hostile than the ones who guarded us while fighting was in progress on Bataan and Corregidor. When there was a changing of the guard, we pressed our liberties as far as we dared, and the new soldiers seemed to assume we had always enjoyed these privileges.

On one of our excursions out of camp, Ralph and I went as far as The Great Stone Face. As we stood on the brow of this formation, we saw a tan Japanese staff car coming around the bend of the Mountain Trail, which marked the western and northeastern boundary of our camp. Just before the vehicle reached the point closest to us, we hurled rocks with all our might at the car—and by sheer luck hit the roof. We were fortunate we didn't hit the windshield. The car stopped and several armed men jumped out, weapons drawn. We ducked down and watched. The car's occupants were obviously alarmed. We didn't wait to see what happened next. We beat a hasty retreat back to camp, making sure that no one saw us. That was the end of the matter. This was the only "aggressive" action Ralph and I took against the enemy during the war.

Although conditions in camp began to improve after the fall of Corregidor, July 1 seemed to mark a distinct transition for the better in our internment experience. This was the day Hayakawa replaced Nakamura as camp commandant. Hayakawa was a younger man, probably in his mid-twenties. He was born in the Philippines, the son of a local Japanese businessman. He was familiar with Americans and their ways, apparently from association with them before the war. He spoke good English and had a laissez-faire way of running our camp. He left our internal affairs in the hands of the Camp Committee, and with rare exception, treated us well.

Fifteen or twenty yards above where the giant eighty-six-ring pine tree had stood was the natural gully we called The Slot. As the trees were felled and tree trunks and large limbs were sawed into rounds eighteen inches long, and smaller limbs were cut into similar lengths, this ravine became a natural chute for rolling firewood into camp. We discovered that by sending a volley of rounds down through The Slot, we seemed to get considerably more wood into camp than rolling down individual chunks. Somehow the larger pieces jostled the smaller pieces and kept the whole barrage moving until much of it reached the bottom.

The men on the wood crew were mostly younger men in their twenties and thirties. They worked under the supervision of Doug Strachan. The wood splitters were mostly older men in their forties and fifties. They worked with John Barrett and Alva Butz by the *nipa* shack nearest the kitchen. The wood stackers were also older men, but included some teenagers, who worked under Richard B. Patterson, Dick's father. They arranged the firewood in stacks in this hut. When the kitchen crew needed wood for cooking, they hauled it to the stoves in a wheelbarrow.

At first, the shack where firewood was stored had a roof and sides made of *nipa*, but as children played around the shack, the flimsy walls got pulled apart, and eventually the side thatching was removed altogether. This facilitated the stacking of wood, and also made it easier to fetch firewood for the kitchen range.

As previously mentioned, life in camp revolved around food. Some twenty men belonged to the "kitchen clique." It included the cooks, bakers, dish washers, kettle washers, servers, and the servers of the children's special diets.

Mary Ogle writes in her book that

> in connection with the kitchen [clique, there] . . . was the dishtowel washing detail. In the early days this was not a very highly respected detail, but after our move to [Camp] Holmes a certain group of two or three miners' wives took over this job and did it all the rest of the time [we were in camp]. They rose early in the morning and got their job done and had the rest of the day to themselves until [it was] time to bring in the "wash" in the afternoon. We had the suspicion that this early morning crew got a few special favors from the breakfast cooks, who also were on the job early. . . .
>
> There were two other large details [that worked] in connection with the preparation of [our] food—the vegetable detail and the rice detail [but they got no extra food. These work groups labored in the kitchen at the north end of the Men's Barracks.] Some forty women . . . [were kept busy at these jobs, but] seldom did they all work at once. . . . [Frequently, it was] necessary to call in extra recruits beyond that number. . . . [These women] would go to work about seven o'clock or seven thirty in the morning[,] . . . stop for breakfast at eight o'clock, and [go] back to work till 10:30 or 11:00.[13]

After we had been in Camp Holmes for several months Dad was asked to take charge of the rice detail. The rice was spread out on tables, and a crew of women workers carefully picked out the bugs and any other foreign particles that were mixed with the rice.[14] When the cooked rice was served, some fastidious campers picked out any weevil that had been overlooked, but most of us figured that a little protein added to our diet wouldn't hurt, so we praticed the motto of, "See no weevil."

In order to speed up the work of cleaning the rice, Mr. Ream invented a clever laborsaving device that we called a "rice shaker." This contrivance helped sort out larger stones and other foreign matter before the rice pickers did the final cleaning.

Activities on Saturday evenings broke the monotony of living in a civilian prisoner-of-war camp. On July 18, 1942, we had our first Saturday-night program at Camp Holmes—a lecture by Dr. Howard Widdoes.[15] The following Saturday night we had an Amateur Night program. "Jim Halsema was announcer for [the] Major Bozo hour,[16] with Concentration Rice the sponsor. [The 'commercial' was a parody,] sung by a quartet to the tune of 'Have you Tried Wheaties.'" The "camp commercial," a takeoff on a Wheaties commercial popular before the war, went like this: "Have you tried rice,/ The best food in all of the land;/ Have you tried rice,/ it's full of grits and sand,/ It's mushy, it's musty, it smells so grand;/ Have you tried rice,/ the best food in all of the land." This was sung by a quartet of missionaries, led by Marvin Dirks. The cereal came "in seven different flavors— burnt [rice], coconut, caramel, perspiration, cockroaches, fish, and syrup."

"Carol [Dickey] sang hillbilly songs and yodeled; little Francine [Juhan] sang 'Smile Awhile,' each winning first and second prizes, which are said to be a ride on the garbage wagon to Trinidad. Rae [Hix] recited her concentration [camp] version of the poem about the tropics, ending, 'Oh, how I want to go home!' Mr. Perry [i.e., Bert Parsons] fluted and Alice [Ziegler] and Gerry [Robinson] sang in spite of an attack of stage fright. . . . [T]he evening [was] a howling success."[17]

On August 22, we were allowed to have another Saturday-night program— a community sing-along.[18] For the next few months these community get-togethers were held about once a month in the mess hall.[19] Later they were held every Saturday night. Many of these programs were lectures by people who were authorities in their field, some were skits, and a few were musicals. All of them were a break from the monotony of camp life.

Charles Wittschiebe put on one series that everyone enjoyed. He showed how that through graphology, the study of handwriting, one could analyze a person's character, disposition, and aptitudes. Internees would turn in a sample of their script anonymously into a box. During the week Wittschiebe would study their penmanship and on Saturday nights would report on his findings. I heard several people remark how amazed they were at the accuracy of his analysis.[20]

Several Saturday night programs were especially memorable. *Our Town,* a play by Eugene O'Neil, was put on by the high-school students and directed by Father Gowen. Another, *Camp Hamlet,*[21] was a satire. Several who have published books about our internment have included Yamato-San's critique of *Camp Hamlet.* It first appeared in the *Camp Holmes Daily News.* Here it is:

Many years have passed since I was interested in Shakespeare's "Hamlet" or Goethe's Faust. This evening [Saturday, July 29, 1944] I had the chance unexpectedly to see Camp Hamlet the tragic - comedy Hamlet. I have not yet acquaintance, though I must, with those persons who acted the roles or the writer of the opera or the musician. Though I had already some "Ahnung" [inkling? hunch?] that it was changed Hamlet from the old drama, I went to see it from curiosity and ennui. Mr. Smith the camp engineer. And lo! There the camp Hamlet was played! Within such limited dining room. With little clothing (except those female persons) and to make matters worse with no curtains or back scene, it must need the most skillful actors and actresses to play its performance. And then, it was played well admiringly well, with profound humor. I like most the Gost's monology those musical melodies. And then all persons sang together in comical yet mournful chorus, tears involuntarily spread in my eyes. It is 'humor' in psychological terminology. All persons roles were performed very well, and each actor or actress having individuality and charmingness. The queens garments were very beautiful as well as the nice gesture of Ophelia. King's comicality and Hamlet's voice, all combined camp Hamlet, the masterpiece was born. It took somewhat longer hours and it made the play more interesting and all passed smoothly except the carrying of Ophelia and doctors treatment. To conclude you are very artistic, musical, profound in esthetics and serene in this living. That is what I cannot help admiring about you. God bless you. Good night.[22]

Before the war Mr. Yamato was a middle-school English teacher in Japan. "He was a very small man, with a copybook command of English, and immediately became a figure of fun to the prisoners, although he was actually in a position to do us harm if he chose."[23] As a member of the staff, he was the camp's "official" translator. Rigid and ineffective, he was a tragic misfit.[24] He was shunned by his countrymen and tried vainly to make friends with us. Most of us did not return his attempts at friendship.[25] Instead, we snickered up our sleeves at his clumsy efforts at communicating. We took the attitude that our nations were at war and he wasn't on our team. As I look back on my contacts with Mr. Yamato, I have mixed feelings about this little man who was so pompous, yet so pathetic.

Another memorable Saturday-night program featured *Pocahontas,* a Thanksgiving skit put on by the high-school kids and directed by Marvin Dirks. For weeks afterward the three- and four-year-olds could be heard going around camp singing, "We will take him to Powhatan,[26]/ We will take him to Powhatan;/ We will take him to Powhatan,/ He will chop his [Capt. John Smith's] head off."

On April 22, 1944, Charlie and I put on a tumbling exhibition for the Saturday evening entertainment. First we walked in on our hands to the front of the stage, turned our backs to the audience, and "bowed" with our legs. (Laughter and applause.) We built up from foot-hand back flips to a full forward somersault. Next I did long dives with rolls onto a mattress pad. Then I did high dives over Charlie standing his full height.[27] The crowd enjoyed the acrobatics. They called for an encore when we went off. We returned and exited doing the "crab walk." We did this by squatting back to back, locking our arms at the elbows, and hopping off stage. The audience thought it was hilarious.[28]

Dick Patterson, who was a year or two younger than I, was the leader of some of the younger teenagers and older children. I was the leader of another group of youngsters. Dick organized his group into a kind of Boy and Girl Scouts Club. We played Capture the Flag[29] a few times out at the rifle range at the southeast end of the parade ground. My headquarters were located in the target area, high up on a clay bank, where we had plenty of red mud with which to defend ourselves. Dick's headquarters were located on a huge rock situated on the lower part of the foothill beyond the camp workshop.

On December 28, 1943,[30] our "armies" engaged in a mud-ball "fight," the only one of its kind we fought, and Dick won.[31] He surprised my team by coming up over the clay embankment that ran parallel with the *nipa* shacks. By attacking from this angle it was impossible for my team to get a clear shot at his "soldiers." The younger "recruits" on our teams made mud balls for the older ones to throw. Annarae Tong-Hunter, who was on Dick's team, still remembers stuffing her mud balls with rocks.[32] It was a dirty fight. Ralph described us in the end as looking like "refreshed carabaos"[33]— but the kids enjoyed it.

When we played Prisoners' Base, Dick sometimes led one team and I the other. We would gather on the parade ground, usually after supper. The players were chosen by the captains, and teams were usually evenly divided. Often we played until after sundown. The game involved a lot of running

Woman standing in line for a Meal
Camp Holmes - July 26, 1942

A sketch by Fern Harrington Miles of Camp Holmes with children playing on the parade ground where the author and Dick Patterson captained Prisoners' Base teams.

and attempts to free our teammates who were captured when they ventured across the center line separating the two teams and were trapped by their opponents. The kids enjoyed the game, and it was good exercise. Little John ("Reamo") Ream and his sister, Katie, were especially good at sneaking around the edge of the field and freeing imprisoned teammates.

The crew that cleaned up Camp Holmes, when our camp moved from Camp John Hay, found softballs, bats, gloves, and other athletic equipment left behind by the retreating Philippine Constabulary soldiers. They gathered these up and stored them in the hope that someday the Japanese would allow us to play *yakyu,* their word for baseball. That day came on November 16, 1942, when the Japanese gave us free access to the parade ground.[34] Sid Burnett, who had a special interest in physical fitness and sports, directed in laying out a softball diamond on the northeast corner of the parade ground directly across the road from the Middle Barracks. He also helped organize several teams. We played as often as weather permitted.

Among the various teams were the Juniors, the Seniors, the Jackrabbits and the Badgers, the Miners, the Hillbillies, the Missionaries, etc. Although the Japanese had adopted baseball as a national sport before the war, our guards never challenged us to a game. And yet, they seemed to enjoy watching us play. I don't know why they never played with us. Perhaps it was because it was a national sport of their enemy, or it may have been because the commandant disapproved of our guards fraternizing, or it could even have been because losing the game would have meant loss of face. I don't know.

I was not an especially good softball player when the first season began. In fact I was rather clumsy. I had lived the earlier part of my life in countries where soccer, not baseball, was the national sport. As a result, I didn't learn to play softball until our family was interned. Although I was never good enough to play in the infield, I did become fairly good in the outfield, and soon learned how to bat, and eventually became a fairly good slugger.[35]

When the rainy season began in the summer of 1943, we had to find activities other than softball because the field became too soggy. At first the rains came as brief showers late in the afternoon. But by July these rains often turned into torrential typhoons. These storms usually peaked in the late summer and early fall. Sometimes they lasted for days, and when they were raging it was impossible to do much except read, play parlor games in the barracks, or gather around the range in the kitchen to get dry and warm. Occasionally, during these months, there would be a break in the weather and we would venture forth to play softball.

By the time the Christmas season of 1943 rolled around, the monsoon rains had passed. The Christmas of 1942 and especially of 1943, were perhaps the most memorable "good times" of our entire internment experience. By comparison, the Christmas of 1944 was quite austere.

On December 24, 1942, the wood crew brought flowers and greenery down from the hills, and the mess hall was festooned with a Christmas tree. The pine-bough arches dripped "with silver bells and colored shining balls." Natalie Crouter continues her description:

> Along the windows at intervals were huge pine wreaths, with red paper bows at the base of Daphne [Bird's] tall painted cardboard candle of silver with red or gold flame set in the center. In between at the upright post hung the branches of red digitalis bells or big clusters of white flowers with buds-like wax orange blossoms set in dark green leaves. At the other end, from the arch, was a small tree . . . trimmed with streamers and a few ornaments. Near the door on a long box with [a] white sheet on it were arranged Santa and his reindeer, trees, animals to entrance the children.[36]

A Christmas Eve pageant was presented across the road from the Sunken Garden on Bottom Side: The simple manger of bamboo [was] covered with pine boughs. The choir sang in the distance, drawing nearer, then the paper star lantern glowed, shone upon Mary [June Crouter] sitting quietly beside the cradle where a soft blue light illuminated the spot where the baby lay. June looked serene and graceful. . . . The choir stopped beside the manger and while they sang the familiar hymns and carols, Wise Men and Shepherds came bearing gifts of gold, frankincense and myrrh to lay at the feet of the baby. A young lamb, bleating and kicking its heels, gave reality to the scene in the dusk.[37]

Early the next morning Marvin Dirks's thirty-two voice choir favored the internees and hospital patients on Bottom Side with Christmas carols. Breakfast consisted of papaya, bacon and eggs, rice, banana bread, and coffee. Alva Butz, with his snow-white whiskers, played Santa Claus, and Sid Burnett acted the part of a pixie. "The two had permission to dress below the guardhouse and pretend to come in from the 'outside' with the bags of gifts." Mr. Butz came onto the parade ground dressed in Doc Nance's red bathrobe.[38]

When Santa and the pixie appeared, the children all let out loud squeals and started running across the parade ground to meet Papa Noel. Santa unloaded the pack from his back and the crowd surged around him. For the very young it was the climax of a perfect day. Santa brought adorable handmade dolls of all sorts, cloth books, doll beds painted blue or yellow, stuffed ducks, horses, and frilled clowns.[39] The gifts Santa passed out were, of course, made by the children's parents.

Christmas 1943 was the most elaborate festive occasion of our entire internment experience. This was just a few days after we received our one and only Red Cross package from America. Ralph and I gathered pine branches from up on the hill for decorations and carried the clumsy things down to camp "till [our] fingers cramped."[40]

"The dining room has *real* curtains made of precious sheets held back by ties," wrote Natalie Crouter.

We . . . [shot] the works on torn ones now that crisp new Red Cross sheets are in the bodega. The dining room is a completely different place. . . . On each table are candles in bamboo sticks, a center tree with icicles of cellophane paper giving a frosty touch. There are pine cones around each tree, a holly spray at each candle. The mantel with [Longfellow's aphorism] "Learn to Labor and to Wait," is covered with holly sprays, red flannel stockings hanging in front of the brick fireplace with logs ready [to be lit]. A clock in the center of the mantelpiece points at 5 to 12.[41]

This was the year that Daphne Bird drew a picture of our camp being liberated by tanks and the marines, in which boyfriend and girlfriend Charlie and Kay were featured prominently.[42] The festivities began Christmas Eve with a beautiful Christmas pageant with marvelous singing by a choir, again directed by Marvin Dirks. Billy Herold played the part of one of the three kings.[43]

Natalie Crouter continues her description:

> The choir was screened so that no light bothered the silent congregation gathered on the terraces just above the sunken gardens. All over was the soft evening fog which drifted slowly away revealing a spangled sky above the dark pines along a mountain skyline.
> . . .
> First [scene]—No room at the Inn, with Joseph knocking at the door and being turned away, Mary [Ruth Zimmerman] kneeling in shadows as her time had come. As Dirks's splendid voice died away on "No room, no room, at the Inn" the light fell on a higher level where the Three Wise Men stood before Herod clothed in rich purples and wine reds. They asked for the new King and were pointed the way by those who asked that He be delivered to Herod when they found Him.
> Again the light traveled to a piece of hilly ground-pasture surrounded by bushes where shepherds stood in long cloaks guarding their flocks. . . . Ann [Gowen] was thrilled to see Bedie [Fred Crouter] in a sack-loincloth, bare from the waist up, holding his crook stead[il]y. The angel, in [a] white robe and shining star crown, came [down] from somber trees bearing glad tidings of a newborn Savior. As the light died, a group of children crept forward to sing in young clear voices before the dark was illumined again on the fourth and last scene—a manger under green pine boughs for [a] roof. Ruth Zimmerman was a serene, gentle Madonna who sang, "Away

in a Manger," to her infant son on the straw bed. . . . The Wise men came, bearing gold and frankincense and myrrh . . . followed by the shepherds with goats, the black one bleating . . . loudly, nearly escaping, but Bedie held on tight till the light went out.[44]

A month after this memorable Christmas, conditions in camp began to change for the worse. By that time the Allied forces under Gen. MacArthur were island-hopping northward, and the prospect that Japan would lose the war became increasingly apparent. As a result, camp regulations became progressively more restrictive. But before going on, we must go back and pick up the thread of other events that occurred in the latter half of 1942 and early 1943.

---

[1]A calm, peaceful period, usually associated with days, as "halcyon days," but figuratively, any period of time so characterized.

[2]Dionysius I, ruler of Syracuse, made Damocles sit in a chair with a sword suspended over his head by a single hair. The realists in our camp believed we would be sitting under a figurative Damoclean sword when America liberated us.

[3]Herold, p. 69, Mar. 25, 1943: "A Jap General and [the] Jap head of [the] Manila camp visited us [and] said we [are] much worse off than Manila. The climate and the scenery are the only things we have, but they are something."

[4]See Cogan, pp. 110-112, for a comparison of conditions in various civilian POW camps in World War II.

[5]*Camote cahoy* was a starchy tuber that grows in the tropics and is known elsewhere as cassava or manioc.

[6]Halsema, Aug. 28, 1944: "Life has a peculiarly numbing quality these days for me—boredom and bad diet are combining to leave me ambitionless, shiftless, touched with a gentle melancholy, tired without having done anything."

[7]D. Mansell, p. 43, Aug. 25.

Foley, p. 214: "The correct word describing the bulk of our wartime experience was not 'exciting' but 'dull'–extremely dull."

In his unpublished diary, my brother, Charles G. Mansell, expressed his melancholic pessimism in these lines:

Weak and weary time shall spell;
In this prison camp we dwell
Far away from any aid;
One by one in earth we're laid,
Till at last alone I'll weep,
Lost in thoughts that once were deep;
Lost in troubled winding thoughts;
Finding misery where I sought.

[8]Foley, p. 200: "Our men . . . kept testing the limits of our guards' tolerance."

[9]Herold, p. 62, Nov. 16, 1942.

[10]Longway, p. [35], Nov. 26, 1943: "With Don and Charlie, go to [the] bottom of Dick [Patterson]'s cave, which goes down and ends in a [a] large, but wet, room. [This was an] adventure in itself, using [a] candle, etc. [We] wander[ed] around . . . [over the surface] rocks and . . . [saw] Joe [Smith]'s cave. [I] found [a] good piece of crystal and coral in various caves. . . . [This was out-of-bounds], but who cares; not us. [We went] back to [our] fire, and stay with Don long after the rest of them go, and read *Lost Horizon*. . . . [Rain threatened], so [we] packed [our] stuff and . . . [hurried] down in a drizzle."

Neither of these caves that we explored was the cave that Ralph dubbed the "Dog Kennel." For some reason Ralph does not describe this episode, so vivid in my mind, in his diary.

[11]Ellen G. White, *Ministry of Healing*, p. 250.

[12]Apologies to The Prudential Insurance Company of America.

[13]Ogle, pp. 193–195.

[14]Ibid., p. 196.

[15]Herold, p. 53, July 17. Ethel Herold gives the date as July 17, and says it consisted of a lecture by Dr. Wilson H. Widdoes. Unless there was a Friday-evening program on July 17, it appears that Ethel is incorrect. Halsema, 1942 diary, Saturday, July 18: "Veteran missionary, Dr. Howard W. Widdoes, 69, lectured on the Ilocanos."

[16]This was a takeoff on Major Bowes Amateur Hour, a popular radio program in the U.S. See Halsema, p. [37]. After liberation I heard that "Major Bowes" was a Nazi spy, who passed secret messages to the Germans via his program until he was caught.

[17]Crouter, p. 73, July 23, 1942.

[18]Herold, p. 56, Aug. 22, 1942: "[We] had another Sat[urday] night program. . . . Hope the Japs don't stop them."

[19]Ibid., p. 58, Sept. 30, 1942. On the 27th "Peggy Whitmarsh talked of her travels." Ibid., p. 60, Oct. 31, 1942: "Billy [played] John Alden; Betsey [Betsy] a pilgrim."

Crouter, p. 110, Nov. 28, 1942: "[John Bergamini gave his] first lecture on architecture, today [Nov. 28, 1942]."

[20]Herold, p. [81], Dec. 14, 1943: "The following is C. E. Wittschiebe's analysis of my page of handwriting:

" 'You have definitely a dual nature that sometimes is cold and indifferent, and at others, tender and sympathetic. Seemingly, you fluctuate between extreme economy and bursts of liberality. You are not easily influenced, but could easily dominate others, if opportunity offers. You are energetic, lively, a quick thinker, enthusiastic. You have a streak of curiosity, strong ambition. Your mind is logical with but slight intuitive leanings. It is capable of fine thinking, quick powers of perception. But other indications are that you are often confused in your reasoning, failing to make proper or sustained use of the powers you have. You have executive ability of an unusual order. ([Have you] ever managed an office or similar enterprise?). Definitely you are of a nature more material than spiritual (like so many women [*sic*]). You show a strong streak of vanity and pride, express your opinion rather decidedly at times. Your imaginative powers are good and lively; you have some humor, and a tendency toward being selfish. Against this, however, you are kindly, relatively good-natured, make a good 'mixer.' "

This was an astonishingly accurate word picture of Ethel Herold's personality.

[21]Foley, p. 220: "The most memorable and moving [of these] event[s] was the high school production of 'Our Town,' followed . . . by 'Our Camp' [i.e., "Camp Hamlet," a] . . . hilarious [satire that] . . . gave us a chance to laugh over our predicament."

[22]D. Mansell, pp. 35, 36, Aug. 2, 1944.

[23]Whitfield, pp. 206, 207.

[24]Crouter, p. 373, Aug. 16, 1944: "Miss McKim says [that] Yamato is really pathetic, he tries so hard to interpret and explain each to the other."

[25]Ibid., p. 364: "Yamato discussed [with Jerry Crouter] how unpleasant it is to have beriberi, for he too has it. When he started to leave he acted as though he wanted to shake hands but was afraid of being turned down. Jerry stuck out his huge paw and the little teacher of middle school grabbed it and hung on in a long shake, loathe to let go."

During the final days of internment I remember him telling a group of us that the Americans were coming very slowly toward Manila "to protect their behinds." I'm sorry to say that we laughed at him, and I was one of them.

[26]The Indian chief's name was pronounced Poe-HOT-un, instead of Pau-huh-TAN.

[27]Ralph commented in his diary: "Don and Charlie did their tumbling very well tonight, very agile, supple pair of athletes, beautiful to watch their complete flips" (Longway, 102, Apr. 22, 1944). "After roll call [I] watched Don & Charlie do cartwheels, handstands, turns in the air, hand-walking, etc., in their traditional style" (Ibid, p. 184, 185], Aug. 25, 1944).

[28]D. Mansell, pp. 18, 19, Apr. 22, 1944.

[29]Longway, p. [48], Dec. 28, 1943: "[We played] capture-the-flag."

Crouter, p. 74 (July 26, 1942): "Bedie was torn between food and a new guerrilla game the boys are playing on the back slope. It is out of bounds but the guards don't seem to mind the youngsters up there and what a thrill for them."

[30]Longway, p. [46], Dec. 28, 1943.

[31]Ibid. Ralph wrote that the teams were "even" and that it "ended in [a] draw," but my memory is that my team got trounced.

[32]Anna Rae [Tong-]Hunter letter to Donald E. Mansell, postdated Mar. 8, 2002: "One of the highlights of our reunion [in San Antonio, Texas] was the chance to reminisce . . . with you and Eloise about baseball games and mud ball fights. . . . Please include all that information in your book."

[33] Water buffaloes. This animal, originally from India, was used for agricultural purposes in the Philippines. To cool off they were allowed to wallow in muddy water.

[34]Herold, p. 62, Nov. 16, 1942: "We can . . . walk all over the parade ground now."

[35]Ogle, p. 240: "The sturdy young Don Mansell hit many a home run."

Longway, p. [81], Mar. 12, 1944: "They wouldn't let us have Don [on our team], he's too good."

[36]Crouter, p. 115, Dec. 24, 1942.

[37]Ibid., p. 116, Dec. 25, 1942.

[38]Herold, p. [65], Dec. 25, 1942.

[39]Crouter, p. 117, Dec. 25, 1942.

[40]Longway, p. [46], Dec. 24, 1943.

[41]Crouter, p. 26l, Dec. 24, 1943.

[42]See p. 11.

[43]Herold, p. 82, Dec. 24, 1943.

[44]Crouter, pp. 261, 262, Dec. 24, 1943.

CHAPTER
17

Two Months Under Virtual House Arrest

On Wednesday, September 2, 1942, when we had been interned for eight months, a rumor swept through Camp Holmes that several internees, including Jim Halsema, the publisher of the *Camp Holmes Daily News*, his parents, his sister Myrtie Legget, along with Betty Foley, Dr. Nance, Gladys Anderson, and several others were to be part of a prisoner exchange and would soon leave for Mozambique[1]—Mom and Dad's original destination. We had been fooled by rumors many times before, but we hoped that we would be among the lucky "some others"[2] who would go. Apparently there was substance to the rumor, for the sailing date actually was set for September 20.[3] Soon we found out that some official was bribed to substitute the names of internees in Santo Tomás Internment Camp[4] in place of people from our camp, and our hopes were dashed.

On September 12 we were told that forty-two missionaries[5] who could support themselves on the outside, would be released to live in Baguio.[6] This included all thirty-two SDAs. We sincerely hoped that the Japanese would not repeat the mistake they had made in January 1942 in allowing us to be released, only to be reinterned the next day. We also hoped that in the near future all the missionaries and other internees would be allowed to live outside of camp.

By the time this announcement was made, Charlie was going steady with Kay. Although the no-commingling rule had been relaxed to some degree, it still had not been lifted on young people. The prospect of a separation that might last for the duration was, apparently, too much for the best friends. They were caught by an overzealous soldier, while simply sitting on a bench just outside the mess hall talking. Charlie was taken to the guardhouse. (Often guards would egg on the teenage boys and girls, saying, "Kisu, kisu.")

News of Charlie's "arrest" and the possibility that our release might be jeopardized, greatly upset Ralph Dinsbier. He came to me and said that

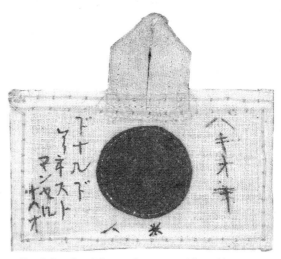

The "dog tag" the author was obliged to wear while released for two months in Baguio in 1942.

if Charlie's breaking the no-commingling rule resulted in the cancellation of our release, we had "better get out the horse liniment."[7] I never saw the man so perturbed. He needn't have gotten upset. Charlie was released later that evening, and the Japanese said no more about the matter. I don't believe they even associated this incident with our release.

On the afternoon of September 15, trucks arrived in camp. We loaded our belongings onto them and were taken into Baguio, where we registered with the Japanese military. Each of us was issued small cloth tags, on which was inscribed in hira gana syllabaries our names, ages, and the fact that we were enemy aliens. The tag was sewed inside a small celluloid jacket, and we were told to wear it at all times and all places. (I still have my tag.)

Major Mukaibo informed us that we were being released under the following conditions: (1) We must not communicate with the Filipinos, except to buy food and other necessities; (2) we could attend church in private homes on Sabbath, or at Carl Eschbach's church[8] on Sunday; (3) we could go to Burnham Park for recreation for a couple of hours each day; (4) we must register with the Philippine civil authorities as soon as possible; and (5) the majority of our time was to be spent at our homes.

In many ways our release was nothing more than a glorified form of house arrest. After we were let out, we discovered that it was safer to be in camp than out of camp.[9] At least in camp we knew whom we could trust and whom we couldn't. Outside there were those who would betray us to the Japanese for a price. Even though the vast majority of Filipinos with whom we came in contact hinted, and even told us openly, that they liked Americans and hated the Japanese, we had to be guarded, lest those who expressed such sentiments be stool pigeons.

The Santoses were surprised and delighted to welcome us "home" when we showed up on their doorstep. As soon as they invited us in and the door was shut, Mr. Santos told us the latest war news. He confided that his nineteen-year-old son had joined the guerillas and was out in the hills "fighting the Japs." He said he got the news every night from KGEI in spite of the prohibition against listening to Allied radio stations on pain of death. He was clearly anti-Japanese as well as being fully informed regarding what was going on in the rest of the world. He told us about the Russian offensive on the Eastern Front the previous winter and confirmed that what the Japanese called the "American debacle at Midway" was really a catastrophic defeat for Japan. He also filled us in on the fierce fighting going on in the Solomon Islands. We were wary to begin with, but by the time he finished, he had so "incriminated" himself that we concluded we could trust him.

That night, after everyone else was asleep, Mr. Santos invited Dad and me to come downstairs and listen to the KGEI newscast. We were so starved for reliable news and felt so sure we could trust Mr. Santos, that we accepted his invitation. As the days went by we learned that our confidence in Mr. Santos was not misplaced, and thereafter we were frequently invited to come downstairs to listen to Allied newscasts. What we heard buoyed up our spirits and revived our faith in the ultimate victory of the Allies over the Axis.

The day after our release Dad and I went to Baguio City Hall to find out about registering as aliens. The official who handed us the registration blanks quietly expressed his loathing for "the Japs." I believe he expressed his true feelings, but we had to be careful. Before we left he told us we would need individual photographs, where we could have them taken, and to return with our pictures to his office in three weeks with the filled-out forms in order to complete registration.

On our way out of City Hall, Dad and I stopped and looked at a bulletin board that had the photographs of fugitives being sought and guerrillas who had recently been captured. Among the latter was a photo of a Col. Nakar and some of his captured guerrilla fighters. They had been caught somewhere in northern Luzon. The caption under the photo stated that the colonel and his men were to be executed, but didn't say when or where.

Our fellow SDAs, whose homes had been damaged by the bombing and subsequently ransacked, found other places to live. The Longways rented a house owned by Joe Rice, a Jewish internee and former real estate agent, who was married to a Japanese woman. This cottage was situated high up on Quezon Hill west of the market. It was at his house that we usually gathered for Sabbath services.

On our way home from church on Saturday, September 19, two Filipino teenagers sped by us going down the hill. They were traveling in a homemade wagon and were going at breakneck speed. Moments after disappearing around the bend below us, we heard a crash. When we came upon the boys, one of them was injured, the other was not. The temple of the injured boy had been gouged by the impact, and he was holding a piece of flesh, which was barely attached to his head, with his soiled fingers. The wound was bleeding profusely. He asked us how bad it was. We wanted to help, but we had nothing with which to administer first aid. The best we could do was to urge his companion to take him to the Baguio General or Notre Dame Hospital emergency room and get the wound treated as soon as possible.

On October 7, my nineteenth birthday, Charlie went to the Baguio market to make some purchases for the birthday celebration. He was gone far longer than we expected, and we became concerned. When he finally got home, he was visibly shaken. He had been forced to watch five guerrillas executed.

As he was going about his business, a couple of trucks with Japanese soldiers drove up. The soldiers jumped off the trucks and shooed everyone out of the market and into an open area across the street, where the guerrillas were to be put to death. One guerrilla was beheaded, three were bayoneted, and the last one was shot. Mrs. Longway also witnessed this execu-

Burnham Park, where the author and his brother used to skate on the cement circles on the left of the photo. This photo was taken September 23, 1947, by the U.S. Army, after much of Baguio had been rebuilt.

tion.[10] I have often wondered if Col. Nakar was one of the condemned men.

Whenever the weather permitted, Charlie and I spent a couple of hours several times a week skating at Burnham Park. Ralph and David Bergamini frequently joined us there. We enjoyed racing around and playing tag in and out of the concrete circles. Four teenage mestizo[11] boys, all of whom were excellent skaters, often came to enjoy the rink. We spoke to them only briefly once or twice, and then only when we played Crack the Whip. In this game, seven or eight skaters would hang on, one behind the other, and race around until those at the head of the line turned sharply and "dug in" their skates. This caused the ones at the tail end of the line to be whipped around. The purpose, of course, was to see who could hang on and who would be slung off.

The reason we didn't talk to these boys was fear that we, or they, might be arrested and questioned by the *Kenpeitai*. As a consequence, it was only after we were re-interned that I learned from Sonny Woodson that these young men were his friends. One of them was the son of John ("Jake") Albright, another was the son of William Grau, both of whom were internees until they were released to live with their Filipino families. The other two boys were the sons of a German immigrant by the name of Möller.

During the fiftieth reunion of internees in Baguio, I met one of the Möller boys and had a pleasant time reminiscing about skating in Burnham Park and other things that happened half a century earlier.

One day two Japanese junior officers in their late twenties or early thirties came to the skating rink and rented skates. It was obvious that they had never been on skates before. They insisted that we teach them how to skate, and we did our best, but without much success. So, we would let them hang on to us and we would pull them around the rink. They enjoyed the free rides immensely.

One day I sat down on one of the park benches with one of these officers and began plying him with questions. He understood a little English, and I knew a few Japanese words and phrases, so I asked him if he was present at the execution Charlie witnessed, and he said he was. I told him that my brother was there too. He didn't seem surprised. Since he was wearing his samurai sword, I wanted to ask him if he was the one who beheaded one of the guerrillas, but decided I'd better not. But I did ask him if his sword was sharp. He said, with evident pride, that it was. At that point I decided I'd asked enough questions.

One day, when these officers came to skate, Charlie got a "bright" idea. Why not invite them to play Crack the Whip with us? Charlie took the lead, and seven or eight of us formed the rest of the whip. The two officers were placed at the tail end of the line. Around and around we sped in and out of the concentric circles. The officers were having great fun. Just then Charlie braked, digging in his skates, as did others at the head of the "whip," and the two officers went sprawling onto the grass between the circles. Fortunately, the grass was soft and neither man was injured and, I must say, they took their fall as good sports and laughed with the rest of us about their spill. But they never came back for more "skating lessons."

During idle hours at our apartment, I spent much of my time drawing pictures. One sketch, dated November 3, 1942, was a picture of Baguio Catholic Cathedral. Occasionally, Ralph and his brother, David, would come over to our apartment and spend the afternoon playing parlor games. Those were the fun times, but most of the time spent in our apartment was boring.

A week after the five Filipinos were executed, the guerrillas took out their revenge on the Japanese by taking over Trinidad Valley town hall under cover of darkness. They also exploded charges on the bridge over the

Trinidad River, and shot into Camp Holmes as they left the area. We on the outside knew nothing about this action, but as a result of it, we were re-interned.

Mrs. Herold, who was in camp when the guerrillas became active, recorded: "[We were] awakened at 1:15 [A.M.] by [a] terrific BOOM and shaking of the building. Before Elmer could get dressed [we heard] another BOOM. . . . [Elmer] went to the guardhouse [and discovered that] the guards [were] as surprised and scared as we women. . . . There were gun-shots in the hills; [and] answering shots. Hayakawa told Elmer to order all [the] men to stay in their barracks; [and] all women to come to . . . [the Middle Barracks]. . . . By 3:30 [A.M. there was] much shooting by our guards; much shooting all around in the hills."[12]

After it was over, the internees learned that the guerrillas took over "the presidencia (town hall) and . . . provincial capitol [sic] of Benguet"[13] for several hours, and partially destroyed the bridge over the Trinidad (Balili) River.[14] The bridge was located about a mile from Camp Holmes on the way to Baguio, and it was here that we dumped the camp garbage.

On November 7, due to the guerrilla activity around Baguio, Carl Eschbach, Arthur Richardson, George Bartter, Woody Bartges, Marshall Welles, Frederick Brandauer, and Leland Johnson[15] "were jailed on the charge of giving help to the enemy." None of the SDAs were taken in for questioning, and we knew that these men "were just as innocent as any of our own. The situation in town became very tense, and so we were almost glad when on the morning of November . . . [13][16] we received notice that all released missionaries were to be returned to camp that afternoon."[17] Of the seven missionaries that were jailed, only Dr. Welles was not interrogated by the *Kenpeitai*.

When Dad purchased our Hallicrafter short-wave radio, shortly before we left Los Angeles, he bought extra vacuum tubes to replace those that would burn out during the time we were in Africa. When we were notified that we were going to be re-interned, Charlie, unbeknown to the rest of the family, stashed away in his mattress some of these tubes, thinking that, because the Japanese had relaxed the rules, his mattress would not be searched. His plan was, once in camp, to turn the tubes over to someone who could use them in making a radio, so we could get the news from Allied radio stations. However, when we arrived in camp, Charlie was shocked to discover that the guards were going through every piece of luggage with a fine-tooth comb. Everything was being searched for forbidden items.

Two Months Under Virtual House Arrest

We were ordered to put all incoming baggage in an uninspected heap. From this pile the soldiers would have us bring over our luggage piece by piece for inspection. Only after it had been examined was it allowed to be taken to the inspected baggage area. As soon as Charlie saw what was happening, he came over to where I was standing near one of the soldiers who was rummaging through one of our trunks. Dad and Earl Roberts (?) were

Taken from a second-story window in the middle barracks, the photo shows Charles Mansell (center left, in plaid shirt) whispering to the author (center, with bandaged hand) that he's afraid the Japanese soldiers will find radio tubes he hid in his mattress pad. He asked the author to show the Japanese soldier (far upper right, bending over) their father's toolbox as a distraction. The Japanese soldier was, at that moment, inspecting one of the Mansells' suitcases. The Mansell boys circled behind the guard, and the author then directed the guard's attention to the Mansell toolbox (upper far right, small dark box). The white-haired man in a black suit (far right foreground) is Ernest Mansell, the author's father. Elder Mansell moved to stand by the guard who was inspecting the toolbox.
Other internees in the picture: The man in white (left foreground) is Buck Parfet, who was beaten up by Sgt. Nobu. Rolland Flory, the man pointing (center background), was later tortured by the *Kenpeitai*. Other internees are Dick Patterson (center foreground, with unidentified child), Walter Neal (in black sweater, upper right), Lyman Jensen (small boy, upper left), Eleanor Dinsbier (behind Lyman Jensen), and Suzanne Derham (in plaid skirt, feet apart).

Taken from a different second-story window, this photo shows Charles Mansell (center left, in plaid shirt) and the author (far left, in black pants) carting off the mattress pad containing radio tubes behind the guard's back. Elder Mansell is standing to the guard's right (in black suit and tie, far left foreground). Beyond the guard is Mrs. Edith Mansell, the author's mother, wearing a black coat and holding a purse. Other internees in the picture: To the right of the stack of mattresses are George Bell and Gov. Walter Hale (with hat). The woman with a light-colored jacket (back to camera) is Frieda Dirks, talking to Gerry Robinson. On the extreme right are (right to left) Sonny Woodson, Walter Smith (with hat), Malcom Mills (in white shirt), Floyd Timm, Bob Corey (in dark shirt), and Paul Peterson. To the left of Mrs. Mansell (in black coat) are Dr. William Mather and his son, Dr. Bruce Mather. Between Charles Mansell (in plaid shirt) and Bruce Mather is Dr. Lloyd Cunningham talking to Frank Knight. Rolland Flory (back to camera) is just beyond the author.

in the process of opening another trunk. At that moment Charlie whispered to me, "Don, I have some of Dad's radio tubes in my mattress pad, and I'm afraid the guard is going to discover them. Get the guard's attention on Dad's toolbox, then come and help me move my mattress pad."

At the very moment Charlie was saying this to me, and unbeknown to us, Rupert Foley, who was at one of the windows on the second floor of the Women's Barracks, snapped a picture of us. Realizing that Charlie would be severely punished, perhaps shot, if caught, I went over to the guard who was inspecting a suitcase near Dad's toolbox and pointed to the little green toolbox sitting on the table. As soon as he opened the toolbox, the soldier was immediately interested in its contents. Then I sauntered over to the uninspected pile of baggage, where Charlie was waiting.

We stood by the pile for a bit, waiting for the opportune moment. In the meantime Dad moved over to the table where the guard was inspecting the toolbox. This diverted the guard's attention from us. At that moment Charlie and I picked up his mattress pad and headed toward the guard. We paused for just a moment behind the soldier's back. Then, pretending the mattress pad had been inspected, we headed toward the inspected area. No one realized what we had done, except, perhaps, Rupe Foley.

At that moment, Foley snapped a second picture of us. It shows Charlie and me starting to set his mattress pad down in the inspected area. We had just passed behind the guard's back and were within arm's reach of where he was standing. Dad is standing at the end of the table, looking down at a clothes hanger and some sheets. The soldier is busy looking at some of Mom's linens, and there on the table beside the soldier is Dad's little green toolbox, which, after being inspected, is closed. Next to Dad, with their backs to the camera, are Dick Patterson and his dad. Mom, in a black cape, is standing some ten or twelve feet beyond the soldier, holding her purse in her hands. The taking of these photos is one of those things that happen once in a lifetime, if that often.

I first learned about the second of these pictures when Jim Halsema showed some slides at a reunion of internees in 1970 in Washington, D.C. I asked him to make me a copy, and he graciously obliged. In 1994, at a mini reunion in San Diego, Dr. Marshall Welles showed me a slide he had gotten, either from Halsema or Foley, of Charlie and me, which I had never seen before. It was the photo of Charlie sidling up to me, whispering for me to get the soldier's attention on Dad's toolbox. It seemed incredible that Foley had taken those pictures of us at those critical moments!

We were forbidden to have cameras in camp, possibly because our captors did not want us to have any photographic evidence to present against them in case they lost the war. At any rate, the Kodachrome rolls on which these and other scenes of life in camp were recorded, were hidden in the bottom of a tin can filled with rice. They remained there for two-and-a-half years and were developed in Australia after liberation. In spite of the time lapse, it is surprising how well they turned out. But this is not the only significant thing that happened the day we were brought back to camp.

Before they were re-interned, Dr. Welles, Frank Knight, Charles Wittschiebe, Ralph Dinsbier, and Leland Johnson purchased nanny goats and had them sent into camp. The fact that they came in when they did was nothing short of providential. The milk from these goats supplied essential nourishment for the babies and younger children, just when the supply of powdered milk was running out in Baguio.

---

[1]E. Mansell, p. [57], Aug. 14, 1942: "Tall rumors: Ships [are] coming for American & British nationals. . . . We're also bound for Manila. We hope it is Mozambique instead." Ibid., p. [58], Sept. 2, 1942: "The Halsemas, Miss Leggett, Dr. Nance, & some others are soon to leave for Mozambique, so we are told. Miss [Gladys S.] Anderson, the Red Cross Nurse, is expected to be evacuated also."

Herold, p. [57], Sept. 8, 1942: "Word came: No diplomatic relations, and the six here [will] not [be] permitted to go to the States. Poor [Dr.] Nance [is] terribly disappointed. Mrs. Halsema [says she is] glad to stay here."

[2]E. Mansell, p. [57], Sept. 2, 1942; Foley, p. 215, mentions that "Jim's name was on the repatriation list and with Mother and Dad's, mine and Michael's (as his relatives)."

[3]E. Mansell, p. 58.

[4]Ibid.

[5]Ibid.

[6]Ogle, p. 188.

[7]This was a horse-and-buggy-days expression, which referred to a semi-liquid analgesic that was rubbed on draft animals that had abrasions from being whipped.

[8]I remember attending Eschbach's church on September 20 and felt blessed by the sermon the pastor preached that day.

[9]Miles, p. 87; Ogle, p. 189.

[10]On Jan. 6, 2002, Ralph Longway told me that his mother was at the Baguio market on the day of this execution and witnessed it.

[11]A person of racially mixed ancestry.

[12]Herold, p. 59, Oct. 16, 1942, underlining hers.

Crouter, p. 98, says: "Awake at 3:30 by the sound of a shot, then more. It sounded below the barracks on the road. Many more shots, up to forty or fifty. From the hill [south of camp] came more gentle 'pings' said to be pistols."

[13]Foley, p. 205.

[14]Hind, p. 70.

[15]Ibid., p. 75.

[16]Miss Ogle has November 11. This is not correct. We were re-interned on Friday the 13th. However, some of those released were re-interned on November 12. See Crouter, p. 105; Herold, p. 61, Nov. 12, 13; and Hind, p. 76.

[17]Ogle, pp. 188, 189.

CHAPTER
18

A Bootlegger Gets
Beaten Up

Not long after we moved to Camp Holmes, some ingenious soul constructed a still and operated it secretly out near the workshop. Much of the spirits distilled by this contraption was consumed at the hospital.[1] In her diary entry for December 3, 1942,[2] Mrs. Herold says that "All along Elmer has been scolded by the guards because liquor gets into camp. . . . The [Camp] Committee [chaired by Dr. Nance] ruled out the still, but it was just moved to another place."[3]

On August 4, 1942, Ethel Herold recorded in her diary that the "cooks [were] all drunk celebrating Alex [Kaluzhny]'s birthday."[4] I remember that night very well. My bunk was situated some forty feet from the cook's room at the end of our barracks, and I heard the rumpus they raised. The revelry went on until the wee hours of the morning and kept us all awake. Rumor had it that some of the guards were accomplices in Clarence ("Frank") Mount's bootlegging operations and were participants at this party.

When gasoline became scarce in the Philippines, the Japanese resorted to using alcohol made from cane sugar to power their vehicles. Charlie Fears, a grizzled old miner who had a thirst for rot gut, used to surreptitiously siphon alcohol from the camp truck and mix it with banana mash. I often watched him in the morning sitting on his bunk with a drinking glass in one hand, vigorously beating his concoction with a fork, then slurping down what he called his "eye-opener."

About noon on December 4, 1942, three weeks after we were re-interned, I was standing on the pitcher's mound at Camp Holmes with Sid Burnett and several young fellows. We were discussing plans for the upcoming softball season, when I noticed a guard walking toward us. This was not unusual, and why I noticed him, I do not know. The soldier was headed toward the Men's Barracks and passed about six feet to my right. We were so busy talking that I didn't look to see where he went. Instead of going to the Men's Barracks, where I assumed he was headed, he must have gone instead to Frank Mount's shack.[5] A few minutes later he passed me going the other way, this time with Frank in tow. This *was* unusual. Mount was known as the camp's chief bootlegger, yet I failed to associate this trip to the guardhouse with his smuggling activities. Perhaps this was because we were so intent on planning for the coming softball games.

Early on in our internment, Mount swore he would never have his hair cut until our camp was liberated. I think he had a "Samson complex." Thus, by December 1942 he was quite hirsute. As he passed us on the way to the guardhouse, I noticed he had on a pair of soiled short pants and was wearing the slouch hat he usually wore when he went on the garbage detail. It was on these excursions that he allegedly made some of his bootlegging deals.

Because it was unusual for someone to go to the guardhouse accompanied by a soldier, we stopped discussing the softball season and turned to see what this trip was all about. As Mount and the soldier approached the guardhouse, we could see Hayakawa, our commandant, standing on the open porch about a hundred yards away. As soon as the soldier delivered Mount to Hayakawa, the commandant appeared to speak to him. We were so far away, we couldn't hear what he said.

Next I saw four soldiers come out of the guardhouse in undershirts with thin bamboo canes in their hands. They began beating Mount about the legs. At first it almost looked comical to see those pint-sized men switching someone much bigger than themselves. Mount danced around from side to side to avoid being hit. As the beating continued, the soldiers seemed to go into a frenzy and began hitting him all over his body. He did his best to fend off the blows with his arms. When the bamboo stick of one of the soldiers broke, he dashed into the guardhouse, picked up a golf club, came back, and began flailing Mount with it. As their bamboo sticks broke, the other guards followed suit and returned with golf clubs. There was nothing funny about the beating now. Suddenly, one of the soldiers dropped his club and ran into the guardhouse. He quickly returned with a baseball bat in hand. In the meantime the other soldiers continued flailing Mount with the golf clubs.

My attention was now drawn to the far side of the parade ground. Doug Strachan was inching his way toward the guardhouse, apparently to get a better look. When he got within about twenty yards of the action, three of the soldiers took out after him. Strachan, who was usually slow and deliberate in his movements, suddenly sprang to life. He turned tail and made a dash toward the Green Barracks. I never saw him run so fast, before or after. By the time he reached the road in front of the barracks his pursuers gave up the chase and returned to their victim. They had no sooner surrounded him, than the guard with the baseball bat took a mighty swing and struck Mount on the back over the kidneys. Mount bellowed and fell forward onto his hands and knees, then slumped to the ground in a prone position.

One of the soldiers now dashed into the guardhouse, while the others continued beating the downed man. The soldier soon reappeared holding by the neck a square-face gin bottle. When he got to where his compatriots were working Mount over, he raised the bottle high over his head and brought it down as hard as he could on the victim's head. Because of a dip in the terrain, I couldn't see if the bottle broke. In any case, Mount uttered no sound. I was sure they had killed him, and so were others who witnessed what happened. We were wrong. Apparently his thick, matted hair absorbed the blow and saved his life.

My attention was again drawn to my right. On the far side of the parade ground, near where Strachan had been a few minutes before, I saw Dr. Nance walking toward the guardhouse, his reddish bearded chin tucked down close to his chest. His stride was rapid and purposeful. The fact that he was chairman of our Camp Committee may have been the reason Mount's assailants didn't take off after him. On the other hand, it may have been his alpha personality. He spoke to Hayakawa briefly and, after a bit, the beating stopped. While Mount was still lying on the ground, Nance turned and walked rapidly back toward the steps that went down to the hospital and disappeared. Within a few minutes he returned with several men and a stretcher. They lifted Mount, laid him on the litter, and took him to the hospital.

One of the ironies of this incident was that some of the guards who beat up Mount were alleged to be his accomplices in smuggling firewater into camp.[6] Renton Hind says in *Spirits Unbroken,* page 80, "A sidelight on the incident was the visit to Mount on the 10th by one of the guards who participated in the beating, stating that he was merely acting under orders."

The liquor traffic slowed significantly after this flogging.

---

[1]Hind., p. 70.

[2]Herold, p. 63, Dec. 3, 1942. The date, December 3, is a mistake. It should be December 4.
Crouter, p. 111, has this happening on "December 4, 1942"; Hind, p. 80, agrees: "Sure enough, on [December the] 4th . . . [Mount] was caught . . . and promptly marched off to the guardhouse."

[3]Herold, p. [63], Dec. 3, 1942.

[4]Ibid., p. [54], Aug. 4, 1942.

[5]Rather than living in the barracks with the rest of the men, Mount lived alone in a *nipa* shack. This hutch was situated across the road that ran in front of the Men's Barracks. He lived here, ostensibly for medical reasons, but more likely because it facilitated his nocturnal smuggling operations.

[6]See Hind, p. 80; Herold, pp. 63, 64, Dec. 3, 1942; Crouter, p. 111, Dec. 4, 1942, for different viewpoints of this episode.

CHAPTER
19

A Meeting With the Guerrillas

The best and last of the good times in internment camp began with the arrival of Capt. Rokuro Tomibe in early November 1943.[1] Originally a businessman from Kyoto, Tomibe was loyal to his emperor and accepted the fact that we were loyal to our country. He treated us fairly and allowed us more liberties than we had enjoyed heretofore. Among the liberties we valued most was the privilege he granted families and small groups of going up on the plateau above camp and having picnics.

As mentioned earlier, on December 1, 1943, the Japanese took over the dark green high-school building by the side of the road that branched off and went to the Baby House and our hospital, and gave us the bodega in its place. Because it would be a month before the bodega was ready for occupancy, classes were discontinued for a while and we high-school students were assigned the job of hauling firewood to The Slot and rolling it down to the wood choppers near the rifle range below. By this time the wood crew was logging off the last of the trees on the mountain east of camp, and we had to haul the rounds considerable distances. We had a couple of beat-up wheelbarrows and a two-wheeled cart in which to haul the firewood. Because the ground up on the hill was uneven, this was hard work. Big Bob Corey, who was 6 feet 4, was the boss of our gang.

About noon on December 4 we had just sat down to rest for a few minutes when we saw two Igorots coming our way.[2] Their pant legs were rolled up and were wet, indicating that they had been walking through dew-laden underbrush. What follows is reconstructed from my diary, pages 87–90, with additions or confirmations from Ralph's diary:

The men greeted us with, "Good morning," and we responded, "Good morning." They sat down and introduced themselves as Felipe and Santiago, apparently their *noms de guerre.* Santiago seemed especially cautious and kept looking around warily.

"Ees Mr. Srachm (Doug Strachan) here?" Felipe asked.

Corey answered, "No."

Santiago wrinkled his forehead. He said that Mr. Herold had sent them up to us.

"Who are you?" Corey asked.

"We are of the USAFFE[3] and we are looking for small arms with which to pight [fight] sepies [spies]," Felipe responded. He then swore us to secrecy.

"Who is your commander?" asked Corey.

"Lieutenant Spencer is our battalion commander. He commands my battalion, sir. We have also Colonels Calvert and Barnett," Felipe replied.

Santiago and Felipe eyed each other for a moment. All at once Santiago drew a handful of papers from his pocket. The first one was signed by Col. Parker T. Calvert and was addressed "To all American citizens and loyal Filipinos." It requested that all arms and ammunition be turned over to the USAFFE.

"We will need it for the coming accion [action]," Felipe said, "and we will pight [fight] to the last man if possible [i.e., if necessary]," he added.

As we sat there, Gene Kneebone, Earl Roberts, Byron Elsley, and Jim Halsema came by with a load of wood in the two-wheeled cart and stood around listening to the conversation.

"Do you want us to call for Mr. Strachm [*sic*]?" Corey asked.

Again the guerrillas eyed each other. Then Santiago spoke. "We weel stay here till fibe o'clock."

"Have you heard any news?" Bob Corey asked. "We've heard that the Marianas Islands have been bombed."

"We hab not heard that, because we receibe typewritten sheet twice a week and I did not read mine this morning," Felipe replied. "Baht [But] our sepy who came from the south told us that Dabao [Davao] had been bombed two months ago.

"There are three riples [rifles] under one of the houses [in the Igorot village], which we hab come to get. We were given limited time."[4]

After arranging for them to meet Strachan and Swick, they left and we went back to work.

The next day, while our crew was back on the hill hauling wood, we got the scare of our lives. Billy Herold, David Bergamini, Ralph Longway, Dick Patterson, and I were on Corey's crew that day.

We had been hauling logs in the two-wheeled cart from the place near where we met the guerrillas the day before and down to the top of The Slot. Just after we had dumped a volley of rounds into camp, Harry Taylor, who was splitting wood down at the bottom of The Slot, hollered up and said, "Doug Strachan is wanted at the guardhouse."[5]

We were stunned and stopped working immediately. After we relayed the message up to the next crew, we sat down and began speculating in regard to what this summons meant. Why did the Japanese want Doug to come to the guardhouse?

Fifteen or twenty minutes later Doug came by us on his way down to camp. As he passed us we asked him why he had been called to the guardhouse. He said he didn't know, that perhaps the guerrillas had been apprehended and implicated him, or it might be something else that they wanted to talk to him about. Corey urged him to let us know what it was all about, and Doug promised he would.

After about fifteen or twenty minutes, Doug crossed the parade ground all dressed up on his way to the guardhouse. As he passed near the bottom of The Slot, he hollered up to us the one word, "Timber."

What did Doug mean by "Timber," we wondered. Timber, of course, can mean wood, but it is also the term woodsmen use to warn people of danger from a falling tree and to get out of the way. We feared the worst and stopped working.

Finally, Corey said, "I don't like the looks of this. Mansell, take the jug and bring us some water, and while you are down there, find out what this is all about.[6] Be sure to be careful who you talk to. It looks pretty bad."

I headed down to camp. The first person I met was Swick. We met right at the front of Frank Mount's shack.

I said, "Herbie, I was on the hill with the wood crew yesterday, and I know you were there too. I met the two guerrillas and understand that you and Doug also met with them. Doug has been called to the guardhouse and, as he walked across the parade ground, he hollered up to us and said, 'Timber.' Do you know why the Japanese called him to the guardhouse?"

Herbie, standing with arms akimbo, never batted an eye, nor did his facial expression change in the least, but I saw the jugular vein on the left side of his neck pulse visibly, and he began to hyperventilate. He said he didn't know why Doug had been called to the guardhouse, and asked me to tell him immediately if I found out the reason. I promised I would. He told me where he would be, then he went his way, and I went into the Men's Barracks to look for someone who had met the guerrillas the day before.

The first person I came across was Byron Elsley, who had been with our wood crew the day before. He was not working that day. I told him what had happened and asked if he knew why Doug Strachan had been summoned to the guardhouse. Elsley was resting in his bunk when I told him this, but suddenly, he was all ears. He said he knew nothing about Doug being called to the guardhouse, and asked me to be sure to tell him what was going on when I found out. I promised I would.

I went out of the Men's Barracks and walked over toward the kitchen. Sy Sorrell was standing there, and I asked him casually if he knew why Doug Strachan had been called to the guardhouse.

He replied, "Sure, the Japs want to talk to him about the wood situation."

I thanked him, but didn't tell him why I asked. To say I was relieved is an understatement. After informing Swick and then Elsley, I filled our jug with water and returned to the top of the hill, where I told our crew that Doug's summons to the guardhouse had nothing to do with the guerrillas. It had to do with the supply of firewood in camp. Our crew was glad to hear this.

In his diary, Ralph wrote: "Man, what a relief."[7]

So, what seemed to be a dangerous situation turned out to be nothing to worry about.

[1]Crouter, p. 235, Nov. 7, 1943: "Tomibe seems to be taking hold so that we are not forgotten any longer."

[2]Longway, Dec. 16, 1943, [p. 43]: "We go to upper slot, where [we] rolled big stuff down for the take-fivers. After half-hour, 2 natives walk by, stop and tell us the latest . . . [news. These are the] first I've ever known as I saw (guerrillo [*sic*]). . . . Hmm, that's a real rememberable. I'll have [to write it] all [up] someday in [a] story. . . . [It was] risky stuff . . . important, but mum is [the] word."

[3]Acronym for United States Armed Forces in the Far East.

[4] D. Mansell notes made soon after Dec. 17, 1943, and D. Mansell diary, pp. 89, 90, Dec. 17, 1944, plus other things I remember about this episode.

[5]Longway, p. [43], Dec. 17, 1943: "From [the bottom of the] slot [there was a call] for [Doug Strachan to go to the guardhouse] and he goes, finally. [This] put us [in a] nonplus mo[od]. [We were] scared as h—, [be]cause if [what we speculated was] so, [I] am up a creek without a paddle. [We] watch[ed] developments from [the] top of the hill, [and] ponder[ed] their meaning."

[6]Ibid., p. [43], Dec. 17, 1943: "[Bob Corey decided to] send Don to see what's up."

[7]Ibid.

CHAPTER
20

Two Men Escape
From Camp

On March 11, 1944, Doug Strachan called all us young men and older teenagers to a meeting in the second *nipa* shack at 5:30 P.M. After we were all together, he said he wanted to discuss something serious and swore us to secrecy. We all agreed to hold in confidence what he was going to talk about. Then he said that when America retook the Philippines, there would be "action," and we needed to be prepared in case the Japanese started a massacre. He said that the guerrillas had already been contacted and hinted that plans were afoot to "defend ourselves" in case the Japanese "start something." Then he said that if this happened, we would be needed as couriers to go to the guerillas for help and, because we were young and healthy, he asked us to volunteer to serve as "runners." We all volunteered.[1]

Months before this secret meeting, Eric Lenze, our camp blacksmith, made a nine-inch utility knife-blade for me from a broken car spring.[2] Some of the other men in camp had similar knives. By doing some scrounging around I found enough worn-out leather soles to make a haft. The scabbard was made out of a wide discarded belt. Lenze helped me make a cap for the haft out of a melted aluminum canteen cup. I fastened the cap to the haft with a rivet made from a tenpenny nail. Because we were forbidden to have weapons of any kind in camp, most men kept these utility knives out of sight. I kept mine hidden in a secure place and took it out only when I had to use it, and referred to it in my diary as "Excalibur."[3] Somehow, I don't know how, Swick found out that I had one of these knives. Perhaps he saw me with it.

On the night of April 2, 1944, after I had scrubbed down the kitchen, Swick talked to me privately and asked me to give him my knife, adding cryptically, "I'll think of you every time I sink it into the belly of a Jap." I never dreamed he was planning to escape and declined his request.

At 4:30 in the afternoon of April 4, I heard Bill Larson remark knowingly that Swick and Green had not been seen all day. Bill was known to exaggerate, so I attached no significance to his observation, but it wasn't long before I discovered that he knew what he was talking about.[4]

That evening we went through the formality of a roll call, although by that time everyone knew that the birds had flown the coop. John Crocker, our monitor, called out, "Green!" a pause. No answer. Again, "Green!" Again, no answer. Carl Eschbach, who was present, reported to the guardhouse that two men were missing. As soon as we were dismissed, I hid "Excalibur" in a well-concealed place—up in a cubbyhole in the eves of the barracks— which I felt was the last place our hosts were likely to look.[5]

By the time I went to clean up the kitchen, I noticed that the guards were already snooping around. Carl Eschbach told us to go to bed. At 10:45 P.M. things began to pop. At 12:30 cars drove into the camp, and men got out and scoured the grounds with flashlights. Everyone was awake and tense, but pretended to be asleep. Swick lived downstairs, but because my bunk was so close to Green's, I was especially apprehensive.

Soon we heard the scuffing of hobnail boots. The lights came on. Carl, Miss McKim, Mr. Tomibe, Hayakawa, and the head of the *Kenpeitai* inspected the bunks of the two escapees. They carted off Green's expensive leather suitcase, and I heard later that they took Swick's hat. Gene Kneebone, Tony Zagar, Anders Lofsted (Green's cubicle mates), and John Crocker, our monitor, who bunked directly below me, were taken to the guardhouse. However, they soon were released and returned to the barracks. Nothing more occurred the rest of the night, and we went to sleep.[6]

School began as usual the next morning, and we hoped that further action by the *Kenpeitai* would go away like a bad dream. Everything seemed normal until 9:15, when all occupants of the Men's Barracks and the high-school boys were ordered to go to the mess hall. After being seated at the tables, we counted off. A few minutes later we counted off again, and our numbers changed. The first time I was number 73, then 71, then some other number. Eventually, I lost track. I noticed that people whose numbers were 10, 20, 30, etc., kept switching positions. Perhaps they feared they would be decimated[7]. The *Kenpeitai* arrived at 10:00. We counted off once more. Again, I had another number.

When Mr. Tomibe walked into the mess hall, we stood and bowed as he entered. In a barking staccato, which Miss McKim interpreted, he said he sympathized with our situation, but that rules must be obeyed. There would be no more picnics up on the hill. He would personally take roll call from now on. There would be no more going outside the fence for any reason. Adult male internees must stand guard at night and would be held responsible for anyone who escaped.

Commandant Tomibe was obviously in trouble up to the hilt. Most of us sympathized with him. He concluded his remarks by asking us if we had any idea why the two men left camp. Father Robert Sheridan wisecracked that they didn't like the food. Tomibe and Hayakawa smiled, and we all laughed. This broke the tension. Walter Tong suggested in a more serious vein that Swick and Green were tired of three years under duress.

Many of the women had their noses pressed against the window screens while Tomibe spoke. After the meeting was over "Hayakawa was reported to have remarked that the men had gone too soon—he could . . . [have told] them when to go, if they had waited!"[8] Apparently he could see the handwriting on the wall—and was probably trying to ingratiate himself with us in preparation for the turnover.

In an interview with Swick on August 8, 1989, in which he told John ("Reamo") Ream what happened after he escaped, he recorded Swick as saying:

> I had a job working in the kitchen . . . [as well as another job working] on the garbage crew. . . . One day I recognized a Filipino scout that I was sure was with some Americans that were still out in the mountains. So I asked him, "Where is Colonel Calvert?" He says, "He is right out here in the mountains, and I'm with them and I'm on my way back to their camp now. . . ."

I arranged to have an interview with Colonel Calvert, who came as close to the camp as he could at night. . . . Doug Strachan [went with me]. . . [Colonel Calvert] said they needed all the help they could get, so my escape [from camp] was all set up. I met Calvert one more time, just to set up the date and time of my escape. The time was 9:30 at night on April 4, 1944. . . . Richie Green escaped with me. . . . Calvert had cargadores outside of the camp waiting for us to take us to his camp. We went down beyond the rear barracks, right over about a four foot high fence. . . . We only traveled at night, and it took us three nights to get to Calvert's headquarters. . . .

The only ones who actually knew that I was going to leave were Doug Strachan and Bill Moule. . . . Doug went out with us . . . helping us carry out mostly medical supplies [which he got from the camp's head pharmacist]. . . . Bill Moule knew all of my plans to escape. . . . He knew more of my plans . . . than Green did. The night that I was going to escape . . . I said, "Bill, this is it."[9] . . .

When [we] got to Calvert's camp . . . he sent Green to join Colonel Barnett, who was commanding officer of the 121st Infantry in the Province of La Union. I was sent north to join Don Blackburn . . . in the Province of Ifugao. I was there for about two months . . . [with the] Bontoc and Ifugao [tribesmen]. . . . They were the most loyal people to Americans I . . . ever met out there. . . .

I was sent by Blackburn north to reorganize the guerrillas. . . . While going through . . . villages I would . . . give . . . [a] short speech assuring them that the Americans were coming back. In the meantime . . . submarines . . . brought a lot of radio equipment, small arms, and a lot of book[s] of matches with MacArthur's photograph on it . . . to distribute along the way. . . .

I went . . . into Cagayan [in northern Luzon] organizing this battalion of the 11th Infantry. After I got [them] half way organized (we were armed mostly . . . [with] Jap arms . . . gotten from small ambushes). . . I started with one company on the northern coast of Luzon at a town called Sanchez Mira . . . [where] we were really welcomed as heroes. . . . Many citizens . . . [kissed] our hands. I started from there to wipe out the Jap garrisons and from there I moved up to Ballesteros and wiped . . . out [the Japs there]. . . .

While at Ballesteros we rested up [for] a few days. . . . [One day] we . . . happened to be looking out at the ocean. I had a lot of troops stationed right there, just for our safety. . . . [Th]ere were Jap ships out on the ocean and here comes a bunch of Japs. . . . We spotted them coming in. . . . [T]his was the best ambush that we ever had. We waited until those boats practically got on shore [before we fired on them]. We killed over 100. . . . [They were] part of the [Japanese] navy, and they didn't know anything about guerrillas being in that part of the country.

I continued from there over to Aparri, wiping out the Japs, but I could not take Aparri on account of . . . [it being] too well fortified. . . . Colonel [Russell W.] Volckmann . . . [called me] to come down to Bessang Pass . . . [which] sort of overlooks the city of Cervantes, and that was one of the biggest battles we had. The battle had been going on for at least a month before I got there. . . . I took over . . . a provisional battalion . . . attached to the 121st Infantry commanded by Colonel Barnett. . . . [My] battalion was one of the first that broke through the Japs to take Cervantes. . . .

From Cervantes I went north and took . . . Tadian . . . then went on to Sagada. . . . [F]rom there I went on to Bontoc, where we had a fairly good size battle. . . . Then I pushed southeast to Benaue [where I met the] . . . 6th Division of the American Army. . . . I was attached to them and . . . we pushed towards [General] Yamashita's headquarters. . . . That's where I ended up fighting. Yamashita surrendered.[10]

The guerrillas under 2nd Lieutenant Swick rendered invaluable service to the American and Philippine forces in the reconquest of the Philippines and, after liberation, he was decorated by the Philippine government with the Legion of Merit and with the Legion of Honor, "which is . . . [equivalent] to our Silver Star."[11] After his return to the States, Swick made the army his career and rose to the rank of Lieutenant Colonel.[12]

What happened in camp after Tomibe's meeting with the men in the mess hall? In his book, *God's Arms Around Us,* Bill Moule records that

about eleven o'clock [on April 6] . . . the Japanese sent word from the guardhouse that they wanted [to question Tony] Zagar. We watched Zagar walk out to the guardhouse, and a few minutes later he came back. As he was walking back to the barracks he was looking over the small groups that had . . . [gathered on the parade ground]; and when he saw us [Moule and his wife, Margaret], he headed our way. When he reached us, he said, "Bill, you're the one they want."

Margaret was scared, and she asked me what I wanted to take. I said, "Just my sweater," as I thought I'd be back before night.

Mrs. [Helen] Johnson came over and gave me a small paper sack. "Here, take this with you."

I thanked her and put it in my pocket. Then Marg and I walked out to the guardhouse where Ray Hale was waiting in the truck for me. Our commandant [Mr. Tomibe] told me I would be taken into the Japanese [Kenpeitai] Headquarters. He wouldn't look at me. He seemed more concerned than I was. I kissed Marg good-by and climbed on the truck.[13]

That little paper sack that Mrs. Johnson gave Moule proved to be a very thoughtful gift.

On April 7 Gene Kneebone, Andy Lofsted, and Tony Zagar were called to the guardhouse again. Zagar was detained only briefly. Lofsted was released in Baguio and returned to camp the same day with a group of internees who had been sent to dismantle some cottages on Bokowkan Road that belonged to the Presbyterians. But Kneebone, who was taken to *Kenpeitai* headquarters, didn't come back that day. Three days later, on April 10, Jim Halsema was detained by the *Kenpeitai*.

---

[1]D. Mansell, p. 12, Mar. 11, 1944: "Doug Strachan wants to see us boys at 5:30 in the farther Nipa Shack. I think he wants to tell us something confidential. Chuck Lerberg thinks he just wants to talk to us about boxing." Because being involved in such an organization could have deadly consequences, my diary entry about this meeting is very brief, but my memory of what transpired is very clear. The words in this paragraph that are within quotation marks are words I distinctly remember Strachan saying.

Herold, p. 94, Aug. 23, 1944: "Dugg [i.e., Doug] Strachan on 'secret' stuff. Billy volunteered to be a courier. All of us secretly told to get emergency supplies of food and clothing to be off at a moment's notice."

[2]Ibid., p. 1, Jan. 2, 1944: "I went out to the blacksmith shop and worked putting on a handle on my knife made from a car spring. I heard a noise outside, and thinking it was a guard, I hid the

blade in my [pants] pocket, then looked out to see who it might be. It was [five-year-old] Mike Derham. I began to chase him [off] and stabbed . . . [my right forearm] with the end of the blade. It severed a small vein. . . . Doc [Paul] Martin fixed me up. No stitches. (I still have the scar.) By the time I crossed the parade ground [and went] to the aid station in the Green Barracks the bleeding had practically stopped."

³The name of King Arthur's sword.

⁴William R. Moule, *God's Arms Around Us* (Nevada City, Calif.: Blue Dolphin Publishing, 1990), p. 326: "The next morning [April 5, 1944] when Swick and Green didn't show up for kitchen duty the word spread like wildfire that they were missing. Carl Eschbach asked Jack [Pearson], Harry [Barz], Johnny [McCuish], and me if we knew where they were, and we said we didn't, which we didn't by then.

"Carl said, 'We can give them a couple of more hours, but after that, we will have to tell the Japs.' " All quotations from *God's Arms Around Us* reprinted with permission of the publisher.

⁵D. Mansell, p. 15, Apr. 5, 1944.

⁶Crouter, p. 318, April 6, 1944.

⁷A practice in the Roman army of putting to death every tenth man for mutiny.

⁸John Ream, unpublished tape-recorded *Interview With Herbert Swick*, on August 8, 1989, at Los Angeles, Calif., transcribed by Renee Ream, pp. 3–5. (Hereafter designated Ream interview.)

Moule, pp. 322, 323: "Swick had made contact with . . . [Col. Parker T. Calvert]. How he did it was his secret. . . . At that time we weren't guarded too closely; therefore it was quite simple to step in and out of camp so long as you showed up in time for roll call. I was sure that the mine superintendent from Big Wedge [Doug Strachan] was doing a little night work by the caliber of the chow he cooked up occasionally. . . . . Swick ventured the information that he had contacted Colonel [Russell W.] Volckmann and the colonel told him to stay in camp until he gave the word, and in the meantime pick up any information that might be useful. Herb said he was going to ask Volckmann permission to take Green with him."

⁹Ream interview, pp. 5–7.

¹⁰Ibid., p. 12.

¹¹Ibid., p. 9.

¹²Ibid.

¹³Moule, p. 327.

CHAPTER
21

Tortured by the Kenpeitai

As I previously mentioned, my rafter-slung bunk was situated in the cubicle immediately adjacent to the cubicle occupied by Gene Kneebone, Andy Lofsted, Tony Zagar, Joe Scotty, and Richie Green, and was directly above John Crocker's bunk. Because I was of military age and had volunteered to be a courier, and these men had been called to the guardhouse for questioning, I feared the *Kenpeitai* would summon and grill me. They never did.

About April 1, 1943, the Moule family, who had been out in the hills with the guerrillas, had been brought into camp. Two weeks later, on April 14, the father, William ("Bill") Moule came down with polio.[1] When he recovered enough to walk, he hobbled around with a distinct and painful limp.

In his book, *God's Arms Around Us,* Bill Moule describes in graphic detail how the *Kenpeitai* tortured him:

> The guard took me into the cell block—[there were] five cells, each one eight feet wide and ten feet long. The bars ran from the floor to the ceiling and were an inch-and-a-half in diameter. The front was all bars, except for the small doors that led into the cells. The guard told me to take off my shoes and empty my pockets. Then I was escorted upstairs and into an apartment. Seated behind

a desk was . . . [Capt. Shimpei Hamada.[2] He was flanked by two non-commissioned officers.[3]]

The interpreter told me the captain wanted to question me about Swick and Green. I was brought over to the desk, and if looks could kill, I'd have died on the spot. Finally, he yelled at the interpreter. The first question the interpreter asked me was where Swick and Green had gone. I told him I didn't know; and when that choice morsel was relayed back to the captain, he jumped up and came around to my side of the desk and commanded me to sit on the floor. As I sat there, he took one of his leather sandals and walloped me first on one side of the head and then on the other, until I thought my eardrums were broken.

Then he went back and sat down. The interpreter told me to get up. The next question was whom . . . [Swick and Green] were going to meet and why they went out. I got along with that question as well as I did the first one, and the same procedure continued. When he got back to his seat, he had worked up quite a sweat. He asked me again about Swick and Green, and again I said I didn't know where they were. The captain barked out a command, and we all went downstairs in front of the cells. My hands were handcuffed in back of me. There was only one link of chain between the two cuffs, and they held my arms almost in a rigid position. As this was going on, I noticed that the cells were pretty well occupied.

After the handcuffs were secured, a guard went over to a filing cabinet, pulled the drawer open, and took out two coils of very small Manila rope. He unrolled it, and threw one end up to a guard standing on the mezzanine floor. Then he started doing something with my thumbs. I hadn't the slightest idea of what was about to take place, but I soon found out. He put a double loop around each thumb and at a given signal I was hoisted up until I was almost off my feet, and I had only one [good] leg that would support my weight. I tried to stand on the toes of my good foot to relieve the pain on my thumbs and shoulders. [This form of torture is known as "The Parrot's Beam."] The pain was so intense that I could hardly grasp what was happening to me, and in all that agony the interpreter kept asking me questions. I yelled and asked to be let down. In desperation I raised myself as high as I could on my toes and at the same time did a "skin the cat," bringing my arms back over my shoulders. But because of the handcuffs, I couldn't complete the "skin" without dislocating my shoulders.

I fainted and was just coming to when they threw a bucket of water in my face. They jerked me to my feet and took me upstairs, put my arms in back again, and started questioning me. The same old questions were asked; and if I had played it smart, I would have told them I knew Swick and Green were going out. But I didn't and consequently they started to work on me again, this time with an ammunition belt, sticks, bayonet scabbards, fists, and open slaps. None of this was pleasant, but I thought I could stall them off and escape

Sketch by George Mathis of William Moule being tortured on "The Parrot's Beam" by the *Kenpeitai*. Used by permission of Blue Dolphin Publishing.

the ropes. I had no business trying to think, because by now the captain was a madman.

The beatings stopped while preparations were made to hang me again. Pulleys were hanging from the ceiling between the hallway and the main room. The ropes were threaded through them, and then tied to my thumbs. Again my arms were pulled until I was standing tiptoe. [Oh,] . . . how it hurt! It felt as if my thumbs were coming off and my shoulders were being pulled out of their sockets. Again I screamed, yelled, cussed, and prayed—all the while the interpreter was trying to interrogate me. I told him I couldn't talk while I was in so much pain. After he passed the message on to the captain and his helpers, they went into a rage and started to beat me. Their beating didn't bother me in the least. All I could feel was the terrible pain in my thumbs and shoulders. I stood it as long as I could and again brought by arms right over my head. When my arms came back into place, I momentarily blacked out and fell to the floor. They jerked me up to my feet, unlocked the handcuffs, put my arms in back of me, and locked them again. When I brought my arms over my head, my wrists turned inside the cuffs and it took off most of the skin because they clamped them on so tight.

There was no questioning that time. When the ropes were in place, they made me stand on a chair, then pulled me up until I was tiptoeing. To my dying day I will see that chair being kicked out from under me. Although I was pulled up tight, I still dropped over a foot when the chair went out and I was swinging in midair; my feet dangled just above the mop boards. The pain was excruciating. I know I must have screamed bloody murder. I prayed and cussed and prayed again. I asked them to please let me down, that I couldn't stand the pain. "I'll tell you anything you want to know about Swick and Green. Only let me down."

I couldn't concentrate on the questions because of the pain, but they still wanted me to talk while I was hanging. When the door would open I was in hopes that it was somebody sent by God Himself to stop all this, but usually the visitor would join them and beat me. As I hung in that position, my face was forced forward and downward. Most of the blows were landing on the top and back of my head. Ordinarily, they would have been quite painful. Now they meant nothing. If only they would knock me out. My thumbs felt as if they were being pulled off. The pain in one was especially intense. The rope had cut through one of them and the ends of my thumbs were becoming big knobs. I pleaded with them to let me down. I thought, "Maybe if I faint or pretend I've fainted, they will drop me."

The moment I relaxed and pretended to go into a faint, I could feel those ropes around my thumbs ten times worse. I was conscious of somebody running over to the desk and back. I knew he was standing directly in front of me, and before I had time to think what might take place, he lit a match and stuck it up my nose. I came out of my faint and went back to my pleading. The captain decided to let me down. As they dropped me down the same thing happened. Every time the shoulder blades came back into their sockets out I went. But it was only momentarily, and they got me to my feet again. The captain continued the interrogation. . . .

Now they wanted to know about an organization that was formed outside of camp and connected with the camp. For the life of me I couldn't get the connection. If there was any organization, I didn't know about it.[4] . . . I tried my best to ward them off and give them some kind of an answer, but at a signal from the captain those two guys would move in on me and down I would go. . . . I very hastily moved toward the wall where I could get up. I was in an awful plight because my hands were still handcuffed . . . [behind me], and I had only one good leg [on which to stand]. About the only way I could help myself up was to get against a wall and use my head to help support me. Many times I would almost be on my feet when one of the Japs would give me a blow that would send me falling again. . . . That went on time and time again before I was able to gain my feet. . . .

Once again on my feet, in front of the Japanese captain's desk, the question was the organization and who was the head of it? Again I told the interpreter I didn't know anything about it. So help me God, they started to hang me again. The same procedure began; and when the guard twisted the rope around the open flesh on my thumb, I bolted, but not for long. All during the preparation and up to the time I was lifted onto the chair, I was begging them to let me tell them everything I knew and that I wasn't lying to them. But to no avail. The guard in back of me pulled the ropes through the pulleys. . . . The captain started kicking the chair out from under me. I begged God to stop them, and all the while I was pleading with the interpreter. . . .

I dropped to a sudden stop as the ropes cut into my thumbs, and my arms felt as if they were being pulled from my shoulders. I yelled at the top of my lungs. I was afraid my thumbs would come off. I was desperate. If nothing else, I had to provoke them into killing me. The interpreter stood alongside of me and started the questions. Again I told him I knew nothing about an organization, and couldn't talk in this condition. He interpreted that, and the captain and his helpers sprang to action. One raised my head with an uppercut to the mouth, and a belt cut the bridge of my nose. . . .

The interpreter asked me again about the organization. I went into a yelling rage. "Tell the . . . [S.O.B.] I can't talk like this. Tell him to kill me."

"Do you want me to interpret that?"

"No! Please don't! I'm sorry!"

My fit was short-lived. My only hope was in God and this interpreter. . . . I rested my foot on the top edge of the mop board and raised as much weight as I could off my ropes. . . . A guard discovered my little trick and kicked my leg away. As soon as he did so, I put it back. He went out and returned with a piece of pine stovewood and knelt down and beat my leg off the mop board. . . .

At every question the interpreter asked, I answered as fast as I could and ended up pleading with him to let me down. He looked at me and said, "Please answer the captain's questions. I do not like to see you suffer like this."

I thought, "Dear God, this is the first ray of hope I've had." Then I pleaded, begged, and promised such as I hope I'll never have to again as long as I live.

The interpreter turned to the captain and talked. Then I asked him what he said, "The captain is mad. You will have to wait."

"Wait. God have mercy." I was at the point of exhaustion. . . . After what seemed like an eternity, the captain barked out a command and a guard loosened the ropes. My arms came down and once again I blacked out. I was pulled to my feet and the ropes taken off my thumbs. They shoved me up to the desk. As I was trying to catch my balance some of the blood from my face splashed on the desk. The two helpers were apparently angered at that and both clipped me about the same time and down I went. It was getting more difficult for me to get up. As time went on . . . I had a mortal fear of ending up on the ropes again. . . .

The grilling went on for hours. My interpreter, who I believed was a Jap civilian . . . knew I was doing my best to answer the questions. I talked freely about the guerrillas, as I knew nothing they didn't know already. I didn't tell them I was an officer [in the USAFFE] and wouldn't, unless it meant another hanging. I knew that if I told them that, I was done for. But I believe if I had to make a choice I could have faced gunfire, a bayonet, or clubbing to death rather than another hanging.

Tortured by the Kenpeitai

The questions about the organization[5] were my downfall. To this day I don't know what they were after. . . . I was at the point of exhaustion. Fortunately, the Japs have to eat and at seven o'clock it was called off. I had arrived at the hall [the *Kenpeitai* headquarters] at twelve o'clock and I'd been worked on until seven. Less than seven hours before, I had walked into the place, confident I could hold up under the best they could dish out. Seven hours later I was almost afraid to be alive. As I was being led down the stairs the thought occurred to me that if I was brought up again, I'd throw myself over the stairway. It wouldn't kill me, but it might stop them from hanging me. . . .

When we got back to the cells, one guard unlocked the door and another took the handcuffs off. I had a hard time bringing my arms around in front of me again. . . . I crawled through the door into the cell and sat down against the wall. Later on that night a Filipino told me that I would have to massage my thumbs or I would lose them. . . . I was for just sitting awhile, but my benefactor couldn't see the delay, so he took my hand very gently and started to rub my thumb. It hurt so . . . bad I decided I'd lose them. . . . Then he showed me how to get my arms up. He put his fingers against the wall and moved . . . [them] up the wall until he had his arms over his head. I tried this maneuver a couple of times and it just didn't make sense. . . . I asked the fellow if I [had] missed chow, and he said I hadn't. The Japs were feeding the prisoners now. He warned me about talking when the guards were near.

The thing that bothered me now was my tongue. It had begun to swell, and I needed water badly. The guard opened the little trap door and passed in rice and water. As I went up to get mine, he made me move back. All it was was a few little ounces in a tomato sauce can, but I was terribly disappointed when I didn't get any. . . .

That night was a nightmare. The pain in my head and legs joined my wrists, shoulders, and thumbs. . . . But my prime concern was water. I stretched out on the floor like the others. Sleep was impossible. The Japs brought in some Filipino prisoners and hung one outside our cell. It was gruesome. All I could do was pray for him. . . . [H]e was worked on for over an hour. Then the ropes slackened and he slumped to the floor. . . .

Daybreak! I was thankful the night was over, but dreaded to face my accusers again. I knew I wouldn't last long unless I got some water. I noticed my good Samaritan squat down near the bars and say something to a native woman. . . . Apparently she was being held hostage for her guerrilla husband. A few minutes later she returned. She glanced down the corridor and then slipped a rag through the bars. It was quickly handed to me with the instructions to suck on it. . . . I put it in my mouth, while my accessory to the crime waited in tense fear. I sucked every drop of water out of that mop rag [and] gave it back to the Filipino. He in turned passed it out the bars. The Filipino lady took it quickly and started mopping the floor with it—not a second too soon.

As we were waiting for roll call I remembered the bag that Mrs. Johnson had given me before I left camp. I stuck my fingers into my pocket and without the use of my thumbs worked the bag out. I asked my friend to open it. It had been two hard boiled duck eggs. They were smashed, but my friend peeled the pieces of shell off the white and gave it to me, and he ate the yoke. It made the saliva return and I lost that horrible feeling that I was going to strangle. Some day I hoped I'd be able to do a favor for Mrs. Johnson. . . .

After roll call the thing I was dreading happened. The captain came in and spoke to the guard. He unlocked the cell door and pointed to me. As I left my cell I prayed to God that something would happen so I wouldn't get hung again. I was taken into the room on the main floor. I had the same interpreter, and he told me, "The captain wants to know the answer to these questions, and you know the consequences." To punch-note the sentence he nodded to his two helpers.

When they asked a question, I tried my best to answer it. . . . Fortunately, I could talk very freely about the guerrillas and not hurt them, and I felt I might do myself some good. . . . The captain was persistent about the [to me] unknown organization; and whenever he came to that, I was stuck for an answer. . . . The interpreter and the captain conversed, then the interpreter drew an imaginary circle on the desk. In the center of the circle he put a dot. "The captain says this is where he wants to go," and he pointed to the dot inside the circle, "but you keep going around here," and he indicated the outside of the circle. . . .

I told the interpreter, "Please tell the captain that I am telling him the truth and that I don't know any more about this organization or about the guerrillas than what I've told him." A noble and pathetic plea, but it must have lost its appeal in translation because the interpreter was still talking when the captain went into one of his tantrums.

He was gaining momentum, when an orderly came in with a . . . stack of mail and started passing it out. The captain and the interpreter received several letters, so I was forgotten about while they read their mail. . . . Then they got back to the business at hand. . . . The captain and the interpreter talked for a while and pretty soon the interpreter turned to me and said, "You go back to your cell."

"Thanks, God, I knew You could do it!"

The guard very obligingly opened my cell door and let me in. . . . That afternoon at one o'clock they gave us our meal. I allowed my water to slop around in my mouth before I swallowed it. I took the rice and gave it to my Filipino friend and adviser. . . .

On the fourth day, the guard took us out in back. Several native women were sitting at a table preparing vegetables—more guerrilla hostages. My cell mates immediately dropped their shorts and picked up a water hose and began bathing themselves. I was going to skip the strip-tease act, but my guards made sure I wasn't. . . . So, off came my clothes and at last I got to drink all the water I wanted. . . .

The fourth night the Japanese and interpreters had somebody going up on the ropes all night long. . . . When they got through with him, they shoved him in with us. . . . I about had heart failure when a short time later a guard came to the window and yelled at me to come up front. I went up and the captain looked me over and then said something to the guard. . . . My only hope was that they would send me back to camp. At four o'clock the guard opened the door and motioned for me to come out. When he finished locking up the cell, he turned to me and said, "Holmes—five o'clock."[6]

Gene Kneebone was taken in for his inquisition by the *Kenpeitai* on April 9, and Jim Halsema was summoned for the same treatment the next day. Kneebone sustained a broken rib. It was from him that I first heard the expression, The Parrot's Beam, applied to the form of torture to which he and Moule and Halsema were subjected. Moule and Halsema were returned together to camp on April 13. Kneebone was brought back the next day.

Moule describes the meeting with his wife, when he was returned to camp, and his subsequent meeting with Capt. Tomibe:

> [W]hen the truck pulled up the incline into camp, I spotted Marg. I realized the last six days hadn't been easy for her. She threaded her way through the guards; and before we met, her eyes had confirmed her fears; and as we melted into each other's arms, she muttered a curse.
>
> "Marg, I never thought I'd ever hear that from you."
>
> "They're worse than that. What have they done to you?"
>
> We were making our way toward the camp when suddenly a guard stopped us, and I was told [that] Mr. Tomibe wanted to see me. I stood in front of him while he looked me over. Six days earlier I stood in front of another Jap officer, and he so held me in contempt that hate literally radiated from him. Now, as I was standing in front of this one, I actually detected tears in his eyes.[7]

The contrast between *Kenpeitai* inquisitor Capt. Shimpei Harada[8] and his henchmen,[9] and commandant Capt. Rokuro Tomibe, was the difference between night and day.

---

[1]Moule, p. 306: "We had been in camp two weeks. April 14, 1943, I came down with polio."

[2]Halsema identifies this officer as "Captain Shimpei Hamada. His assistant was Corporal Tomomi M[i]yaki. The interpreter seemed to be a Japanese who had lived in the Philippines prewar." Halsema, 1944 Diary, p. [41], Apr. 10, 1944.

For further information concerning these men, see endnotes 8 and 9 of this chapter.

[3]Apparently Cpl. Tomomi Miyaki was one of these two noncommissioned officers.

[4]There was such an organization in camp. It was led by Doug Strachan, who, apparently, kept this information from Moule. (See pp. 191, 193-195 in this chapter.) It is astonishing that Strachan, who was the ringleader of this organization, was never called by the *Kenpeitai* and given the third degree. If he had been summoned and tortured, and had revealed that such an organization ex-

isted, we young men who had volunteered to be couriers would have been compromised and doubtless would have been tortured too.

⁵Apparently, the Japanese must have gotten wind of Doug Strachan's organization but were never able to find out anything more about it.

⁶Moule, p. 337. Moule states that "one of the cruelest Japs I saw in the whole outfit was a young fellow about eighteen years old. With one particular prisoner he had the guards pull him up until he was tiptoe, then he told the prisoner he was going to the *cine,* and after he got back he had better be ready to talk. That poor creature hung there praying, pleading, and yelling in agony for two hours while that b . . . . . . went to the show. During the time he was hanging, he put his feet against the bars, and several times tried to 'skin the cat.' Before he could get over, he would slip down. Then he would moan, pray, and scream. The guard would tell him to be quiet, and in the same breath give him a smack with an ammo belt. There were times I wished they would kill him; it would have been more merciful. I couldn't stand to look at him, and yet I couldn't keep from looking. The last time I looked, blood and sweat were dripping from his face. He was pleading as I had done to let him down or kill him. They did neither. They just beat him until he was a screaming maniac." Gene Kneebone witnessed this hanging and told me about it after he was returned to camp.

⁷Moule, p. 340.

⁸Halsema, ibid., pp. [44, 45], Apr. 16, 1944. Crouter, p. 303, Mar. 15, 1944: Natalie Crouter says that Capt. Tomibe "related [to Nellie McKim] an argument [he had] with Lt. Harada [apparently before Harada was raised to the rank of Captain] on how to treat internee visitors at Christmas. Harada was very officious, herding them together, making them stand in line over here or over there, pushing their lunches around. Tomibe said it was no way to do it. Pointing to Harada's shoulder insignia, he said emphatically, 'If you are of that opinion, you had better take off the insignia of rank and go back to Japan!' Whereupon Harada shouted back at him, 'And if you are of that opinion, you had better take off your insignia of rank and go back to Japan!'"

⁹"On July 19, 1947, President Manuel Roxas of the now independent Philippines convened military commissions to try the remaining [war crimes] cases, including that of Harada. He was specifically charged with causing the death of 18 Filipinos and his staff for other crimes. His subordinate, Tomomi Miyaki was accused of torturing among others, Kneebone, Moule, and myself. All pleaded guilty. Harada admitted: 'While I was the Commander of the Baguio Military Police detachment my duty was to maintain peace and order in that area. For that purpose, I thought we had to destroy the guerrilla members as quickly as possible. I believed that by doing so I was contributing to win the war under such circumstances. I had to order my men to do those things.' In 1952 Philippine President Elpidio Quirino granted 'conditional' pardons to the Japanese war criminals in the Philippines on condition that they leave the country for Japan upon their release. One of them was Harada. Eventually he found a job with Northwest Airlines in Tokyo."

In an email to me dated Sept. 19, 2002, 2:06 P.M., Halsema states that "Harada was not in Baguio in early 1942. I [Halsema] encountered him in 1944. His face was unmarked." If so, Harada could not have been the man who killed Rufus Gray. See chapter 10, p. 103.

CHAPTER

22

Plans to Escape

On April 9, five days after Swick and Green escaped, the Japanese military reinforced the garrison at Camp Holmes with thirty new soldiers. Besides the taking away of privileges, such as picnics up on the hill, there would now be new onerous regulations. On the 17th Capt. Tomibe announced at roll call that all knives (excluding table knives) must be turned in. Those failing to comply would be considered outlaws and would be dealt with as such. "Excalibur" was hidden in a safe place so that, even if it were found, it could not be traced to me. I discovered that it was getting rusty, and secretly cleaned and greased it, and put it back in its hiding place.[1]

At a meeting of the Camp Committee with the commandant, Tomibe asked, " 'What will you do when the Americans come back?' The Committee . . . answered, 'We will stay here.' [To this] Mr. Tomibe . . . [repeated the warning about knives in camp], 'Any armed civilians in this camp will be considered combatants.' "[2] Capt. Tomibe was simply reinforcing what the Japanese military had instructed him to say.[3]

As I mentioned earlier, our halcyon days came to an end in February 1944. Things began to get tough soon after General Morimoto visited our camp. An *"Important Notice,"* which appeared "on the [Bulletin] Board" on February 13, stated that, "Effective Sunday February 20,

1944, no more bags [of food] will be permitted to come into camp." It was also announced that we could not "listen to the guardhouse [radio] anymore."[4] A couple of days later on February 22 we were each given a sheet of paper on which was printed an oath, which we were required to sign, which stated that we would not attempt to escape from camp. The same day we saw posted on the bulletin board "Rules and Regulations issued by the Commandant's Office," which imposed on us some 18 rigid rules.

About a week later on March 2, the wood crew was "ordered to cut 300 fence posts."[5] On May 25 the Japanese "brought in a load of . . . bamboo [to be woven into] a lattice."[6] *Are they going to use it for a fence?* I wondered. I had guessed correctly. When completed, it was two "5-[strand] barbed wire fence[s]."[7] The outer fence was to be covered with a wall of bamboo lattice made after the bamboo was split, to make it more difficult to escape.[8] I have wondered if the ordering of the 300 fence posts had anything to do with Swick and Green's escape a month later. I would not be surprised to learn that it did.

The two fences were completed on June 28. To drive the posts into the ground "four soldiers would raise a log block, to which four handles had been attached, and would pound them in while they chanted something that sounded [to me] like, 'Ichi, no, san, yo!' "[9] The next day Elder Frost had a chat with me in the *nipa* shack. He said I seemed to be slipping spiritually. I acknowledged that this was true. He encouraged me to maintain my Christian principles. I said I was young and wanted to enjoy life. I acknowledged that I had been letting down the bars, and said that I felt that the Japanese would not let me get out of the camp alive because I was of military age.[10] He wept when I said this, and although I did not promise to change my ways, his words had a profound effect on me and in time they bore fruit. I consider that I am a Christian today because of that talk.[11]

I was not the only young man who felt he would not survive the war. On May 23, 1944, Ralph wrote: "I'll be glad if I'm alive 26 years from now.[12] I have a vague premonition that I'll never get out of here."[13] In his entry for June 29, he says: "Don shares my philosophy of not surviving the war. We face in our minds premonitions of certain death. . . . Religion we discussed, & how hard [it is] to be true [to Christian principles] when you believe your days are numbered."[14]

By the time I had the visit with Elder Frost on June 29, 1944, I was thinking of escaping. I said nothing to him about this idea, of course. Also, I said nothing to Ralph, because I did not want to have on my conscience what might happen to his mother and brother if we escaped and they were tortured or killed.

On July 4 to be exact, I had a scary dream about escaping and joining up with "Captain Swick and Lieutenant Green."[15]

In the evenings Ralph, Sonny Woodson, Mike Shaffer, and I would frequently walk up and down the road from the barracks to near the guardhouse and back. One night in late July, when Ralph wasn't with us, the subject of escaping came up. We were serious. We thought we could see a bloody turnover when the Americans came back, so we laid some tentative plans. A couple of days later, when Sonny and I again talked about escaping, we decided we could not risk taking Mike with us. We felt he was not physically up to it. So, we quietly dropped the subject in our conversations with Mike,[16] and it never came up again.

My diary says that the results of a blood test our family took in June showed that my "red blood cell count [was] 4,600,000; [my] hemoglobin 89. That's tops for this place. Charlie: R.b.c., 4,300,000; hemo., 70; Mom: R.b.c., 4,000,000, hemo., 84; Dad: R.b.c., 3,200,000."[17] On August 27 "Sonny had a physical examination. . . . He told me that he . . . [was pronounced] in excellent physical condition, except for his teeth."[18] His blood count, as well as mine, was so good that we were on the camp's list of donors.[19]

I chose Sonny as my escape partner because he was physically strong, he was born and reared in the Philippines, he knew Northern Luzon well, and he spoke Ilocano, the local dialect. As our plans matured we met secretly in the *nipa* shack and discussed the problems that faced us. On the night of September 9, "we talked until 1:45 A.M."[20]

Our most desperate need was shoes. After almost three years in camp, our shoes were in tatters. But Sonny had a solution. Many of the gold miners in camp had worn but excellent boots. He would borrow pairs that fit us, saying we needed them for a skit the young people were going to put on.[21] In the meantime Sonny and I had been working secretly on our backpacks.[22] So far as food and other necessities were concerned, we had our Red Cross supplies. In addition we had been toasting a portion of our rice ration on the kitchen range in the evening. Our plan was to escape via the septic tank overflow ditch behind the Men's Barracks. Once out of camp we would hike up the Mountain Trail until daylight and hide during the day.[23]

Sonny told me he was not Bertrand Woodson and that his real name was Clinton L. Ivanhoe, so he had no qualms about leaving his family.[24] I was not so "fortunate." I had parents and a brother in camp. I told him I could not leave without telling my mother goodbye. I hoped that, since the Japanese had killed no one for escaping up to this time, they would spare my family the death penalty, but I knew this was by no means certain and that they would be tortured.

On the evening of September 10 I told Mom I was planning to escape. She was shocked and asked me if I was serious. I said I was. She said that the Japanese would probably kill Dad and Charlie and begged me not to go.[25] She was not thinking of herself, although, if I had escaped, she would doubtless have been tortured, if not killed. She was thinking of others. This brought me to my senses. I promised not to go. This was the hardest decision I ever made in my life. From that moment on, and for many hours thereafter, my mind was a whirl of confusion. When I told Sonny my decision, he was sorely disappointed. I shall never forget his words: "Think and you hesitate; hesitate and you are lost." Well, thank God, I thought and hesitated. Instead of losing my life, I probably saved it, as you will see.

That evening, after scrubbing the kitchen, Mom came in and again made me promise not to escape. I repeated my promise that I wouldn't.[26]

Curiously, Sonny, who was so determined to escape, gave up on the idea, because "he didn't want to go alone."[27] My decision not to escape resulted in a parting of the ways with him.

In 1977, thirty-two years after liberation, I met Herbie Swick for the first time at the Internees' Reunion in San Francisco. I asked him what our chances would have been, if Sonny and I had escaped. His terse reply was, "Zilch. You would have been shot." I was surprised and shocked.

"Why would we have been shot?" I asked.

"Because you had not made prior arrangements to escape.[28] In the first place, you would probably have been turned in to the Japs by the Filipinos. But, even if they didn't turn you in, and you succeeded in reaching our camp, we would have suspected you of being sent by the Japs and we would have shot you. The guerrillas had a rigid policy regarding unauthorized people coming to their hideout: Shoot first; ask questions later."

I have a merciful God to thank for being alive today, as well as a loving mother, who kept me from doing something that had a great probability of ending tragically.

---

[1]D. Mansell, p. 30, July 5, 1944.

[2]Ibid., p. 18, July 18, 1944.

[3]Herold, p. [92], July 8, 1944: "Even if . . . [Tomibe] wanted to treat us better, he would not dare to, or the [Japanese] army would fix him."

[4]Crouter, p. 288, Feb. 13, 1944.

[5]Ibid., p. 295, Mar. 2, 1944. Cf. Ibid., p. 291, Feb. 22, 1944: "The Japanese have sprung a mean and ominous one [on us]. They want us to sign a paper that we won't try to escape no matter what the conditions"; ibid., p. 314, Mar. 31, 1944: "Some internees in Santo Tomas, for instance, were reported to be leaving the camp and later returning. Because of this, internees in that camp have had to get out of bed for unannounced roll calls at 2 A.M. The order for our fence came as a result of such rule-breaking."

[6]D. Mansell, p. 20, May 2, 1944.

Longway, p. [120], May 25, 1944: "[I] saw 9 trucks come in, one after another, filled with bamboos, long, thick ones. Strangest cargo I've seen for awhile, but they may use them for [a] fence. Had everyone guessing as the 1000 or more long bamboos were heaved out on the parade ground (in r[ight] f[ield,] incidentally)."

[7]Herold, p. [88], Apr. 19, 1944.

[8]Ibid., p. [90], June 11, 1944: "The guards are splitting the long bamboo poles and making a high criss-cross fence to extend above the outer barbed wire fence. It may be 30 ft high in places, but our mountain set-up permits us to look over it and still enjoy our pretty view."

[9]D. Mansell, p. 28, June 28, 1944.

[10]Ibid., p. 28, June 29, 1944.

[11]In 1958 during the General Conference Session in San Francisco, I met Elder Frost for the first time since internment and told him that his talk led to a turning point in my life.

[12]Ralph was alluding to his mother's 26th wedding anniversary.

[13]Longway, p. [118], May 23, 1944.

[14]Ibid., p. [141], June 29, 1944.

[15]D. Mansell, pp. 29, 30, July 4, 1944.

[16] When I related at the 1990 Internees' Reunion at the University of Southern California, that Sonny Woodson and I planned to escape from Camp Holmes in the fall of 1944, Mike Shaffer, who was acting as program chairman, spoke up and said, "Don, you've forgotten that I was going with you." This was true. I did not comment on his reminder, because I did not want to offend Mike by telling the reason in front of everyone. At our reunion in San Diego, Calif., in 1999, I explained briefly why we had left him out and apologized. Mike said he understood and told me that, soon after we had talked about escaping, he had decided not to leave camp.

[17]Ibid., p. 27, June 20, 1944.

[18]Ibid., p. 44, Aug. 27, 1944.

[19]Although we were on the donors' list, we were never called upon to donate blood. About this time Carroll Hinderlie and Ernest Smith got stomach ulcers and were on the verge of death because of loss of blood. Dr. Welles has told me since that what these men needed most was milk, not

blood, and this is the reason we were not called. At this critical juncture our camp cow was attacked by the camp hogs and stopped giving milk. However, *in answer to prayer*, a young milch cow showed up near the goat pen, and supplied the milk needed to save these men's lives.

[20]Ibid., p. 48, Sept. 9, 1944.

[21]Ibid., p. 49, Sept. 10, 1944.

[22]Ibid., p. 39, Aug. 20, 1944.

[23]Ibid., p. 50, Sept. 10, 1944.

[24]Ibid., p. 48, Sept. 9, 1944.

[25]Ibid., p. 50, Sept. 10, 1944. "Mom looked me straight in the eye and asked, 'Do you know what they will do to your father and your brother?' I said I did." In my mind I hoped that, inasmuch as the Japanese had never carried out their threat to execute five men and five women at random, if someone escaped, they would not kill anyone if Sonny and I escaped.

[26]Ibid, p. 50, Sept. 10, 1944.

[27]Ibid., p. 52.

[28]Ream interview, p. 4. Swick said to John Ream: "I learned [from the fact that] 'all the Filipinos . . . were scared of us (due to the Japs) . . . that if and when I escaped, I would have to contact somebody I could trust before I escaped."

CHAPTER

23

Fowl
Play

Food became increasingly scarce from March 1944 to February of 1945.
During that year there were times we got so hungry that it was a temptation
for internees to steal food, especially protein. But even before this year of
famine, there were times when we got hungry enough to steal. September
10, 1943, was one of those hungry times. That evening Ralph and I stole a
chicken, which we planned to cook and eat.[1] As we were in the process of
purloining the fowl, Les Wüttrich almost stumbled onto us and we had to
scram. Luckily, he didn't see us. After he left we caught Dinsbiers' red hen,
"meshed her in wire," and hid her under what Ralph called the "Carabao
Tree."[2]

The next day, Saturday, we transferred the chicken from the "Carabao
Tree" to the top of the hill and hid her under the "Fowler's Tree."[3] Doing
this made us late for Sabbath School, but we stayed for church.[4] The sermon must have had a beneficial effect on me, because that evening Ralph
wrote in his diary, "Don backed down . . . [on the chicken affair because it
bothers his] conscience."[5] So, we "return[ed the] chicken" to the hen house
the next day.[6]

I'm glad we didn't follow through with our selfish plan. If we had, one
wrong step could have led to another, and who knows how it would have
ended?

Thirteen months later, on October 11, 1944, Ralph and I heard that Shorty Wilson[7] had gotten caught red-handed cooking a camp rooster.[8] Jim Halsema wrote in his diary, "Doc Skerl . . . found . . . [the rooster] cooking in the pig pen shed, underneath another pot, and tended by . . . [Shorty]. Old [John 'Pop'] Nill . . . [and Jake Mason] are involved."[9]

A week or so before, Shorty had tried to get Ralph and me "in on his raid," but we refused to get involved. We warned Shorty that "he would get caught if he tried it." Some time during the morning of October 11, Jake invited Ralph to a feed in his dugout that night. I was not invited. At 2:30 Sandra Blake, accompanied by Carla and Nellie Day, asked both Ralph and me to come to the party, even though Shorty, who by then was being investigated for stealing the chicken, was one of the invitees. We pointed out that if we attended, and Shorty also came, we would be considered guilty by association. Sandra agreed with us for a while, but when Carla pointed out that, although Shorty was being investigated, he still had not been charged and could mingle freely with us, Sandra switched abruptly and said, "What the heck, take the worry later."[10]

Ralph and I smelled a rat. After Sandra, Carla, and Nellie left, Ralph and I walked on the parade ground and discussed what to do. I told Ralph that I couldn't see selling my soul and reputation "for a mess of pottage."[11] For me the solution was simple. I had not been included in the original invitation and I had a good reason for turning down this belated solicitation. With Ralph it wasn't so easy. He had accepted the original invitation. If he reneged now, he would be "ostracized for the duration." On the other hand, if he attended, he would be judged guilty by association. We wrestled with his problem and asked others for advice, but as late as supper time Ralph was still undecided.[12]

Ralph had earlier written in his diary, "Thievery is rampant, & I keep my fingers clean. . . . Things are disappearing, light bulbs, etc., & people are crazy with hunger." This was true. At the end of our conversation, Ralph decided to attend the party. However, after supper he met Elder Frost (who would be one of the judges at the upcoming trial). He convinced Ralph that he shouldn't go.[13]

Ralph felt I had refused the girls' invitation to the party too rashly and had unnecessarily caused hard feelings. I surely had. He was by nature more diplomatic than I was, and when he explained his concerns privately to Jake and Carla, they said they understood, and cancelled the party altogether.[14]

Meanwhile, Shorty was going around bragging about what a good time he would have had, if he hadn't gotten caught.[15] Not only was I undiplomatic, but I acted like a self-righteous prig, letting it be known that I would tell the truth about anything I knew concerning the chicken affair. When Lizzy Wilson, Shorty's sister, heard about this, she sought me out and, quivering with rage, gave me a tongue-lashing. When she finished, I knew I had an enemy.[16] Fortunately, I was not called to testify or I would have had more enemies.

Jim Halsema wrote in his diary that "nine chickens have gone down the . . . [Wilson] gullet. Carl [Eschbach] asked Art [Richardson] to serve on the special investigating committee. He refused [saying,] 'When you had a pork chop case against the kitchen crew,[17] you were afraid to prosecute. Now you've got a bunch of high school kids—you're safe to go ahead.' "[18] This was true. It was a case of the teenagers being made an example to the rest of the camp.[19] Generally speaking, adults caught stealing got away with it, although in one or two cases, *individual adults* convicted of stealing, did serve jail time.

A hearing was held on October 13, at which Shorty and Jake "pleaded guilty to the judiciary committee. During the hearing they said that they had promised the wings and neck to [Pop Nill] the man who took care of the pigs, for the use of his stove. The boys were sentenced to . . . solitary confinement on limited rations for [five days and two days, respectively]."[20] Pop Nill served two days and lost his job as swineherd.

This trial was not the end of chicken stealing. Ethel Herold says that

> One day . . . Billy [her son] and David [Bergamini] had a good chance to catch a Jap chicken. It seemed that the chickens did not know where the prison territory began and sometimes wandered into our pigpen, hoping for a scratch in our manure. Billy said it would be easy enough to pen a chicken in our pig shed, then that night catch it and kill it. I warned him not to as it was too dangerous. Our own Camp Com[mittee] might accuse him and David of stealing [a] camp chicken and punish them; or the Japs might catch them and punish them even worse. But that night, after dark, here came those two boys with a little chicken

all cleaned and skinned. . . . It was up to me to get it cooked. The smell of cooking chicken would have been like the sounding of trumpets, and the consequences really something to explain. [So] I thought it easier to risk it on . . . the open-air little kitchen. . . . [A]ny smell would be wafted away. . . . [N]ot so in the big closed in kitchen.

The chicken was small and young and tender. I put it in the bottom of my precious kettle, covered it with the last of the little *camotes* [that Billy and David brought back from Trinidad Valley], and covered that with the hot water allowed me for my bath ([I] skipped my bath), put the hot pot on the stove, took some kitchen mending with me to sit right there and guard every second. Even . . . [so], [Mrs.] Teddy Tyson took off the lid and exclaimed, where did we get all those little *camotes*. I made [up] a big story . . . [about] them and told the others to let them alone, as I wanted them to boil as fast as possible. An hour's boiling was too much for the *camotes* and about right for the chicken. . . . I got it upstairs without detection of contents. David had been invited to come to our place to eat. The chicken was divided . . . in half. David took out the breast for his mother; Billy likewise gave me his share of the breast ([which I] divided with Betsy and Elmer). Then the two boys really feasted. But poor David went home and vomited his all up.[21]

In my diary, under the date of October 13, 1944, I wrote: "For some time past I have been a 'sin-sick soul.' Recently I have heard that still small voice calling. It seems to say: 'This prison camp is part of a plan. Son, you will get out of it OK.' "[22]

In his diary, under the same date, Ralph wrote: "After roll call, [I] walked with Don for 2 hours on the old road. We discussed everything from brains to girls, & I was amazed to find what a vast spiritual change has come over Don. . . . [It coincides] with my own." We both had the feeling that God had a hand in our internment experience.[23]

Because I was taking his class in anatomy and physiology, Dr. Welles invited me to watch Lizzy Wilson undergo an appendectomy on October 14. When I arrived at the hospital, Carla was standing over by a window. I went over and asked her if she was angry with me because I refused to attend her party. She said she was not, and was genuinely glad to see me. She was subdued and told me she had decided to tell the whole truth about the chicken affair. About this time Lil Dosser called Carla over to tell her something. When Carla came back, she said Shorty did not want me to be present during his sister's operation. I said that that was all right with me and started to leave. In the meantime someone must have told Doc Welles about Shorty's objection.

I was on my way out when Doc Welles came in and said, "None of this, 'over my dead body,' and no back talk, Shorty." At first I didn't understand what Doc Welles was talking about. It didn't dawn on me that someone had told him about Shorty's objection, and that the doctor was bawling him out, when he said what he did. So, I stayed and watched the procedure.[24]

After the operation Carla told me Jake had "decided to reform." She said he probably would never again eat a bite of chicken without thinking of the "fowl affair."[25]

---

[1]Longway, p. [12], Sept. 9, 1943: "Don and I plan . . . to kill Dinsbier's chicken." Ibid., p. 13, Sept. 11, 1943: "Don and I go for the chicken. [We are] scared [out] by [Les] Wüttrich once and scram, but finally get Dinsbier's [Rhode Island] Red from the goat pen house."

[2]Ibid.: "[We] mesh her in wire and hide her under the Carabao Tree."

[3]Ibid., p. 13, Sept. 11, 1943: "[We manage to] elude Carroll [Walker] and go to [the] Carabao Tree, [then we go] to the top of [the] hill with it and hide it under the Fowler's Tree."

[4]Ibid.

[5]Ibid., p. [13], Sept. 11, 1943: "Don backs down by conscience on chicken business."

[6]Ibid., p. [13], Sept. 13, 1943: "Up early and . . . [go] up to [our] chicken cache . . . and return chicken, 'cause Don backs out.' "

[7]The names of the teenagers involved in this episode have been disguised.

[8]Longway, p. [230], Oct. 11, 1944.

[9]Halsema, 1944, p. [114], Oct. 11, 1844.

[10]Longway, p. [231], Oct. 11, 1944.

[11]Genesis 25:29-34. Longway, p. [231], Oct. 11, 1944: "Don says he doesn't want to sell his soul & reputation 'for a mess of porage.' " I said pottage, not porage.

[12]Longway, p. [231], Oct. 11, 1944.

[13]Ibid.

[14]Ibid.

[15]D. Mansell, handwritten diary, Oct. 11, 1944. (Hereafter designated D. Mansell, handwritten.)

The handwritten version of my diary contains things that do not appear in the transcribed version. When I disembarked in San Francisco on Mar. 30, 1945, the FBI asked us to turn in our diaries and assured us that they would be returned to us. I wasn't sure I wanted to trust the FBI, so

I handed them my mother's diary. They returned it to me after several months. Thus they have no record of my diary.

[16]Ibid.

[17]Longway, p. [131, 132], June 14, 1944: "[The] cooks were caught last night [June 13, 1944] frying up camp pork steaks. All of the cooks will be kicked out soon."

The cooks were never disciplined. Art Richardson was right: It was easier to prosecute callow youths than adults.

Halsema, diary, p. [69], June 23, 1944: "[The Camp] Committee heard from [Chief of Police, Col.] Dosser that all pork chop evidence was hearsay: no one was willing to testify. They voted (not unanimously) not to issue minutes. 'It might seem like we were exonerating them,' was [Carl] Eschbach's excuse."

[18]Halsema, p. [115], Oct. 12, 1944.

[19]Longway, p. [242], Oct. 20, 1944: "All that the Camp [Committee] ever does is crack down on us minors, just because we don't have the connections that the wily rulers have."

[20]Miles, p. 145.

[21]Herold, p. 99. This entry is undated, but it can be bracketed as having occurred in the late fall of 1944.

[22]D. Mansell, handwritten, Oct. 13, 1944.

[23]Longway, p. [234], Oct. 13, 1944.

[24]D. Mansell, handwritten, Oct. 14, 1944.

[25]Ibid.

CHAPTER
24

The Last Months
at Camp Holmes

A couple of weeks after Swick and Green escaped, Jim Halsema wrote in his diary:

> A gang of short brown men in bright blue denim fatigue clothes and wash basin sun helmets [our guards] [began] pounding in fence posts on cemetery hill above . . . [the Men's] barracks. . . . Five strands of barbed wire are encircling the camp; patrols with fixed bayonets tramp our walks; sentries stand by the pig pen looking across at the camp— the place is beginning to look like a concentration camp.[1]

But even before these regulations were put into effect, lean-tos, which eventually would be outside the camp perimeter, were ordered dismantled. Thus, on April 12, Ralph "heard that [a] new fence [was going] to be constructed" just beyond the workshop. This meant that he and Charlie, and others who had shacks out near the pig pen, would have to tear them down. As soon as the new rules were announced, it became more difficult to get access to the garden area and salvage materials before a guard ordered them to leave.[2] Some guards were strict about enforcing the new rules, others were lenient—and we took advantage of them.

The same day, April 12, Charlie asked the guards at the bodega for two planks. The guard gave permission, and he came away with four, including a good door. He and Ralph piled two pieces of galvanized iron roofing on the door, and deposited them near the nipa shack where the firewood was kept. That afternoon they searched for a place to rebuild their shack and selected a spot near the septic tank behind the Men's Barracks.[3]

The next day, right after roll call, Charlie and Ralph leveled off the site they had chosen for their shack. In the meantime they got David Longway and Curtis Tong to tear down what remained of their shack and transport it to the new location. When Charlie and Ralph finished leveling off the new foundation, they sought and obtained permission from the guards to bring back loads of planks and other materials left behind by other shack owners to use on their new shelter. By dinner time they had brought "every stick and nail" they could find to the new location.[4]

About this time Jim Thompson decided that a dugout under the Green Barracks would be a fine place for his new abode, so he began excavating a rectangular hole between the grid of piers that held up that building. By April 18 he had it well on the way to completion and invited his wife, Marie, and Natalie Crouter "to see the cubicle . . . [he had] built" "in three days" from "odd pieces of tin and board and logs, picked up from discarded heaps."[5]

The Thompson dugout must have inspired the Crouters to build a shanty of their own,[6] for soon after, they laid claim to a spot near the south end of the Green Barracks, adjacent to a storage area that had been dug out before the war and was used for storage and, during our first months at Camp Holmes, was used by John Duty as the camp's shoe shop. This area had a barbed-wire fence around it, and Jerry Crouter began to excavate a dugout for himself and his family in the area adjacent to it.

On May 6, Ralph and I observed that some of the "catacombs" under the Green Barracks were "really nice,"[7] and we decided to construct a dugout of our own. The piers supporting the barracks were some twelve feet apart, so we staked out our "claim" in the area between the four piers next to the Crouter dugout and set to work excavating the dirt. There were only about three feet of clearance between the ground and the barracks' floor joists. So, we first had to dig a hole two-and-a-half to three feet deep in which to stand before we could dig from a more comfortable stance. Excavating that hole was back-breaking work. We had to use a pick and shovel bent over and on our knees, until the hole was scooped out deep enough to stand in.

The day after Ralph and I began to dig, Dad became interested in our project and joined us in excavating.[8] The location of our dugout was directly under the bunk space in the Green Barracks that Mom shared with Marie Thompson and Edna Miller.

One evening, four days after beginning our project, Emil Jorgensen gave me a soggy piece of rice bread to eat. I woke up in the middle of the night feeling dizzy and bilious.[9] I suspect that the bread had something to do with this. For some reason, these dizzy spells lasted off and on for some time, and I was unable to work with Dad and Ralph when these waves of wooziness hit me. As a result, they did most of the digging until I got over those bouts.

On May 25 Ralph decided to excavate a dugout of his own for his mother and brother, and he began excavating the area between the next set of piers adjacent to ours. The space under the barracks was poorly illuminated. So, we scrounged around down in the abandoned Igorot village and found several lengths of insulated electrical cord and carefully connected them to the electrical system of the Green Barracks, and, presto, we had lights.[10] We added walls and doors from materials that we found at the Igorot shanty town, and we soon had comfortable dugouts. The great advantage of these "subterranean" refuges was that they gave us places where we could get away from it all.

Commenting on this advantage, Natalie wrote in her diary: "This dugout is heaven—to get out of that room. . . . I am out of the stream, where I need to be right now. . . . No two dugouts are alike. [The] Mansells' is huge. [It] has a window with two panes of glass, a door, curtains, [a] couch [made out of a bedstead, and a] chair, all on a grand . . . [scale]."[11] Other "catacombs" were far more lavishly furnished than ours. For example, Natalie wrote that millionaires Phil and Peg Whitmarsh made their dugout look "like the saloon of a ship."[12] It was far more extravagantly equipped than ours.

Ralph fashioned a couch from packed earth and covered it with a blanket. Dad helped the Longway boys make a table out of scrap lumber.[13] By August 30 Charlie and Kay, who by now were seriously considering marriage, "[had a] nice little place [under the Green Barracks]. . . . [It had] whitewashed walls and a roof." Ralph and I were invited to their "cubicle-opening party."[14]

As far back as March of 1944, when it became apparent that it was only a matter of time before America retook the Philippines, a controversy began to rage over whether families should live together. This project became known as "the Family Unit Plan," or "the Cubicle Plan." Ever since Capt. Tomibe had taken over as commandant, couples had been allowed to associate together freely during the day. Envy by those who didn't have a dugout, and the lack of room for more subterranean sanctuaries, fueled the controversy.

Because by now it had become impossible for every family to have a dugout under the Green Barracks, the idea was born of rearranging the living spaces in the Middle Barracks, so that families could live together. This, of course, would mean a lot of shifting around and crowding to accommodate the incoming husbands. Many of the women opposed the Cubicle Plan because it would mean rearranging their living space to make room for their spouses. But there were more compelling reasons for their opposition to the plan.

The furor lasted for months. The principal argument of the anti-cubicleers was that it would result in accidental pregnancies. The main argument of the pro-cubicleers was that times were getting increasingly dangerous, and when the turnover came, it would be best for husbands and fathers to be with their families. Eventually, with the concurrence of the commandant, those in favor of the Cubicle Plan won out.

At 3:00 P.M. on July 6, 1944, the men were ordered to assemble in the new schoolhouse for a spiel by a new commandant. We lined up in four rows. When the Japanese officers strode in, Yamato led the way, followed by Capt. Tomibe, then Lt. K. Oura, and finally Lt. Sakashita. After facing toward us, Yamato-San shouted, "Sarrute!" (Salute). It sounded like, "Cheroot!" and we either didn't understand what he said, or, more probably, purposely misunderstood. In any case, we didn't move. Yamato repeated his command. We continued to remain as we were. Finally Capt. Tomibe took the lead and bowed, and we bowed with him.

Capt. Tomibe gave a short speech in which he formally turned the camp over to the new commandant, Lt. K. Oura. At the close of Tomibe's speech, Yamato again shouted, "Sarrute!" This time we bowed—to Capt. Tomibe.

Oura was tall for a Japanese, almost six feet. His head was clean-shaven, his black beard showed a couple of days' growth, his mouth was tight-lipped, and he had a mean look about him. He began speaking, with Yamato interpreting.

As best as I can remember, his speech, as rendered by the camp's official translator, went like this: "We, de Imperiar Japan not have riving spasu (living space). About four souzand (thousand) years ago de great Nippon sutarted (started). Before the war de Hiripine Airands (Philippine Islands) were corony (a colony) of the United Statesu and not produce materiar, (hence the shortages we were experiencing)." As he continued, the tone of the speech became threatening: "You must not run way. Must not repeat bad examper (example) once more. If you do, you must eat poory (poorly)."

Later, while I was studying in our high-school study hall room, I heard Lt. Oura tell our Camp Committee through Miss McKim (they were meeting in a classroom on the other side of a bamboo wall) that the reason our rice ration had recently been cut was because Japan had conquered a large part of India and was having to feed its starving millions.[15] After the Japanese left, I could hear the committee members snickering among themselves over this claim.

By July 26 the outer fence with the woven bamboo lattice was complete. This reduced the area of our camp by a third. It cut out the workshop, "garbage districts" (we were now burying our trash, rather than dumping it in the Trinidad River), the goat and hog pens, and the entire hillside.[16] Four days later Oura began to exercise command. It appears that Capt. Tomibe was demoted to Second Lieutenant and placed under Oura.[17] We felt sorry for Mr. Tomibe. But no matter what the Japanese military might do to him, he would remain Capt. Tomibe to us.

On August 2 Oura decreed that we could spend only fifty *pesos* a month at the camp store. Because of burgeoning inflation fifty pesos was hardly enough money to buy food for a person for two days,[18] much less a month. On August 8, as if in response to the commandant's new restriction on buying at the store, the Igorots[19] kindly donated a thousand pounds of *camotes* to our camp.[20]

The day these *camotes* came in, supper consisted of "ground creamed beef, rice & camotes." This was more food than we'd had for quite a while.[21] Were it not for these occasional good meals and our Red Cross supplies, we would have fared much worse than we did. On August 26, for instance, our ration was a mere 860 calories.

Before morning roll call on September 15, a rumor swept through camp that Capt. Tomibe was leaving. The rumor was true. "Tomibe in khaki riding breeches, open collar, white shirt with sword and cap with chin strap, came up the road, [and] stopped in front"[22] of the Middle Barracks by the side of the road. After roll call, we all gathered at the crossroads and Tomibe spoke, with Miss McKim translating. He said he had been with us for almost a year and had received orders to go to Manila. During his stay "we had become friends under [the] difficult conditions of war and [he] hoped that after peace we could be friends again under better . . . [circumstances]."[23] He said he was sorry we were subjected to the conditions in which we found ourselves and urged us to take care of our health. He ended with, *"Sayonara."*

We burst into spontaneous applause and shouted back, *"Sayonara!"* At first Capt. Tomibe seemed startled by our response, then pleased.[24] We continued to clap for quite a while. A few disapproved of this gesture and moved indignantly indoors at the conclusion of roll call. Capt. Tomibe then left in the camp truck, which the Japanese staff apparently considered was a suitable send-off.[25] "Tomibe is a real gentleman,"[26] I wrote in my diary. We were sorry to see him leave. With his departure, what would things be like? It didn't take long for us to find out.

September 22, 1944, was our one-thousandth day of internment. At 9:30 A.M., Charlie and I were taking a test in General Science, when we heard three distant detonations. Gene Hungerford, our teacher, remarked that it didn't sound like blasting to him. As we looked out the window of our high school, we saw Harold Fildey and Paul Peterson over on the northwestern edge of the parade ground above the sunken garden.[27] They were pointing out toward the China Sea, twenty miles away. We concluded that Paul Peterson, who was blind in one eye, must be observing something with his good eye—something that was worth seeing. Gene dismissed us from class to take a look for ourselves.

When we got to where others were gathering, we could see only two planes. They looked like a couple of mosquitoes flying north, parallel to the coast. Suddenly I saw four specks flying in the opposite direction. The two lower planes of this formation suddenly disappeared, and just as suddenly, at least twenty planes seemed to swarm out of the haze.[28] Someone, I think it was Gene Kneebone, who had a spy glass, claimed to have counted as many as forty aircraft. We could hear the deep sound of exploding bombs, followed by "a fluttering undertone of what [old] Col. [James M.] Love . . . [called] .50 cal[iber] machine gun thwatting."[29] This activity continued for about half an hour.

When the "show" was over, we were thrilled. The guards out near the pig pen appeared nervous, and the soldiers up on the hill blew whistles and wigwagged their concerns with semaphore flags to their countrymen below. Over near the guardhouse we could see Yamato. He was just standing, pensive, listening.

Later, Gus Skerl, who watched the action with us, told us that the Japanese staff was jittery. He also said that Mr. Furuya, the Japanese civilian who supplied our store, told him that American planes had bombed the waterfront at Poro on the coast and that as soon as this news reached the Baguio market, prices sky-rocketed. All this buoyed up our spirits. Mike Shaffer is quoted as saying that "internees are going around as if they'd swallowed canaries." But it wasn't long before most of us realized that the coming of our countrymen would mean harder times. Things would get worse before they got better.

Some internees celebrated by splurging on corned beef or spam. "I decided not to. It may be a long time yet before we get out," I wrote in my diary.[30] A few weeks later, two American planes flew over camp, and we were again overjoyed. Nevertheless, I wrote gloomily:

> Once again the world seems bright,
> But our faith must be discreet,
> Shattered hopes like broken lanterns
> Lie in fragments at our feet.[31]

Lt. Oura's reaction to the appearance of the planes on September 22 was swift and decisive. That afternoon he told Carl Eschbach that internees must make blackout curtains, and we, not the Japanese military, must supply the material for them.[32] We gladly complied with his order, because it meant that the tide had turned against Japan. By the evening of the 23rd "every light was hooded with some kind of contraption,"[33] wrote Ralph. Yet, strangely, Oura left the lights burning around the camp perimeter.

The more evident it became that the war was going badly for Japan, and that it was only a matter of time before America retook the Philippines, the more irrational, irascible, and erratic Lt. Oura became. Our rice ration had been cut, and now weevily field corn was substituted in its place. Yet, in spite of our steadily deteriorating physical condition, Oura demanded more work from us, and longer hours at the garden. Our situation was growing desperate. The only thing that kept our spirits up was the occasional American planes that flew over.

On October 18 our Camp Committee wrote the following letter to "His Excellency, Highest Commander of the Philippine Islands. Your Excellency: We the undersigned, members of Camp Holmes Civilian Internment Camp No. 3, respectfully submit this urgent appeal to you for assistance in obtaining enough food to keep us alive. . . . At present we are not receiving the essential foods in sufficient quantity to sustain life; anemia and other illnesses resulting from malnutrition are increasing at such an alarming rate our doctors state that unless immediate steps are taken to obtain more food the damage to our health will not only be irreparable, but death will follow."[34]

Oura turned a deaf ear to our requests, taking the stand that all orders regarding the camp food supply originated at Manila army headquarters and he, merely a good soldier, had to obey those then in effect. Proof of this was once again forthcoming on October 31, when our corn ration of 150 grams per capita, daily, was reduced to 100 grams.[35] Probably because Ralph and Charlie and I put in long hours at night scrubbing and cleaning up the kitchen, Bob Brown, our boss, told us on October 30 that "Doc Welles had given permission for . . . [us boys] to eat a bit of corn mush after work."[36] We didn't need to be given permission a second time. Although the mush had weevils floating throughout, we closed our eyes and ate the extra amount allowed us with relish.

On November 13 the menu for the next day that appeared in the *Camp Holmes Daily News* read as follows:

Breakfast: Rice
Tea
Lunch (?)
Supper Rice (?)[37]

Were it not for our hoarded Red Cross packages and the occasional large supply of *camotes* and vegetables that Sgt. Sugano was able to purchase in the Baguio market, the prediction of death by slow starvation envisaged by our Camp Committee would surely have come to pass. Because my digestive system seems to have been more efficient than that of many in camp, I was one of the few who managed to maintain a fair degree of health in spite of reduced rations and loss of weight. Many of those less fortunate suffered from vitamin deficiencies, such as beriberi and pellagra.

On October 3, Lt. Oura and Saito-San went to Manila and Los Baños in the camp truck driven by Ray Hale.[38] The Lieutenant and Hale returned two days later with Yoshio Mazaki, the son of a Japanese general, who proved to be a real friend to us.[39] As soon as Ray arrived in camp, he reported that U.S. planes bombed Clark Field on the way down, and that, while in Manila, he learned that on September 22, 23, and 24 "American . . . carrier-borne dive bombers, deck attack bombers, and twin-engine fighters roared over . . . [Santo Tomás] internment camp, waggling their wings in greeting."[40] This was electrifying news. Our countrymen were on the way. How soon would they reach us—and would we be alive when they arrived?

Oura returned from Manila a sick man. I was told he had kidney stones. Whatever his ailment, he took to bed when he got back to camp. In his diary, Jim Halsema, wrote: "This peasant [Oura, originally a farmer, is] afraid of modern inventions, but not of calling our doctors fools. . . . [He gets] no sympathy from 468 internees or his staff."[41] The last two words in this description are significant. Even the members of his staff disliked him.

On October 9, I wrote in my diary: "The Camp Committee talked to Lt. Oura, who, for the first time, seems satisfied with the garden project. He is reported to have started out by apologizing for the rough way he has spoken to the Medical Committee and Miss McKim. He said that his recent kidney stone attack was due to the angry way he had spoken."[42]

According to the grapevine, Oura told Miss McKim that her God had punished him for the way he had been treating us. Whether or not this was true, the next day he allowed a Safety Committee to be formed. The purpose of this committee was to look after our safety if fighting occurred.[43] Oura even said we could paint a red cross on one of our buildings. But alas, his change of heart was neither lasting nor consistent. By November 13 "he utterly refuse[d] to let us purchase food from the natives." Fortunately, Lt. Sakashita promised to secure food from farmers coming down the Mountain Trail on their way to the market.[44]

On November 30, Thanksgiving Day, a "Civic Service" was held in the Sunken Garden to celebrate the day. It began at 10:00 A.M. Several of our leaders spoke. At the close, "we sang the two 'N' [the forbidden national anthems]"—"The Star Spangled Banner" and "God Save the King."[45]

That afternoon Charlie and Kay were married.[46] Natalie Crouter describes the wedding:

> Kay and her beloved Charlie were married at a small wedding by Carl at 4 P.M. today. The bride wore Daphne [Bird]'s lovely white organdy print. There were about 16 guests at a dinner afterward, including a wedding cake. . . . [The reception] was [held] in two cubicles in the Ark. The Dawsons gave up their cubicle for one night [for] honeymoon quarters. The aids all attended the ceremony

and Kay is happy, cannot imagine herself married to anyone else. So all is serene and the couple settled for life.[47]

Ralph and I were ushers; Vadna Fildey was matron of honor; Charlie Wittschiebe was best man, Carl Eschbach tied the knot,[48] and Harold Fildey assisted. As soon as the ceremony was over and the wedding party got to the "Ark," it began to rain heavily.

Charlie and Kay took up residence in the Middle Barracks along with the other married couples.

Early in December a group of Japanese officers made a complete survey of the camp's buildings—taking measurements, computing floor space—and on the 8th, the third anniversary of the attack on Pearl Harbor, our hosts informed our Committee that they were taking over the hospital building. They told us to prepare to vacate the patients to the Green Barracks on Topside.[49] On the 20th this communication became an order. It almost sparked a riot. The hospital staff threatened to resign, but there was no way they could stand up to the Japanese military. The staff had no choice but to knuckle under. For the next week our camp was in chaos. Making a place for the hospital patients and staff involved major adjustments that affected everyone in camp to a greater or lesser degree. The south end of Green Barracks had to be cleared in order for the hospital patients and staff to find other places to live. The remaining segregated couples were merged into family cubicles and housed in the mess hall, which was converted into living space.

With the dining room gone, the kitchen staff gave out dishes and cutlery to each internee. They served us at meal time, and we ate at our bunks. On December 23 the last of the hospital patients were transferred to their new quarters.[50]

December 25, 1944, was very different from the two previous Christmases. No friends or families of internees were allowed to visit us. Unlike previous Noels, I did not go caroling with Dirks's choir. Breakfast was a double portion of rice, instant coffee from Red Cross packages for coffee drinkers, sugar, and a banana. Lunch consisted of a mixture of rice, corn flour, onions, soy sauce, and who knows what else—but it was food.

At 10:00 A.M. Charlie Fears, dressed in a red suit and wearing his long white, tobacco-stained beard, again played Santa. He sat in a cart drawn by a rather uncooperative horse, led by Louis Robinson. As "Santa" came up the road from the guardhouse and the children saw him, they let out a whoop. Santa dispensed to each child some chewy candy supplied by the Japanese, a handful of roasted peanuts, a piece of *bucayo*,[51] and a banana.[52]

I had supper with Mom and Dad on the sidewalk between the Middle Barracks and the Green Barracks. We had rice, gravy, candied *camotes*, small hamburgers, boiled onions, and ersatz coffee. We supplemented our fare with gravy that Mom made. Those who wished (and who didn't?) could have seconds of rice and gravy. I saved my seconds of rice and toasted it.[53]

Wrote Natalie Crouter, "[Only] three small trees glittered with lights again as on Christmas Eve, symbols of the shrinkage in size, manner and content of all our celebrations this year."[54] The scantiness of the decorations was symbolic of the hard times that had slowly, but now swiftly, came upon us.

---

[1]Halsema, 1944 diary, p. [46], April 20, 1944. See p. 199.

[2]Longway, p. [96], April 12, 1944.

[3]Ibid., p. [97], April 12, 1944.

[4]Ibid.

[5]Crouter, p. 330, Apr. 18, 1944.

[6]Herold, p. [88], April 19, 1944: "Natalie Crouter, Cubicle cartoons: [A] man and woman and 3 kids in swung beds. Greater East Asia cans of milk, save milk. 3 male and 3 female heads looking out from . . . the commingling quarters, some are really swanky."

A quip by Fr. Clifford Nobes: "New York before the stork."

[7]Longway, p. [110], May 6, 1944.

[8]D. Mansell, p. 21, May 7, 1944.

[9]Ibid., p. 22, May 10, 1944.

[10]Crouter, p. 341, May 14, 1944: "The new Underground cubicle town . . . is even being wired for electricity."

[11]Ibid., p. 343, May 17, 1944. Ibid., 341, May 14, 1944: "Mansells looted tin [from the former Constabulary officer's village, which was] full of holes [and put it] on the North Wall, with charming runo sticks held together by woven string on the South Wall."

[12]Ibid., p. 343, May 17, 1944.

[13]Longway, p. [147], July 9, 1944.

[14]Ibid., p. [188], Aug. 30, 1944.

[15]See also Longway, p. [145], July 6, 1944; Halsema, diary 1944, p. [74], July 6, 1944; Hind, p. 199, for different versions of what Yamato translated.

[16]Longway, pp. [159, 160], July 26, 1944.

D. Mansell, p. 34: "A new fence has been built at the far end of the parade ground. This is to keep people who have no business at the workshop away from there. It cut out some 3 or 4 acres of ground. It feels as though slowly but surely the barbed wire noose is closing in on us."

[17]Crouter, pp. 366, 367, July 31, 1944.

[18]Longway, p. [165], Aug. 2, 1944.

[19]We knew that, had it been possible, these mountain people would have been willing to supply us with the food we needed. But, of course, the Japanese would never allow this. The

friendliness of these mountain people toward Americans undoubtedly galled our hosts.

[20]Ibid., p. [185], Aug. 26, 1944.

[21]Ibid., p. [171], Aug. 8, 1944.

[22]Halsema, diary 1944, p. [99], Sept. 15, 1944.

[23]Crouter, p. 385, Sept. 15, 1944.

[24]Halsema, diary 1944, p. [100], Sept. 15, 1944.

[25]Ibid.

[26]D. Mansell, p. 52, Sept. 15, 1944.

[27]Ibid., p. 54, Sept. 22, 1944.

[28]Ibid.

[29]Halsema, diary 1944, p. [104], Sept. 22, 1944.

[30]D. Mansell, p. 55, Sept. 22, 1944.

[31]Ibid., p. 79, Nov. 25, 1944.

[32]Halsema, diary 1944, p. [105], Sept. 23, 1944.

[33]Longway, p. [207], Sept. 23, 1944.

[34]Crouter, pp. 400, 401, Oct. 25, 1944.

[35]Hind, p. 223.

[36]D. Mansell, p. 70, Oct. 30, 1944.

[37]Ibid., p. 76, Nov. 13, 1944, copied from the *Camp Holmes Daily News*.

[38]Halsema, diary 1944, p. [110], Oct. 3, 1944.

[39]Halsema, p. [112], Oct. 6, 1944. "[Dr.] Dana [Nance] writes from Los Baños (Sept. 26): 'Mr. Masaki [i.e., Mazaki] who brings this note is entirely trustworthy and will, I am sure, do everything in his power to make internment as reasonable as possible. He is a gentleman in every sense of the word—our loss is your gain.' "

Herold, p. [97], Oct. 7, 1944. "[The] son of Gen. [Jinzaburo] Mazuki [i.e., Mazaki] is here (very young) officially; [he] speaks English and seems nice. It seems his Dad was purged some years back for being too civilized in the Western manner."

Yoshio Mazaki was killed in the fighting in the mountains east of Manila sometime around April 10, 1945. Although he was our friend, we respected him for being loyal to his emperor.

[40]Ibid., p. [111], Oct. 5, 1944.

[41]Ibid., p. [113].

[42]D. Mansell, p. 61, Oct. 9, 1944.

[43]Halsema., p. [114], Oct. 10, 1944.

[44]D. Mansell, p. 76, Nov. 14, 1944.

[45]Ibid., p. 80, Nov. 30, 1944.

[46]The only other wedding in camp was that of Carroll E. Dickey and F. Wilma Park, which took place on March 23, 1944.

[47]Crouter, p. 417.

[48]On July 13, 2002, Charlie wrote me: "Carl Eschbach tied a great marriage knot between Kay and me. It is as strong today as it was 58 years ago."

[49]Hind, p. 239. Hind says December 9; Longway, p. [303], says December 8, 1944. Longway is correct.

[50]Miles, p. 146.

[51]Coconut candy made from grated coconut mixed with *panocha* sugar.

[52]Crouter, p. 431, Dec. 25, 1944.

[53]D. Mansell, p. 96, Dec. 25, 1944.

[54]Crouter, p. 432, Dec. 25, 1944.

25

Our Camp Moves to Manila

The day after Christmas, roll call consisted of the announcement that all available men were needed to help move the hospital equipment to the Green Barracks on Topside. I carried ten loads and strained my back on the last load. I rested in the afternoon to let my muscles recuperate.

That evening after supper I heard that Mr. Yamato had come running to our shoe repair shop and demanded his boots, whether they were ready or not. Soon after, he told Miss McKim that orders had been received that our camp was to move somewhere right away. But where? The news spread like wildfire. "What now?" I wrote in my diary. "We just moved."[1]

The Camp Committee immediately went into session and made plans for our exodus. We heard that 60 percent of the camp would move on Thursday, 40 percent on Friday, including the hospital patients. Ralph came up to my bunk and said he saw Sgt. Sugano near the kitchen. He was drunk and kept urging Warren Graham to have a drink of *sake*.[2] "Sampru, sampru," he insisted. "Arr go Manira." But he didn't say where in Manila.

All kinds of rumors were flying: We were going to be repatriated.[3] No, we were going to Los Baños. No, we were going to[4] Bilibid. But was it Old

Our Camp Moves to Manila

Bilibid in downtown Manila, or New Bilibid, situated at Muntinglupa outside of Manila? We hoped it would be the latter. Our captors wouldn't or couldn't tell us which. We were limited to a half cubic meter of baggage, a bedroll, and a lunch for the trip.

We didn't know it at the time, but after the war Jim Halsema discovered the reason why our camp was moved:

> General Tomoyuki Yamashita[5] was given control of Japanese forces in the Philippines [on] October 2, 1944, only days before the Americans began their liberation of the islands by landing on Leyte island. His superiors insisted that . . . [the invaders] be driven off. . . . He was sure that by now his opponents had such overwhelming strength in the air and on the sea that his only hope was to build fortifications in the mountains of Luzon, where infantry could be effective. . . . But it was not until December 20 . . . [that] he received permission to follow his plan. The barracks at Camp Holmes would be very useful. Trucks taking men and supplies northward could bring the internees to Manila on their way to make another supply run.[6]

The foundations of the barracks at Camp Holmes, after the camp was destroyed by the U.S. Air Force on January 7, 1945. This photo was taken in 1947 by Mrs. Inez Longway, while on her way to China with her husband and their son, David.

Our move to Manila ultimately worked in our favor, although we didn't realize it at the time. Had we stayed at Camp Holmes, we might have been bombed out of existence.[7] Also, an American ship carrying aviation gasoline was blown up just at this time. This resulted in the U.S. Air Force being short on fuel,[8] which prevented American planes from doing bombing and strafing runs *on the three critical days during which our camp moved from Camp Holmes to Old Bilibid Prison in Manila.* Were these mere coincidences? I don't think so. I happen to believe that God's hand was in this. Had the American planes been able to bomb and strafe during those days, our trucks moving south could easily have been inviting targets for American planes. Our airmen, flying high in the sky, would not have been able to distinguish our trucks loaded with civilians from enemy trucks loaded with soldiers.

On the night of December 26, I stayed up until 3:00 A.M. helping around the kitchen, then went to bed to rest my sore back. Many stayed up all night, slaughtering chickens and livestock, grinding cereals and peanuts, baking, and cooking. I got up at 6:30 A.M. Breakfast was served early: Rice and veal gravy, and plenty of corn mush—all we could eat.

After breakfast, I began separating those things I could afford to discard from those I couldn't do without. I packed sheets and blankets in a duffle bag; my books and next most important things in an army footlocker and a suitcase. The most essential things—my drawings and my diaries, I rolled up inside two blankets and carried them, along with an aluminum canteen, on my person. The deadline for having our things at specified locations on the parade ground was set for 11:00 A.M.

During the night the Camp Committee organized the first contingent of internees into nine groups. At 10:30, in spite of my sore back, I toted my things out to the parade ground. This done, I went over to help Mom and Dad. After that, I helped the Douglases with their luggage. When we finally lined up by our belongings, our family (not including Charlie and Kay, who were assigned to the second contingent) were in the eighth group. Frank Knight was the leader, with Eric Little, his assistant. We were to travel together to an unknown destination somewhere in the Manila area.

By noon I was tired, irritable, and hungry, and my back hurt. Lunch consisted of beef broth and rice—all we wanted. In addition, we were given soft rice and boiled rice. I took my ration of rice and toasted it. By mid-afternoon it looked as if it was going to rain, so we covered our things on the parade ground, but the clouds passed on. In the meantime, Mom gave me a haircut, and I took a shower.

Later that afternoon I sold my two mattress pads to Hayakawa, who had set up a booth near the flagpole and was buying them. There internees could dispose of things they couldn't take with them. I sold my bedstead for 150 inflated *pesos*. This was the equivalent of US$75 before the war. Now all I could buy with them when we got to Manila was nine coconuts.

Late in the afternoon I went to the garden with Ralph and dug up about forty pounds of *camotes* in half an hour. These tubers were very immature and watery. Supper that night consisted of mashed *camote cahoy*, chicken, and gravy. We were served all we could eat. In addition, after evening roll call, each internee was given a ration of sugar and some hastily cooked meat.

While we were packing, Japanese officers began appropriating our medical supplies for their own use. There was nothing we could do about it. Herbert Derham talked to one of these officers, who told him that the Americans had landed on Mindoro, an island 100 miles due south of Manila. This, as it turned out, was true. But a rumor that went the rounds that the United States had issued an ultimatum to Japan demanding we be evacuated to Manila, was the product of someone's overworked imagination.

This was the 1,096th day of internment. Two months before, on October 24, Jim Halsema had become seriously ill with liver abscesses, possibly due to the maltreatment he received from the *Kenpeitai*, and he was hospitalized. Gene Hungerford took over the publication of the *Camp Holmes Daily News*. With the announcement that our camp was moving, publication of this news sheet officially stopped on December 27.

That evening I felt as if I were coming down with a cold. I took some sulfa pills and aspirin tablets, and I laid down on some discarded bedsprings and tried to sleep. It was too uncomfortable. So, I made a "rat's nest" out of discarded junk and slept on it. I got up at 3:15 A.M. and put the last of my things at the designated place on the parade ground, and went back to "bed." By breakfast time my cold symptoms had vanished.

I ate a big breakfast and felt I'd gained five pounds from all the food we'd been served the last couple of days. We would need this nourishment for the journey ahead. We had roll call at 6:00 A.M. and were supposed to leave at 6:30, but it was eight o'clock before fifteen trucks showed up to transport us to our new location. As soon as they did there was a mad scramble to get everything loaded on. I helped Mom and Dad with their things. Just before we left, Charlie and Kay asked me to save them a place when we got to our destination. I promised I would. Then we were off. In addition to my bedroll with my drawings and diaries, I carried on my person two pounds of toasted rice, ten Red Cross sugar cubes, a can of corned beef, and a quart of water in a canteen.

Two of the four soldiers sent to guard us were nasty. The other two were halfway decent. Everything was piled on our truck slipshod, and the ropes lashing down the baggage on our truck were not properly cinched up. I feared that our things would be jostled off when we started down the Kennon Road zigzag.

As we went through Baguio, the Filipinos looked surprised. We waved to them, and they waved back, but the unpleasant guards said, "No good," and we stopped. I took a last look at the city. From a distance I saw the Santos house and the upstairs apartment we had rented from them—perhaps for the last time.[9] Mentally I said goodbye to all the irreplaceable things we were leaving behind. Our family had been more fortunate than most of the folks in camp who had their belongings looted.

Kennon Road was a mess of potholes, but the scenery was magnificent—rocky crags with deep ravines in between, all covered with seared grass. The road wound back and forth like a gray ribbon hundreds of feet below in places. At several points the road was barely wide enough for the truck to get around the curves. At three places we came to chasms that were hundreds of feet to the bottom. I got on the left side of the truck, next to the mountain, ready to jump at the least hint that we were going over the edge. Fortunately, we made it to the lowlands without mishap.

When we reached the coastal plain, our convoy stopped. Many of the internees headed for the bushes. Fortunately, I had taken care of these needs at Camp Holmes. It was shameful the way some of guards scolded our women folk and chased them back to the vicinity of the trucks, where they were compelled to abandon all modesty. We men simply turned our backs and looked the other way.

Soon the trucks started up again and headed for Rosario. Everywhere, we could see evidences of fierce fighting three years before. At one of the side streets, our truck stopped and we saw a group of Japanese soldiers drilling. They were the most bedraggled bunch of warriors I ever saw. Some appeared to be no older than sixteen. Some had rifles, some staves, and

Sketch drawn from memory on January 6, 1945, of a Japanese sentry standing at a curve on Highway 3, near Rosario, while the internees were being transported to Manila.

some had no weapons at all. Many looked diseased. After a lengthy delay in the hot sun, our drivers backtracked to a crossroads, and we headed south.

About noon our trucks stopped at Binalonan where we could see a gallows, on which, it was said, many guerrillas had been executed. Here we were ordered to offload all our baggage, and our trucks and drivers left us. Apparently, they were commandeered by an officer that pulled rank on Lt. Sakashita. We sat under some trees in a park and began eating our lunches. The meat in some of the lunches had spoiled, but some internees ap-

parently ate it anyway—to their great regret later.[10] I munched on toasted rice and drank water.

Soon Yamato ordered us to stop eating—until permission was given. Some protested, and he relented a bit. He said we could eat "cookies or smarr cakes"—which we didn't have. Later, he informed us that we

The author with his daughter standing at the same spot on Highway 3, where the Japanese sentry was standing on December 29, 1944. Photo taken in February 1991. The author holding an open binder with a copy of the sketch of the sentry.

would be in the park until 3:00 P.M., at which time other trucks would pick us up and take us to Manila.

At 3:00 P.M. nine trucks arrived, not fifteen, the number that had brought us from Camp Holmes to Binalonan. We were told we would have to store our baggage and it would be brought down to Manila later. So, we piled as much of our heavy stuff as we could onto the trucks and followed them with our hand luggage to the municipal building, where we stored everything, except for the few things we carried on our persons. Sakashita assured us we would get our baggage in the next couple of days. But, could we count on it? Would we ever again see the things we were leaving behind?

Within half an hour we climbed aboard the nine trucks—thirty-six persons per truck, including four Taiwanese soldiers who were sent along to guard us. These men were different from the soldiers who had accompanied us from Camp Holmes to the lowlands. At least on our truck, these men took the worst seats. The truck was so overcrowded that I rode almost all the way to Manila on top of the cab. I had to be alert every moment, lest I be thrown off when the truck lurched. There were no handholds up there. It was a never-to-be-forgotten ride. The sun blazed down, the wind was searing hot, and the highway dust, powder dry. These conditions made my eyeballs raw, yet I dared not take my eyes off the road.

Trucks, trucks, and more trucks passed us continually, all going in the opposite direction. Now and again we saw bedraggled soldiers trudging along the highway pulling carts or field pieces. Occasionally we passed a carromata.[11] Somewhere between Binalonan and Tarlac I saw the truck ahead of us hit the wheel of one of these horse-drawn vehicles. The load of papayas and mangoes the carromata was carrying spilled all over the highway. The poor horse, though uninjured, was knocked into the ditch beside the road. Our convoy stopped very briefly and we men scrambled down, helped extricate the animal, commiserated briefly with the owner, climbed back on board, and kept going. We felt sorry for the poor man, but there was nothing more we could do.

We arrived in Tarlac at five in the evening. Lt. Sakashita allowed us to get off the trucks at a place where some vendors were selling food, but he insisted on doing the buying himself. Eggs were selling at twenty-five pesos apiece. Everything would have been just fine, if some of us hadn't disobeyed the lieutenant's order and tried to dicker with the natives. Exasperated, Sakashita made us all get back on the trucks.

On and on and on we drove. Half our journey was behind us, but we still had 118 kilometers to go. Some of Highway 3 was in good repair, especially the concrete portions, but the asphalt sections were in terrible shape. Twice, our driver fell asleep and almost went into the ditch, and once, when this happened, he almost collided head on with an oncoming truck. The other truck almost went into the ditch to avoid a collision. Fortunately, our yelling and pounding on the roof of the cab awakened our driver in time to avert a crash.

Just before we came to Angeles, four searchlights ahead of us and four behind were turned on and probed the murky sky. We were allowed only one rest stop on this leg of the journey. By this time there were people on board who were in desperate need of restroom facilities. One man in the truck just ahead of ours reached the point of desperation. We were speeding along at fifty miles an hour when he threw caution to the winds. What a sight—his trousers at half-mast, while he clung to the back of the truck for dear life. When we arrived in San Fernando, Pampanga, around 8:30 P.M., we were allowed to descend from the trucks to stretch our legs for a few minutes. I walked up to my unfortunate friend and ribbed him a bit. He tried to make a joke of his predicament: "I thought you guys were going to slide off the road," he said. "I'll never live it down. They'll tell their children and grandchildren about it to their dying day." Later I was told that there were similar emergencies on the other trucks.

About 10:00 P.M. it began to drizzle, adding to our miseries. Although I was dead tired, I dared not relax. The rain made the cab slippery. Finally, when we reached the outskirts of Manila, Dad offered to change places with me. I gladly accepted his offer. By that time I had what felt like a knot the size of a goose egg on the end of my spine. I had been on top of the cab almost continually for nearly eight hours. At last we arrived at the front gate of Old Bilibid Prison on Azcarraga Avenue. This was the place where we hoped we would *not* be taken. We were deeply disappointed to discover that this was to be our new home. By now it was past midnight and all of us were exhausted.

After a lengthy delay, during which our driver had trouble starting our truck, we parked inside the prison. Manila was under blackout, making it hard to see anything. However, against the overcast sky, we could make out the outline of the sixteen-foot-high walls surrounding the prison with their grim-looking guard towers at the corners.

After we offloaded our hand luggage and dragged it through a small door in the gate that led into the hospital compound of the prison, Mr. Yamato ordered us to line up for roll call. Always a slave to protocol, he insisted on this. By the time the roll was taken, it was almost 1:00 A.M. There were more delays. Finally, Hazel Trimble became hysterical and cussed out the Japanese. It didn't help. Yamato informed us that there was no food, no hot water, no fire, nothing, but we were instructed to *unroll our mats* (which we didn't have) and "forget in sleep."[12] Only then were we allowed to enter the dimly lit and partially demolished building that bore the superscript, "Hospital: Erected 1908." Yamato gave us twenty minutes to get ready for bed before the dim light in the lobby would be turned off.

After hauling my stuff up to the second floor, I felt around in the dark and stumbled into a camp cot with a board platform instead of canvas. I piled the few things I had with me onto it, then I hurried downstairs to help others with their luggage. It was 2:00 A.M. before I finally got to bed—clothes and all. I slept without a mosquito net over me or a mattress pad under me, and I used the bag with the remnants of my toasted rice as a pillow—and never awoke once until morning.[13]

---

[1] D. Mansell, p. 97, Dec. 26, 1944.

[2] Japanese rice wine.

[3] During our internment many rumors, some ridiculous, some serious, circulated throughout the various camps.

For example, when Father Sheridan came to Camp Holmes, he told how someone at Santo Tomás Internment Camp had joked that the Russians had taken paregoric (an opium derivative used to treat diarrhea) and the rumor went around that the Russians had taken a city by that name.

In mid-June 1943 a rumor went around Camp Holmes that "Turkey [had] declared war on the Axis." (Herold, p. 71, June 19, 1943). Here is how this one got started and grew:

Someone sent a turkey into camp to be fattened up for Thanksgiving. When the fowl arrived on the camp food truck, John Crocker, who helped open the food packages for inspection, casually remarked that a turkey had come in. A five-year-old, who had never before seen a turkey, overheard Crocker's remark and ran to his mother and excitedly reported that "Mr. Crocker said that a turkey came in." A neighbor, who overheard the child's "startling bit of news," spread the word that Turkey had come into the war without verifying what the child actually said. Someone else down the line embellished the story by adding that Turkey had declared war on the Axis.

[4] *Bilibid* means "wheel" in Tagalog. The cell blocks of this prison radiated out from a central tower, like the spokes of a wheel, hence the name.

[5] After his lightning campaign down the Malay Peninsula that ended in the surrender of

Singapore, Gen. Yamashita was lionized by the Japanese press as "the Tiger of Malaya."

[6]Romilda Wilder, *From Brent to Bilibid,* typewritten monograph, copyright 1994 by Romilda Wilder, all rights reserved, p. 36, quoting James J. Halsema.

[7]The barracks at Camp Holmes were bombed out of existence by the U.S. Air Force on January 7, 1945, a week after our departure. All that was left were the foundations.

[8]Betsy Herold Heimke email to Don Mansell, Oct. 24, 2002: "When we ladies were at the First Convalescent Hospital on Leyte we ate cafeteria style with the recuperating GIs. One day my mother was asked by one of the GIs what was the exact DATE of our move to Manila. When she said, 'December 28,' he said, 'Oh, my goodness!!! That was the day we were short of gasoline, so we couldn't strafe those areas you were crossing—Wow! God was really with us.' It is my firm belief that indeed He was."

[9]When I went by the house in 1991 and took pictures, it was still standing and showed no apparent damage, although most of Baguio was devastated by the fighting in the winter of 1945.

[10]Herold, p. 101, [no date, but it was Dec. 29, 1944]: "[At Binalonan] we were allowed to eat our chow, but the rice was sour and the meat tainted. I ate just a bit of rice; Betsey [Betsy] ate a little of the rice and pork; Elmer and Billy were so tired and hungry that they ate our share and also what the Adventists gave us (they not being spoilt pork eaters). . . .

"[While our trucks stopped briefly at a barrio] Betsey [Betsy] tried to vomit, and without permission I took her behind some bushes to go to the bathroom. Something had made her deathly sick. For the next 8 or 9 hours until we got to Manila, she was deathly sick."

[11]A two-wheeled vehicle drawn by a horse.

[12]Crouter, p. 439, Dec. 28, 1944, italics mine.

[13]D. Mansell, pp. 97–105.

CHAPTER
26

Old Bilibid Prison

When the rising sun awakened me on December 29, 1944, I itched all over. I quickly discovered the cause of my discomfort. My cot was alive with bedbugs. There was no way to get rid of all of them short of throwing away my cot, and I didn't want to do that. On the other hand, I had no desire to sleep on the filthy, hard concrete floor as others were doing. I stood up and brushed off as many of the bugs as I could, and picked off as many as I could find on my clothes, and crushed them with my shoes.

Then I looked around and noticed that the windows of our building were merely gaping holes in the walls. Some of these were covered with shutters made from corrugated, galvanized iron sheets nailed to wooden frames, hinged at the top, and propped open at the bottom. Some windows had no shutters at all, and I realized that was not the place to be when the rains came down and the wind blew. I also noticed that colonnades, spaced about twenty feet apart, supported the "roof" of the building.

While I was standing by my cot getting rid of the bedbugs, one of the old timers said that shortly before the war President Quezon had ordered the hospital building torn down, but that the work of dismantling stopped with the outbreak of hostilities. I decided to take a look at the "roof," or third floor, of our building and climbed the steps to see. When I got up there, several other internees were gathered by what remained of the third

Old Bilibid Prison

Aerial view of Manila with an oil fire burning in the port area. Bilibid Prison is the square at the bottom of the photo. Quezon Blvd., down which the First Cavalry tanks came, is on the left. Far Eastern University administration building is the U-shaped structure on the left. The Battle of Manila began when the Japanese started firing on First Cavalry troops, from the upper stories of Far Eastern. The long white "roof" (bottom of photo) is partly demolished Bilibid Hospital. Under the slight projection on the far side middle of the hospital "roof" was where the Mansells and the Longways lived. From a window on the left of this projection is where the author saw the Battle of Manila begin.

To the right is a sketch drawn by the author on January12, 1945, of the same oil fire that appears in the preceding aerial photo. The wind is blowing from a different direction. On the right is the Marco Polo Hotel prior to the firestorm that destroyed Manila.

story wall and were looking over it into the main compound. Our group included several women. Across the wall I saw several long, low buildings radiating out, like the spokes of a wheel from a high guard tower in the center of the compound. This is what gave the prison its name.

Over to the right and about fifty yards away, some twenty military POWs were milling about in the prison yard. They kept looking our way, and some of them waved furtively to us. We waved back. The women in our group were probably the first white women they had seen in three years. No words were exchanged.

While we were waving, we heard the roar of planes and the crumping of antiaircraft ("ack-ack") fire. Looking up, we saw six fighters directly overhead, flying from east to west. Suddenly, puffs of flack began peppering the sky around them. One ack-ack shell burst close to one of the planes. The plane took quick evasive action and apparently escaped harm. About this time our guards down on the ground below saw us up on the roof and yelled for us to come down. We did.

When I walked downstairs, I saw that much of the second and ground floors were littered, inches thick, with debris left by the hospital's previous occupants. I walked on downstairs to the first floor. It too was littered with trash. In the wings of the building, people were waking up who had bedded down on these pads and were discovering to their horror and disgust that they were smeared with dried blood and fecal matter,[1] and like my cot, they were infested with bedbugs and other vermin. Many internees were pitching their pads out the windows. As I walked through the lobby and toward the front entrance, I noticed that on the left were stacks and stacks of these mattress pads, some eight feet high.

I went out the front entrance and down the steps to look around our compound. On the west side of our hospital building, I found open cell blocks with iron bars. Several internees were going from one cell to another reading graffiti on the walls. One poignant message caught our attention. It read:

> Words cannot fully express, nor can the mind conceive, the trials, hardships and tortures we have endured at the hands of the Japanese. We are broken mentally, morally and spiritually at the hands of a nation of perverts. (The Japs.) We leave it to you incomers to wreak our vengeance!!

Bad off as we thought we were, the military prisoners, who had inhabited this hellhole before us, had suffered far more than we had. A calendar for 1944, marked off up to December 23, seemed to suggest that our move from Camp Holmes was contemplated before Christmas.

A sketch of Bilibid Kitchen drawn by the author on January 18, 1945.

After finishing going through the cell blocks, I went to the northeast section of our compound where several internees were reading what was written on a row of crosses. A hundred and seventy-eight graves along the north and east walls attested to the awful conditions these men had endured. One cross marked, "Unknown Filipino," told a tale of silent suffering that ended in death. The date inscribed on the grave marker showed that the soldier died shortly after the fall of Bataan.

We were discovering that the horrible stories we'd heard about the outrages committed against our POWs were true. The data inscribed on the silent crosses and the messages scrawled on the walls of the cell blocks spoke of inhuman brutality. A few of the deceased, I later learned, turned out to be relatives or friends of some of us internees. One of the dead, D. D. ("Fritz") Starr, was a nephew of the Fildeys. Sy Sorrell told me that some of the dead were personal friends. I noticed that the latest date carved on the neatly marked crosses was October 6, 1944.

While we were looking at these crosses, our cooks were preparing breakfast. We first had roll call, then got in line for breakfast. The meal consisted of boiled rice and hot water. I divided my can of corned beef and shared part of it with Mom and Dad, then took what was left and divided it with Ralph, who looked woefully emaciated. He looked like a hunchback and was terribly despondent.[2] The thing that especially bothered him was the loss of his diaries.[3] Somehow most of his belongings, including his precious diaries, had been left out on the parade ground at Camp Holmes at the mercy of the elements. At least my stuff, and Mom and Dad's things, were left under cover at Binalonan and Lt. Sakashita had promised we would get them soon. I offered to divide up with Ralph what few things I had with me, but he said No. I had never seen my friend so utterly discouraged, and it worried me.[4] I did what I could to cheer him up, but he seemed to care for nothing.

In the afternoon I helped grind dried, rotten fish. What a stink! Supper consisted of boiled *camotes,* rice, ground-up fish, and *pichay.*[5] I ate everything that the servers doled out, except the horrible-smelling fish.

After supper, as I walked back toward the entrance to our building, I almost ran into a Japanese soldier coming around the corner from the opposite direction. We both stopped before we bumped into each other. In broken English he told me he was one of the soldiers who took us prisoner at Brent School, exactly three years before. *What a coincidence!* I thought. If he was indeed one of our original captors (and at first I was skeptical), a marvelous change had come over him. There was nothing menacing about him now. Perhaps the way the war was turning out made the difference, I don't know.

We only spoke long enough for me to assure myself that he had indeed been at Brent School when we were taken captive. I asked him a few questions about the rooms to which the men and the women were directed to go. Then he had to leave. His parting words were that he would come back and we'd talk some more. I never saw him again. Why did he want to talk with me? Did he recognize me? I didn't recognize him. Was he the soldier who pointed with his bayonet and made me go with the women and children to Toddler's Dorm? So far as I know, that soldier spoke no English. If he was the one, where had he picked up the little English he spoke? Had he learned it as a guard at one of the POW camps? That is how one of the Taiwanese guards we met at Camp Holmes told us he had learned to speak English.[6] These are tantalizing questions to which I shall never know the answer. (See pp. 51, 52.)

The second lot of internees arrived at Bilibid the following morning, December 30. All the people in this group had red eyes with dark circles under them. Charlie looked pale and emaciated, and seemed almost in a daze. Kay didn't look much better. We who had come in the first contingent set to work scooping and shoveling out the filth on the floor and making places for the newcomers to bed down. Then we gathered the few personal things they had managed to bring with them and set them in the place we had cleaned up for them. The rest of the morning, while Charlie and Kay slept, I helped carry in our baggage that had arrived from Binalonan.

True to his word, Lt. Sakashita had seen to it that the stuff we left in the municipal building in Binalonan got to Bilibid, but much of the baggage that belonged to the second group was left in that town. In taking stock of my possessions, I found I had only lost some books, some maps, and a few odds and ends, all of which could easily be replaced. Ralph didn't get a thing![7]

After the morning's exertions, I tried to get as many bedbugs off my cot as I could and spent most of the afternoon resting. Charlie and Kay slept like the dead. When Kay woke up, she told me that when their group arrived in Binalonan, Charlie made it a point to see that all the things the folks and I had left there were loaded onto the trucks before he put any of his and Kay's things on.[8] As a result, most of their things were left in Binalonan. From the description she gave of their ride, it was far worse than ours. Kay said that Oura acted like a madman. He shoved Carroll Hinderlie around, got angry at Phil Whitmarsh for some unknown reason and cut down his luggage that was suspended from a shoulder pole, and, for no apparent reason, slapped Alex Kaluzhny three times.

The Camp Committee assigned our family to a cubicle on the second floor at the front of the building, next to the balcony, which was above the entrance. The Longways were assigned to living space just across the aisle from us. For supper our family gathered around my cot. We used it as a table and stood around it. The meal consisted of rice, soy bean curd, and *camote* greens. While we were eating, I noticed a couple of bedbugs crawling out of the crack in the boards of my cot. I said nothing. If the others noticed them, they didn't say anything either. It was getting too late to do anything then, but I decided that the first thing in the morning I was going to get rid of those pests. I spent a miserable night in the company of those bedbugs.

Early Sunday morning I took my cot and set it out under a mango tree near the kitchen. The cooks were preparing breakfast and had boiling water for anyone who wanted a hot drink. I got an idea. After breakfast I borrowed a hammer and took apart the three-board platform that was nailed to my cot.

Then I threw the rickety, bedbug-infested cot frame in the trash. When I separated the boards, I found that the grooves were crawling with bedbugs. After scraping off the bugs and their eggs, I stomped on the pesky bloodsuckers, then went to the kitchen and got cupfuls of boiling water and poured it down the edges of the boards. That got rid of the pests. This done, I saved the nails and set the boards out on our balcony in the sun to dry.

Earlier that morning I'd noticed a pile of 5/8-inch-thick reinforcing rods in the prison yard. These rods were twenty-four feet long. Why not put some hairpin bends in one of them, nail the three boards from my cot back together, and lash my platform to a new bed frame? I found a place where some steel posts were sticking up out of a cement slab and went to work carefully bending a reinforcing rod into the proper shape. The rod was so stiff, I could barely curve it unassisted. When I finished, I made sure that my cot boards were bedbug-free and nailed them back together again with the same nails I had extracted from them, then I lashed my now clean platform to my new bedstead with rope I'd brought with me from Camp Holmes. It wasn't long before a few others got the same idea and made their own bed frames.

When I sat on my new cot, I discovered that it sagged too much on the open, unsupported end. I also noticed that the frame tended to flare out at the bottom and spread apart. So, I tied some pieces of rope at strategic points to keep it from spreading apart, but it continued to sag at the unsupported end. There wasn't anything I could do about that. So, I slept with my feet at that end.

Until we rigged up our mosquito nets, the mosquitoes bothered us terribly in the evening, and we worried that we might come down with malaria or dengue fever. Fortunately, most, if not all of us, escaped these mosquito-borne diseases.[9]

On December 31, Miss McKim informed us that we had a new camp commandant, a Major Ebiko.[10] She said he seemed friendly.[11] He proved to be far more humane than Oura, whose power over us was now curtailed.

Several rules were announced at roll call on January 1, among them: No more going up on the "roof" of our building, and no more burning of wood for private cooking. Also, no more making bedsteads out of reinforcing rods. Before the prohibition against private fires, Ralph and I had cooked some of the *camotes* we dug up at Camp Holmes just before we left. The *camotes* we didn't cook soon became moldy and bitter.

During the day flies pestered us terribly, and in the evening and early morning we could see large rats scampering about in our compound. A little investigation revealed that some of these varmints had burrowed tunnels down into the graves along the north and east walls, and were apparently feeding on the dead bodies buried there. At night these filthy rodents had the audacity to invade the first floor of our sleeping quarters.[12]

Mike Shaffer told me that on New Year's Day he found an American POW's diary in the crawl space under the east end of our hospital building. It had obviously been left there by one of the former occupants of our prison. He told me he was passing the journal around to some of our fellow internees, and promised to lend it to me when he got it back. He said it contained a heartrending record of inhuman treatment. I never had an opportunity to see it. It was lost in the upheaval following liberation.

From the back balcony on the northeast side of our building, we could look over the sixteen-foot wall and see Japanese trucks moving northward on Quezon Boulevard. The troop movements we had seen on our way to Manila and large numbers of loaded trucks traveling in that direction should have told me that the Japanese forces were withdrawing from the city.

About 6:00 A.M. on January 2, American planes again flew over camp. They were met by bursts of antiaircraft fire. Almost every day, from then on, we saw the bombing and strafing of Japanese military installations on the outskirts of Manila.

R. Willis Dunne, chairman of our Safety Committee, was the last person to leave Camp Holmes. He arrived at Bilibid on January 3 with the very last things left behind out on the parade ground. Among the things he brought with him were most of Ralph's belongings, but not all. When Ralph checked them over, several important items were missing. Ralph wrote in his diary:

> My little army suitcase, as well as the rest of my luggage, was on board. . . . [After] identifying my stuff, I rushed upstairs to gaze on my given-up-for-lost belongings. . . . My stuff sure appeared as if Noah had discarded it in a hurry. My duffle bag was saturated, all the remaining clothes sour. . . . The bottom of my duffle bag was a mud pan, and only about two-thirds of its original contents [were still in it]. . . . Losses include two shirts, David's clogs, and worst of all, one shoe from each of my lone two pair. . . . All I have . . . [on my feet] is a pair [of] Bill [Herold's] loaned shoes. . . . My feet are such monsters that I can find dozens of discarded shoes and have no use for them.

My large army trunk was intact, waterless, and orderly—[but] all my precious books were gone . . . —all gone . . . [but] what an indescribable relief, when I found my diaries, snug and dry in the difficult place I hid them. That ends a week of worry.[13]

The first truly big air action began about 7:45 on the morning of January 6. We first heard the humming of aircraft in the distance. From stratus clouds on the southern horizon, planes seemed to dart out in groups of two and three. Suddenly, out of the clouds roared at least ten fighters. They circled, banked, and dived. The sky surrounding them was spattered with little black puffs of antiaircraft fire. Our excitement was intense. We hoped none of our fighters would get hit. Our planes were not challenged by what the *Manila Tribune* used to call "Wild Eagles."[14]

About 9:20 A.M. we again heard a deep, steady humming sound. Soon we saw a formation of bombers coming from the southeast. Moments later we heard the rumble of exploding bombs. Suddenly, we could see and hear the *pop, pop, pop* of antiaircraft fire up in the sky. Earl Roberts and I had gone out on our balcony to watch. We counted some seventy ack-ack bursts directly overhead. Twenty-four B-24s moved majestically into the flack. Soon antiaircraft shrapnel began raining down all around us. We were afraid we were going to get hit. The door onto the balcony was clogged with jubilant spectators. Above the staccato of ack-ack, Roberts and I yelled for them to open a way for us to get inside before we got hit by the falling shrapnel, but they seemed transfixed by the events transpiring above them, and didn't budge. So, we dashed the ten feet to the doorway and forced our way inside the building.

When the all-clear sounded, we assembled for church in one of the empty cell blocks. At 11:20 air-raid sirens announced the approach of more planes. Instead of seeking shelter in the main building, we stayed where we were. There was another raid at 12:30, and another at 3:15. Some fifty bombers took part in this last bombing run. They blasted the area to the southeast of us.

At around 10:00 the next morning a formation of twenty-three bombers unloaded their missiles, again to the southeast of us, then they circled to their right and disappeared. Minutes later, as I stood near the kitchen, a formation of twenty-one B-24s unloaded their cargo to the northeast of us. Flack filled the sky from time to time. A piece of shrapnel hit the roof of the kitchen about ten feet from where I was standing. Peter Herklots, who was next to me, made a mad dash for it, but I reached it first and kept it as a souvenir.

A few minutes later a formation of twenty-five bombers roared in from the southeast and veered slightly to its right as it progressed northward. The violence of the exploding bombs made the earth shake. Another wave of bombers flew over about this same time. I counted approximately forty seconds from the moment I saw a flash until I heard the first reverberations of the exploding bombs, and calculated that the target was about eight miles away.

Between 1:00 and 2:00 P.M. we watched five fighters strafe the area to the north of us. They would come in one after the other, peel off, and swoop, machine guns blazing. They circled their targets like birds of prey looking for a meal. Not a single antiaircraft burst managed to hit any of them. But it wasn't long before we awoke to the realization that our planes were not immune to enemy antiaircraft fire.

At 10:05 on January 8 we heard air-raid sirens wailing. I watched from the prison yard, just to the east of the hospital entrance. A formation of twenty-four B-24s approached inexorably, flying from southwest to northeast. As they neared the zenith, bursts of antiaircraft fire began peppering the sky overhead. I noticed a burst of flack just behind one of the planes at the right of the formation. Next instant there was another burst, this time near the engine on the right side of the plane. For a brief moment there was a trail of what looked like whitish smoke, which instantly burst into a sheet of bright orange flame that swept the length of the fuselage. While the bomber could still be controlled, the pilot managed to get the mortally wounded plane to veer to the right and out of formation, apparently to spare the other bombers.[15] The rest of the formation flew impassively on. We watched in horrified fascination as the bomber exploded in a huge ball of fire. Some of the women wept.

Out of the crew of eleven,[16] "4 or 5 parachutes billowed out and gradually descended on the city. . . . One of them . . . [must have snagged on the burning wreckage of] the plane and flamed, the man falling to a horrible death."[17] Such were the horrors of war we witnessed that day. I watched as one survivor floated down in his chute to the southeast of us. As he drifted down, the flaming wreckage of the bomber descended in pieces to the east of us.

The next day, and the days that followed, saw more military action. On the 10th of January two P-38s roared down Rizal Avenue at rooftop level and dropped leaflets. Only one fell into our compound. Billy Mather picked it up.[18] He showed it to me and let me have it long enough to read it and make a couple drawings of scenes it depicted. The main part of the leaflet bore the following message:

> When General MacArthur left Corregidor, under orders from President Roosevelt to proceed to Australia and organize the offensive against Japan, his last words were, "I shall return."
>
> From that moment his one driving ambition has been to get back to the Philippines, to drive out the Japanese, and to restore the legitimate government of the Philippines.
>
> Today General MacArthur is back in the Philippines. He has returned as he promised. His great task is now entering its final phase. The forces under his command are assailing the Japanese invaders throughout the Philippines. With those forces General MacArthur will accomplish the liberation of the Filipino people.
>
> But that liberation can be accomplished more quickly, and at less cost in American and Filipino lives, with your help and co-operation. General MacArthur will tell you, over the radio, in proclamations, and by leaflets exactly how and when you can help. Watch closely for these instructions.

To say we were thrilled is an understatement. After completing the drawings, I returned the leaflet to Billy. Meanwhile, we tried to live our lives as normally as possible. On the 14th a copy of the *Manila Tribune* was smuggled into camp. It stated, among other things, that a convoy of 100 ships was lying off Lingayen Gulf. According to this paper, Japanese planes had been sent to repulse these ships. The paper also spoke of one spearhead thrusting south toward Cabanatuan, where many American POWs were imprisoned. Another was moving on toward Manila. It was surprising how free from Japanese propaganda the *Tribune* was in reporting this news.

At night we frequently heard shots being fired and, on the 15th, members of the Japanese staff admitted that guerrilla units were active in the city. Many staff members expected that the Americans would arrive at any moment, but the days dragged on with no sign of the U.S. Army.

On the 17th Ralph and I were standing at the gate of our compound with several other internees, including Father Sheridan. The priest was plying Mr. Yamato with questions about the American landings and the progress of the fighting. Yamato cagily parried the questions, but he did concede that the Japanese newspapers were full of propaganda. Father Sheridan picked up on this remark and, for the benefit of the rest of us, interpreted Yamato's statement to mean that "Japanese papers tell lies." Yamato did not reply, but he changed the subject and said we were happier than he was. He said he could not return to Japan alive. He must follow Japanese custom and go to his destiny. I have to admit I felt sorry for the little man.

Father Sheridan asked Yamato if he was a Christian. He said, "Sometimes." This amused us, but he was apparently dead serious. After making some empty promises, he saluted us and left. Ralph and I discussed Yamato's remarks and concluded, not surprisingly, that he saw the handwriting on the wall.[19]

On the 28th Yamato told the Committee that there was much guerrilla activity in Manila. Later that same day Sgt. Sugano told our Committee that he was having difficulty getting food for us because of guerrilla activity throughout the city. He said that, because of this activity, he could go out only at night to get food supplies from the Japanese army warehouses. According to him, Rizal province was full of guerrillas. On the night of February 2, we were awakened several times by detonations that sounded like artillery shelling nearby. I was convinced that it was fighting between the Japanese Army and guerrilla units.

Late in the afternoon of February 3, we saw nine Corsair fighter-bombers swoop over Santo Tomás Internment Camp[20] a quarter of a mile to the northeast of us. This had never happened before.

After a scanty supper and evening roll call, I went up to our cubicle, sat down on my bed, and began to write up the exciting events of the day. Gradually, I became conscious of a roar of motors coming from the north. At first I thought it was the sound of planes, but as I listened more carefully, it was a different sound. Dad and I decided to investigate. Others must have had the same idea. We hurried to the northeast balcony, where perhaps a dozen others had congregated and were peering northeastward onto Quezon Boulevard. Hordes of Filipinos were coming out of the houses and running up the boulevard in the direction of the sound. Suddenly, I saw two tanks rumble into view as they came down Quezon Boulevard, where it intersected with Calle España. Behind them were trucks loaded with men dressed in olive-drab uniforms, wearing pot helmets, which in the diminishing twilight looked similar to those worn by our guards. All at once the whole procession stopped. Some of my fellow internees declared that they were American troops. Still skeptical, I assumed that they were Japanese soldiers taking up positions to wipe out the guerrillas. I wasn't the only doubter.[21] Out of the turret of the lead tank popped a soldier's torso. The tank's gun swiveled, and the soldier must have yelled something to the crowd surrounding the tanks, because they melted back into the houses.[22] Others more sanguine and with better information than I had, such as Betty Foley, declared that they were American tanks and soldiers.

Suddenly I heard a shout down in the prison yard below us. The sergeant of the guard was yelling something in Japanese, and at the same time was motioning vigorously for us to get off the balcony. Before I left, I saw our guards donning helmets, fixing bayonets, and slinging bandoliers of ammunition over their shoulders. I returned to my bed, sat down, and began writing about the exciting events transpiring just a few hundred yards away. As I did so, I heard the tanks rumble down the boulevard about a block. By the sound of things, they had halted just north of Far Eastern University, 200 yards away.

Suddenly, every doubt was blasted from my skeptical mind as Mom shouted above the staccato of machine gun fire, *"The Battle of Manila is on!"*[23]

---

[1]I recently learned that these mattresses had been used by military POWs suffering from cholera, as well as bacillary and amoebic dysentery. It is a wonder an epidemic of intestinal disorders didn't break out. As it was, a number of internees did come down with dysentery. Because I apparently had better than average resistance to the "bug," Dr. Skerl assigned me and Adeline Fairchild the task of washing the soiled linen of these patients—a most distasteful job. Apparently, Adeline was also resistant to the disease.

[2]D. Mansell, p. 106, Dec. 29, 1944. Longway, p. [334], Dec. 29, 1944: "Don tells me my shoulders were bowed low, and I felt like they certainly were, and as if I were 1,000,000 years old. Too much true utter exhaustion yesterday, the worst I've ever felt in my life."

[3]Longway, p. [343], Jan. 2, 1945: "Still no sign of Willis Dunne [the last man to bring things from Camp Holmes], still no inkling as to the fate of my diaries, somewhere between here and Trinidad. Losing them would be veritably like losing a member of the family."

[4]D. Mansell, handwritten, Dec. 29, 1944: "[Ralph is] despondent and it worries me."

[5]A Chinese vegetable, pronounced "peach-eye."

[6]On October 15 and 16, 1944, Ralph and I worked in the vegetable garden area making a path for the guards. One soldier who was Taiwanese came over where we were working and talked with us. He spoke English surprisingly well. We asked him where he learned it. He said he learned it from the American POWs at Cabanatuan.

[7]Longway, p.[339], Dec. 31, 1944: "I worried today like a stockbroker over my few remaining

earthly possessions, so paltry, yet so precious. I hear they've been sitting on . . . [the] parade ground . . . [at Camp Holmes] for 3 days and it's rained every day, so, I imagine [that] if I ever receive them, they'll . . . [look] like they've been on the wrong side of Noah['s flood], but still I wait."

[8]D. Mansell, handwritten, Dec. 30, 1944: "Charlie did me the best turn in all his life. He saw to it that my stuff and Dad's and Mom's stuff were on the truck before his own. In fact, he and Kay left [in Binalonan all their possessions in the big steamer trunk that Dad gave them]."

[9]Cogan, p. 278, quoting Halsema, *Bilibid Diary*: "Many internees . . . had dengue fever, the usual hypoproteinosis, beriberi, and other maladies."

[10]He is not to be confused with the infamous Lt. Abiko, of Santo Tomás Internment Camp. Cogan, p. 273. Cf. p. 277, which speaks of Maj. Ebiko. Abiko was killed during the fighting at STIC.

[11]Longway, p. [344], Jan. 3, 1945: "Just before [Major] Ebiko, our new boss, climbed the stairs, the foolish order was passed around that all men wear shirts. . . . All our shirts were hurriedly buttoned on in time to stand and bow to our replacing commandant. He is a pleasant appearing fellow, informal and facile, but not dressed like a sluggard as was Oura. . . . Anyway, he can't be any worse than Oura and chances are he's better than that unshaven [shavetail]"—a low rank, newly commissioned army officer, especially a second lieutenant.

[12]Crouter, p. 451: "The rats in Bilibid are very annoying at night. . . . They squeak loudly and scamper along the bags and tile shelves, knocking over bottles, rattling cups and poking into tin and paper. We have to cover all food and soap."

[13]Longway, p. [346], Jan. 3, 1945.

[14]Ralph called them "Mild Eagles." The term was appropriate. The only time these enemy aircraft flew over the city was at sundown, at which time they could be seen scurrying over the city at treetop level.

[15]Hind, p. 256: "Suddenly one of the planes was hit, began to trail smoke and was soon on fire. It slowed down after having maneuvered out of range."

[16]Halsema, diary, 1945, p. [1], Jan. 8, 1945.

[17]Longway, p. [356], Jan. 8, 1945.

Halsema email attachment to D. Mansell, Oct. 12, 2002, re: Yoshio Mazaki: "[On Jan. 14, 1945] Masaki [i.e., Mazaki] said two of the four [American, *sic*] parachutists were dead from burns of the explosion [of their B-24 when hit by AA fire], one was badly burned but alive in the hospital. The fourth is in good shape."

Hind, pp. 256, 257: "Four of the crew began bailing out. Three of them were soon clear of the plane and their parachutes began functioning. The fourth fouled his parachute on the plane and could not free himself." Halsema, diary, 1945, p. [1], January 8, 1945: "Two of the crew of 11 seemed to parachute down successfully."

D. Mansell, pp. 117, 118: "I had taken shelter in the inside corner, formed by the building and the balcony, because of the falling flack, so I did not see all that happened next. Afterward, I wrote: "Soon pieces of flaming wreckage floated down to the east of us, and a column of black smoke began rising from the area. After a bit two parachutes could be seen deploying. Some said they saw as many as five. One of the two airmen [I saw] was falling very fast and I soon lost track of . . . [him]. The other chute floated down normally. We could see the airman swing back and forth under his chute. He disappeared to the southeast of us."

I believe that Mazaki's account in Halsema's email attachment and Longway's account are the most accurate.

[18]Halsema, *Bilibid Diary*, Jan. 10, 1945: "Bobby Patton found our first American propaganda: a leaflet extolling the virtues of Doug MacArthur."

Either Halsema confuses Bobby Patton with Billy Mather, or I am mistaken about only one leaflet falling into camp.

[19]D. Mansell, pp. 127, 128, Jan. 17, 1945.

[20]William A. Breuer, *Retaking the Philippines* (New York: St. Martin's Press, 1986), p. 146.

[21]Crouter, p. 466, Feb. 3, 1945: "At first some people said it was Japanese tanks, for they thought they saw Japanese characters on . . . [them]. . . . Denki [Camp Committee Vice Chairman, Phil Markert] was at our space trying to fix the burning electric wire before nightfall, so that they could turn on the current before dark. Like so many of us, Denki could not believe the Americans had come. His lip curled in doubt as he said, 'Nonsense! There are lots of Japanese tanks in Manila. This may be some in retreat from somewhere. It can't be an American one.' He turned back to his wire and I did not try to convince him. I wasn't sure Bedie was right myself." Ibid., p. 467: "Everyone went around talking about whether it was or wasn't the American Army. It wasn't very long before we were sure."

[22]Miles, p. 161: "Two of the American tanks got separated from the others and came down the street [Quezon Boulevard]. . . . One [tank] stopped, and an American soldier stuck his head out and yelled, 'Hell, Harvey, we're on the wrong street!' "

Moule, p. 370: "Gene [Kneebone] had been too optimistic all during the war, something like myself. He had us out [of camp] every week from the time this thing started, and I had swallowed it too many times. Later the same day I heard another rumor. 'Doc Walker was out by the wall, and he heard something slam; then in good old American English he heard someone say, "Harvey, we came down the wrong road. Turn back." ' "

"I found Doc Walker and sure enough it was true."

Halsema, 1944, p. 6: "There were distant hollow machine gun sounds plus shots closer by to the north. A tinny siren down Rizal Avenue. . . . Sounds of a tank making the corner, then a burst of fire across the wall. Sentry put on his tin hat, left to get his pack. Meanwhile, Betty [Foley], watching traffic on Quezon . . . [Boulevard, from the balcony on the second floor], noted Filipinos scurrying up side streets for cover. 'It was just like a movie,' [she said]. A large and several small tanks covered with men, what looked to Cam [Gray] like jeeps with 37 mm cannon, and 10-wheel trucks swept down the road. Guns popped, upstairs residents scurried down. [Doc] Walker and [Clark] Carter, on the roof, claim they heard a Southern drawl shout, 'G———t, Hahvey,' and saw F[ar] E[astern] U[niversity] building riddled with fire."

Herold, p. 106, Feb. 3, 1945 (The Herolds who lived on the northeast end of the second floor probably had the best view of the action of anyone in camp): "At dusk we 4 [Herolds] were sitting on our bunk just wondering when we noticed through the crack in the window that the Filipinos in the street were running. . . . A huge tank appeared slowly rolling down Quezon Blvd. Then another one following. Elmer said he was sure they [were] American make (perhaps stolen by [the] Japs). Then another tank. The men on them were huge, with strange helmets, and dark uniforms. Japs could not be that big, they must be Americans—eight tanks rolling powerfully along—we were breathless. Billy was standing on the window sill looking from the top of the crack. Others were coming to see what the Herolds were looking at. Billy burst out, 'My God, they are AMERICANS.' We were almost petrified with joy. This news spread like wildfire. THE AMERICANS HAD COME. Truck loads of soldiers and jeeps followed the 8 tanks. No shooting did we hear until they got even with the Jap G[eneral] H[ead]q[uarters] at the Far Eastern Univ[ersity building] across [the boulevard] from us. The Japs fired on them, then our tanks let them have it. Our Camp Safety . . . [Committee] called us down stairs."

[23]Based largely on D. Mansell, pp. 105–142, Feb. 3/4, 1945.

CHAPTER
27

Liberation!

It was more than twenty-four hours after the Battle of Manila began before the first American soldier set foot inside our part of Bilibid Prison. That was on the evening of February 4, but it was a month before the last Japanese resistance was finally crushed on March 3, 1945.

"Despite an order from Lieutenant General Yamashita[1] *to retreat* from the city, [Rear] Admiral Sanji Iwabuc[h]i, the local commander, ordered 20,000 Japanese sailors and naval troops, along with a 1,600 rear guard[2] army infantry *back into* Manila."[3] "Iwabuchi's men . . . fortified [the city] with barbed wire entanglements and barricades of overturned trucks and trolleys. Houses were converted into machine-gun nests, with their entrances sand-bagged, stairways barricaded and walls ripped open for firing slits. Big guns . . . removed from Japanese ships in the harbor . . . were dug in on strategic street corners."[4] The admiral also ordered his men to set fires to various parts of the city.

Thus, as February 4 dawned, fine ashes and cinders sifted down on our compound and covered everything. Outside, the battle raged with varying intensity. We were fortunate to have thick, sixteen-foot-high walls surrounding our prison, interposing between us and the battling armies outside. We were also fortunate in that the Americans didn't breach those protecting barriers. During the night of February 3 the Japanese rolled a barrel of gasoline into our compound and set it up near the north gate, then piled it high with explosives. (I heard that Lt. Oura was the officer who ordered this done.) Apparently, they intended to detonate it, if the Americans tried to come in. When I looked for it in the morning, it had been removed. (I heard that it was another lieutenant, who outranked Oura and was friendly toward the POWs across the wall, who ordered it removed.)

As soon as it was light enough to see, I found a quiet corner in our building and finally wrote down the happenings of the past thirty-six hours. About 7:00 A.M. there was a lull in the fighting and the Safety Committee allowed us to go upstairs, but we were warned to come down immediately if fighting resumed. Someone told me that a dead Japanese soldier was lying on Quezon Boulevard where it intersected with Calle España. I went upstairs to the northeast end of the building and looked out the window toward the spot where I first saw the tanks coming into the city. The dead man had been stripped of his clothes and shoes and was beginning to bloat. It was macabre.

At 11:30[5] we were all called down to the lobby of our building for an announcement. Carl Eschbach stood on a table and read a message he had just been given by Major Ebiko. Its essential part said that our guards had been "assigned to another duty and . . . [would] be here no more."[6] Then someone shouted, "Gangway." We all opened a passageway and presently we heard the clank of hobnail boots.[7] Then, before our unbelieving eyes, eight of our guards marched out through the path we had opened for them. They looked straight ahead and said not a word—and neither did we. Most of their faces had a "sunk and trapped" look.[8] I shall never forget the expression on one young soldier's face as he passed me. He looked to be about eighteen and was carrying a box of grenades in his outstretched arms. Our eyes met for an instant. The best way I can describe what I read in that glance is that he had a sick, wan smile.[9] When the soldiers reached the door in the gate to the main compound, they lined up single file. The sergeant opened the small door in the gate, and our guards marched out single file. The sergeant was the last man to leave. Just before he closed the door, he turned and gave us a hate-filled glance, *then he was gone!*

As soon as that door closed, we cheered and cheered. Then we sang "God Bless America" and "The Star-Spangled Banner." Carl, still standing on the table, unfurled the forbidden flag, "The Victory Parade Flag," which the women in camp had made. It was handed to Pop Claunch and Gus Skerl. These men headed up the stairs to the balcony. Charlie and I joined them, and helped tie the flag to a bamboo pole. When the flag was raised, the military prisoners across the wall joined us in cheering. Suddenly, shots rang out. A POW officer across the wall, shouted, "Get that flag down! It's just a target." We quickly hauled down the colors and took the flag inside. Moments later, those of us who were on the balcony were flattened by a terrific explosion a few hundred yards to the south. A piece of steel two inches wide, five inches long, and an inch thick struck the wall next to the window where the Longways lived. Fortunately, no one was hit.

About one o'clock the tanks on Quezon Boulevard began blazing away at the northwest corner room on the second floor of the Far East-

A photo of internee children with parents taken February 6, 1945, by a U.S. Army photographer.

Dr. Gus Skerl greeting Brig. Gen. Fellers at the entrance to the Bilibid Hospital. From the left: Dick Patterson, Stella Herklotz (holding rag doll), Wilfred Poirier, unidentified person, Josephine McKenzie, Robert Tangen, Elsie Sharp, and Fred ("Bedie") Crouter. U.S. Army photo taken February 5, 1945.

ern University building where the Battle of Manila first began. The Japanese answered with a 37-millimeter cannon. This duel went on for several minutes. During a lull, I noticed a rifle sticking up behind one of the window sills. Then I saw a Japanese soldier's helmet projecting just above the sill. The man raised his head higher and peered down on the boulevard. To my utter astonishment, he stood up, calmly climbed out the window and onto a projecting ledge, crept to a projecting corner of the building, raised his rifle and fired a shot down at something or someone on the boulevard. Then, as calmly as he went out, he retraced his steps and climbed back into the building—unscathed! Why the Americans didn't shoot him is a mystery to me. Perhaps they were busy loading their guns. All I can say is that that soldier was brave—and lucky. After we were liberated I spoke to a GI, who was one of the first soldiers to enter that room on the second floor of Far Eastern. He told me the Japanese dead were stacked six and seven deep and that their 37-millimeter cannon was a total wreck.

About 3:00 P.M. I went up to the "roof" of our building. As I peered out over the city, I counted thirteen separate fires and wrote in my diary, "The sun was a blood red behind the pall of smoke hovering over the city. It was symbolic to us internees. It wasn't the rising sun anymore, but the setting sun."[10] Not wishing to become a target of a sniper, I went downstairs. Down on the first floor Herb Loddigs was telling a group of internees about his

Gen. Douglas MacArthur, surveying the graves of the soldiers buried in Bilibid Prison. From left, internees are Carroll Dickey, Robert Tangen, Charles Mansell, Carl Eschbach, John Renning (?), Joan Turner (?), John Hind (?). U.S. Army photo taken February 7, 1945. The author was standing with a group of internees on the balcony above Gen. MacArthur when the tanks of the First Cavalry Division came down Quezon Blvd.

experience with the *Kenpeitai*. His story, which I have related on page 101, gushed out in a torrent of words.

When he finished, I went looking for Ralph. When I found him, I suggested we go to the little door that led from our compound into the main part of the prison. The ranking officer of the POWs across the wall had given orders for his men not to come into our compound, and Carl Eschbach had taken similar action with respect to our going over there. But we could stand at the door that separated our compounds and talk to one another.

Ralph and I, and four or five other internees talked with several of the POWs who had gathered at the gate. One of them was a young POW in better physical shape than most of the others. He introduced himself as Jim Bray[11] of the 4th Marines. We waited and talked with the POWs the rest of the afternoon and into the evening. We were determined to be foremost among the internees to greet the first American soldier who came into our compound.[12]

About seven o'clock there was a hubbub over by the POW barracks, and Bray went over to see what the commotion was about. He was soon back with the news we all wanted to hear. "Well," he said, "the boys are here! The boys are here—tough and sweaty, and I mean tough."[13] Then followed the story of what happened:

There had been some sniping on Rizal Avenue, and soldiers of the 37th Ohio Division, who were preparing to bivouac, were ordered by one of their officers to rip away some boards that covered a large hole in the prison wall and find out what was beyond. When they tore the boards away, they were dumbfounded to find American POWs on the other side.[14]

One of us passed this news to Carl Eschbach and Phil Markert, who went to meet the officer in charge of these men.[15] We waited at the gate for two hours before Carl and Phil returned. Carl then told us they had met Major Wendt[16] in the Bilibid Prison office. "The major is a real fighting man," Carl told us. The officer was all grimy and sweaty, and had lost his upper bridge a few days before in the fighting up north. As a result, he said he couldn't make a speech to us, but he promised to put a company of soldiers around us, and said he would send an officer to meet us.[17] Carl stimulated "our imaginations with his description of the first Yank that he had seen . . . [in] 3 years."[18] Then our chairman and vice chairman went

Bilibid internees signing up with the Red Cross. From the right: June Knight, Errol ("Jerry") Crouter, William Junkin (? sitting), Dr. Bruce Mather, Ruth Culpepper (back to camera), Hugo Culpepper, Vadna Fildey, Harold Fildey, Vere Derham, Ward Graham, Sue Graham, Robert Dyer, John Bergamini, Mary Hinderlie, Clifford Nobes, Betsy Herold, Carroll Hinderlie, Ray Hale, and Mary Kneebone. The person beyond Jerry Crouter's hat is almost certainly Eugene Hungerford.

into our building to tell the good news to the internees who were still awake. A group of internees joined us at the gate.

Ralph wrote in his diary:

> Twenty minutes later, down the road [of the main compound] ambled a huge shape. The great bear of a fellow stuck his head . . . [through the gate of our compound and said], "Howdy, boys. I'm Lt. Wooster from the 37th Ohio National Guard." . . . [I]t was good to see his huge frame, covered with the new American uniform and their stuccoed helmet, gun over [his] shoulder, ammo [belt] about his waist. Immediately a crowd gathered around our prize exhibit.[19]

We said, "We've been waiting for you for three years." He replied, simply, "We've been looking for you for three years."[20]

Words cannot adequately describe nor express our feeling of being free at last. It was something that had to be experienced to be fully appreciated. We were grateful, of course, for the protection of the brave soldiers who surrounded our compound. But our supreme thanks went to God, whose "everlasting arms" were ever "underneath,"[21] and kept us from being crushed under the heel of a defeated and desperate enemy!

---

[1]Gen. Yamashita, as senior commander in the Philippines, was held responsible for the atrocities committed by Adm. Iwabuchi's forces in the so-called "Rape of Manila." After the war, Yamashita was tried, convicted, and hanged. We internees probably owed our lives to the fact that he ordered us moved to Manila. It is a wonder that a man of Iwabuchi's temperament and spirit didn't order the execution of all POWs in Manila as part of his scorched-earth policy.

[2]Of these 21,600 Japanese servicemen, only a handful were taken prisoner.

[3]Cogan, p. 119, italics hers.

[4]Rafael Steinberg and the editors of Time-Life books (Alexandria, Va.: Time-Life Books, 1980), p. 115.

[5]D. Mansell, handwritten, Feb. 4, 1945.

[6]Ibid.

[7]Crouter, p. [469], Feb. 4, 1945.

[8]Ibid.: "They and we were silent, their faces looking sunk and trapped. The corporal's [I thought he was a sergeant] fat face was sullen and defeated."

[9]Ibid., p. 469: "One short, beady-eyed pleasant fellow looked at us with a timid friendly grin—a good sport to the end."

[10]D. Mansell, handwritten, Feb. 4, 1945.

[11]Jim Bray appeared with his son on the History Channel several years ago—I believe they were celebrating the 50th anniversary of Jim's liberation. It showed father and son visiting several camps where Jim had been a POW.

[12]Longway, p. [400], Feb. 4, 1945: "I longed to see a real dough boy (now G. I. Joes) and had my fondest wish fulfilled, for 20 minute later, down the road ambled a huge shape. The great bear of a fellow stuck his head in the door with, 'Howdy, boys, I'm Lt. Wooster from the 37th Ohio National Guard.' This was my first encounter with an . . . American soldier. And did he look tough, and the sweat rolled down from him, he stank like a steer, but, oh Lord, it was good to see his huge frame, covered with the new American uniforms and their stuccoed helmets, gun over the shoulder, ammo about his waist. Immediately a crowd of people gathered about our prize exhibit."

D. Mansell, handwritten, Feb. 4, 1945: "I waited at the gate. Carl [Eschbach] and Phil M[arkert] went to meet the Major. I waited first in line for 2 hours before Carl returned. When he came he told us that Major Wen[d]t was a real fighting man from the 37th Ohioans. . . . A while later I met my first real Yank in three years. [He was] big, tall, and pleasant. [He was carrying] a short gun [a carbine, he was wearing an] O[live] D[rab] uniform, and a pot helmet. He was Lieutenant Wooster

[Worcester pronounced Wooster(?) and said he was a member] of the 37th Ohioans. I was among the very first [internees] to greet him. [I believe we let Bill Moule be the first one to shake his hand because of what he had gone through.] We said, 'We've been waiting for you for 3 years.' He replied, 'We've been looking for you for 3 years.' "

Moule, p. 371: "Some time that night [Feb. 4, 1945], and I wouldn't attempt to say whether it was 10:00 P.M. or 2:00 A.M. [it was much closer to 10:00 P.M. than 2:00 A.M.] . . . a commotion at the gate drew my attention, and, as I was on a binge of emotions, I investigated. There he was like a man out of Mars, our first American soldier! We shot questions at him a mile a minute. His name was Kinkaid [error, his name was Wooster, or Worcester, pronounced Wooster], and he was from Arizona [error, he was from Ohio]. His gear and dress was of special interest to us. The last helmet we saw was the old World War I type. This fellow had a helmet that came down over his ears, it had a liner in it and could be used for a wash basin and to carry water. . . . He had on overalls that had pockets for knives, hand grenades, first-aid kit, and food. His weapon was a short automatic carbine, and he wore a new type boot."

[13]D. Mansell, handwritten, Feb. 4, 1945.

[14]Ibid.

[15]Ibid.

[16]Halsema, 1944, p. [8], Feb. 4, 1945: "[The first officer within the walls of Bilibid was a Major Wendt from Cleveland of the 37th Division, an Ohio National Guard unit.]"

[17]D. Mansell, handwritten, Feb. 4, 1945.

[18]Longway, p. [400], Feb. 4, 1945.

[19]D. Mansell, handwritten, Feb. 4, 1945.

[20]Ibid.

[21]Deuteronomy 33:27—"The eternal God is thy refuge, and underneath are the everlasting arms."

If you enjoyed this book,
you'll enjoy these as well: